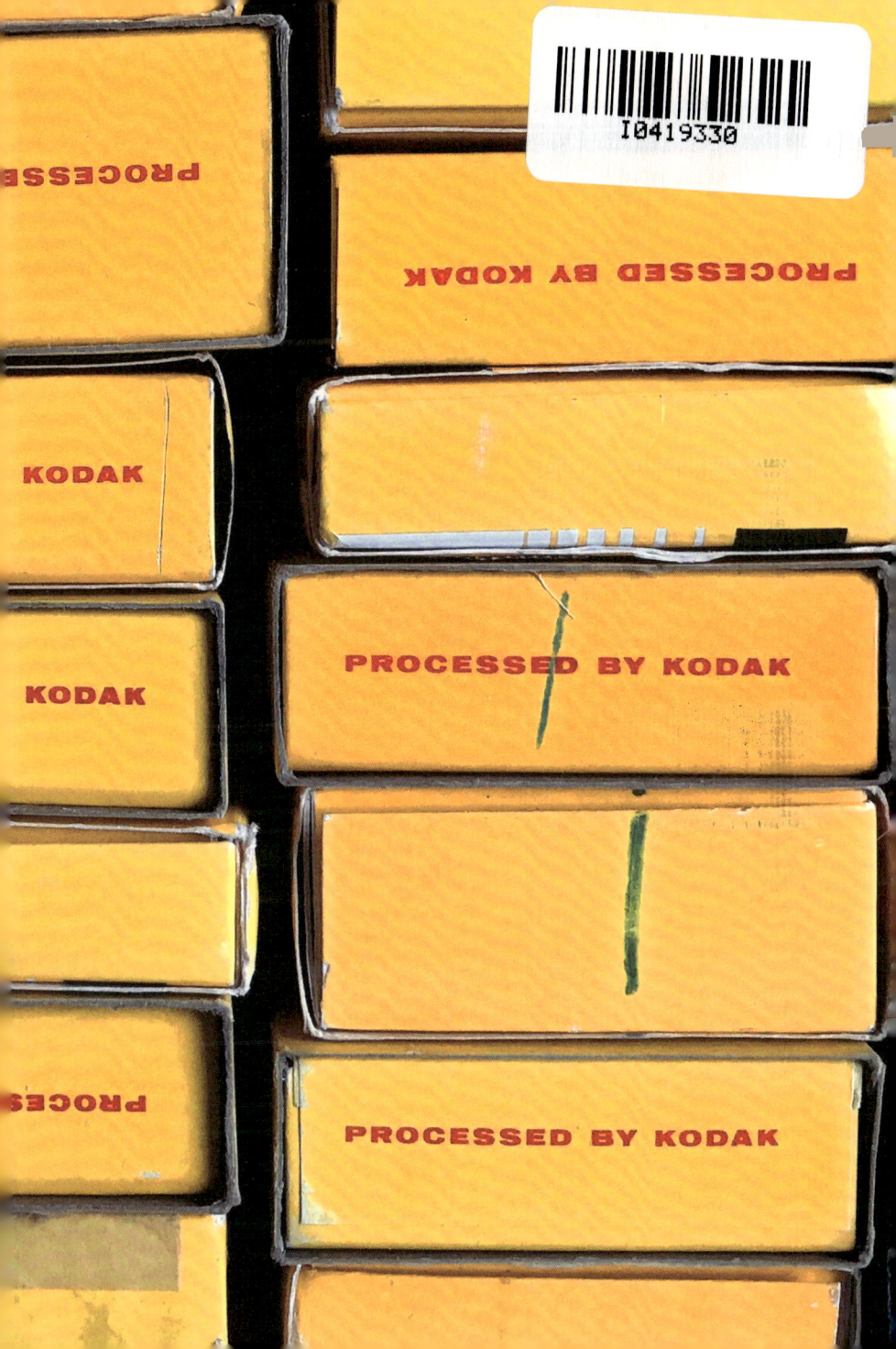

PROCESSED BY KODAK

PROCESSED BY KODAK

KODAK

KODAK

PROCESSED BY KODAK

PROCES

PROCESSED BY KODAK

I0419330

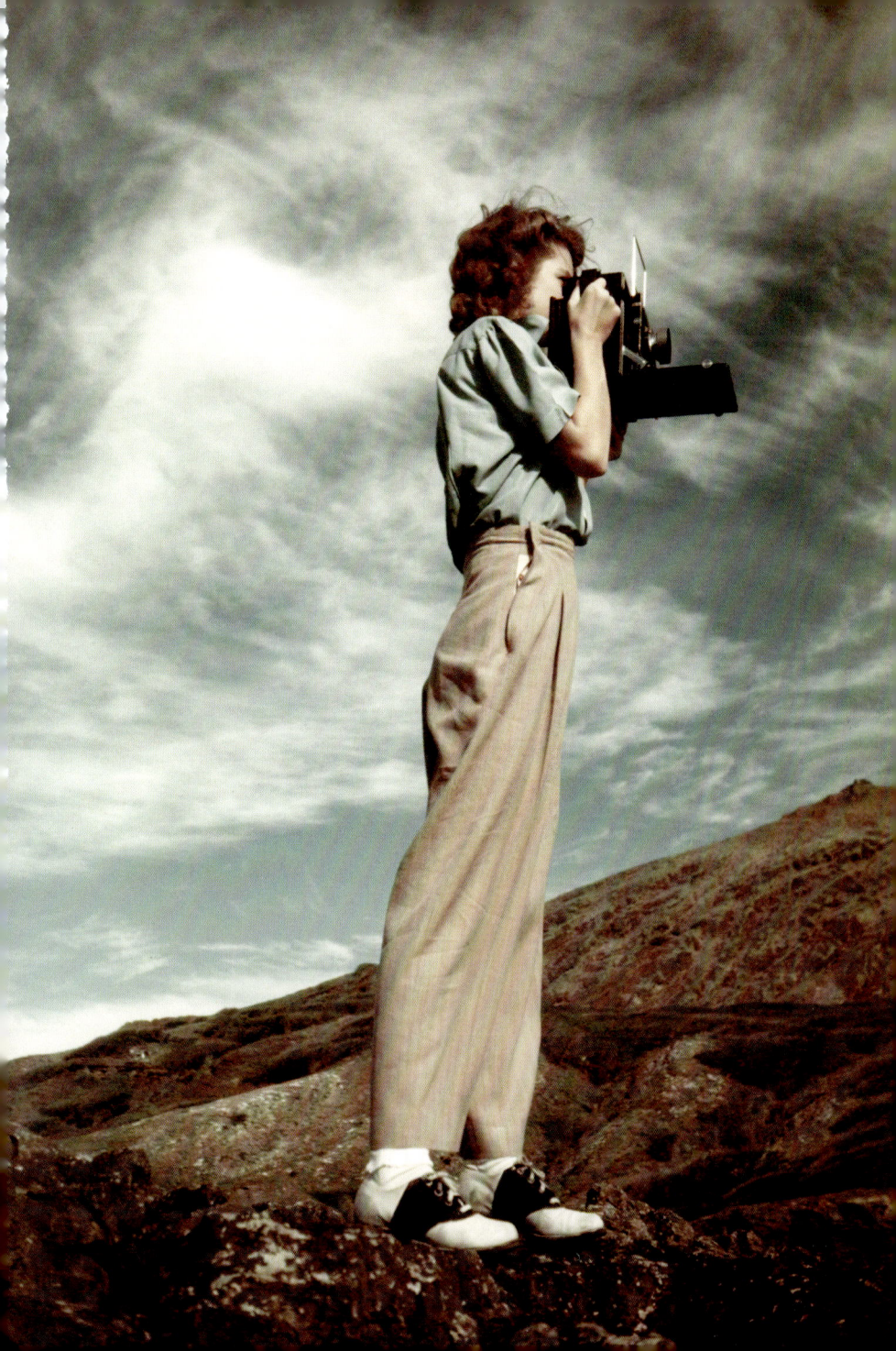

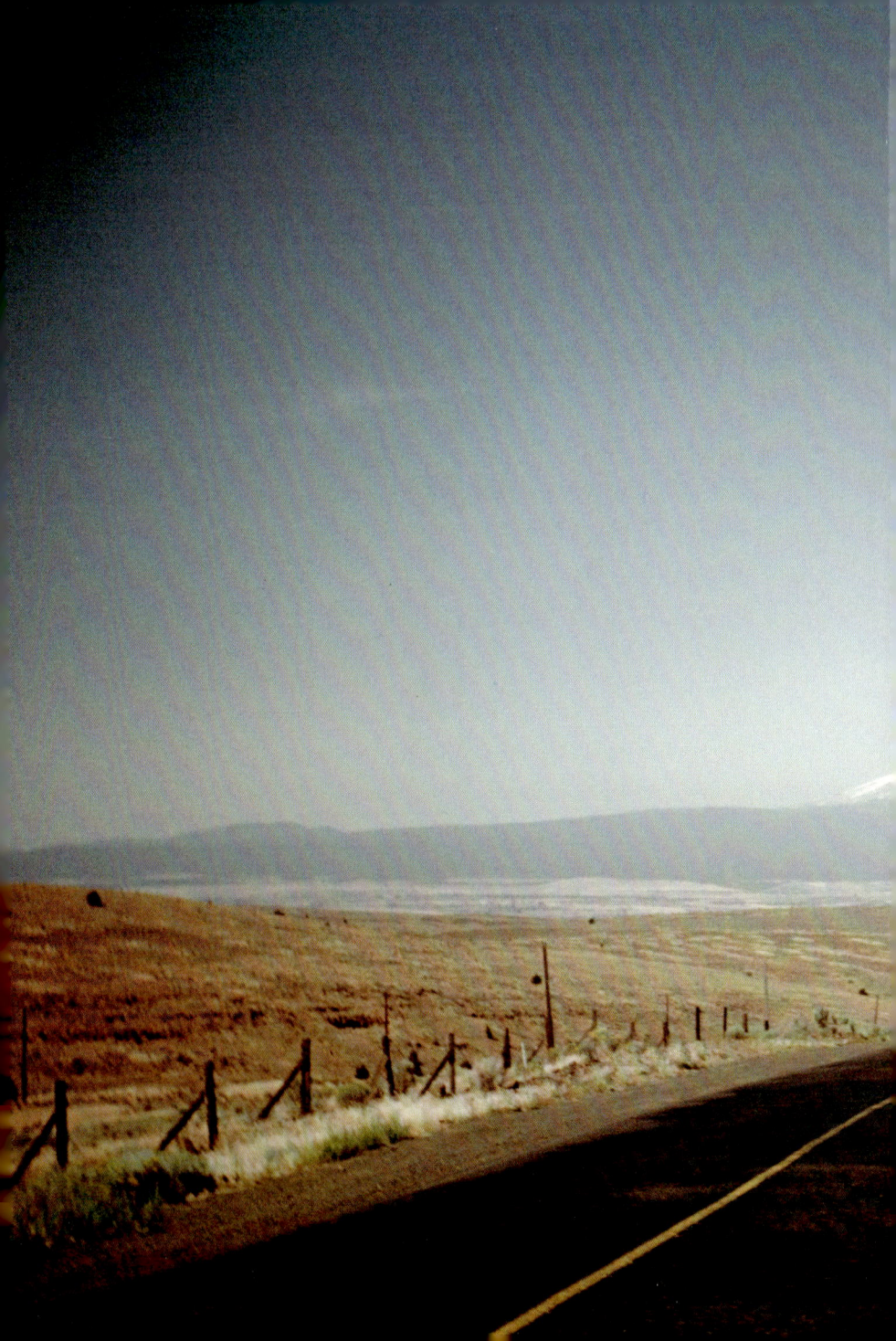

Lee Shulman

The Anonymous Project

Midcentury Memories

Edited by Reuel Golden
Essay by Richard B. Woodward

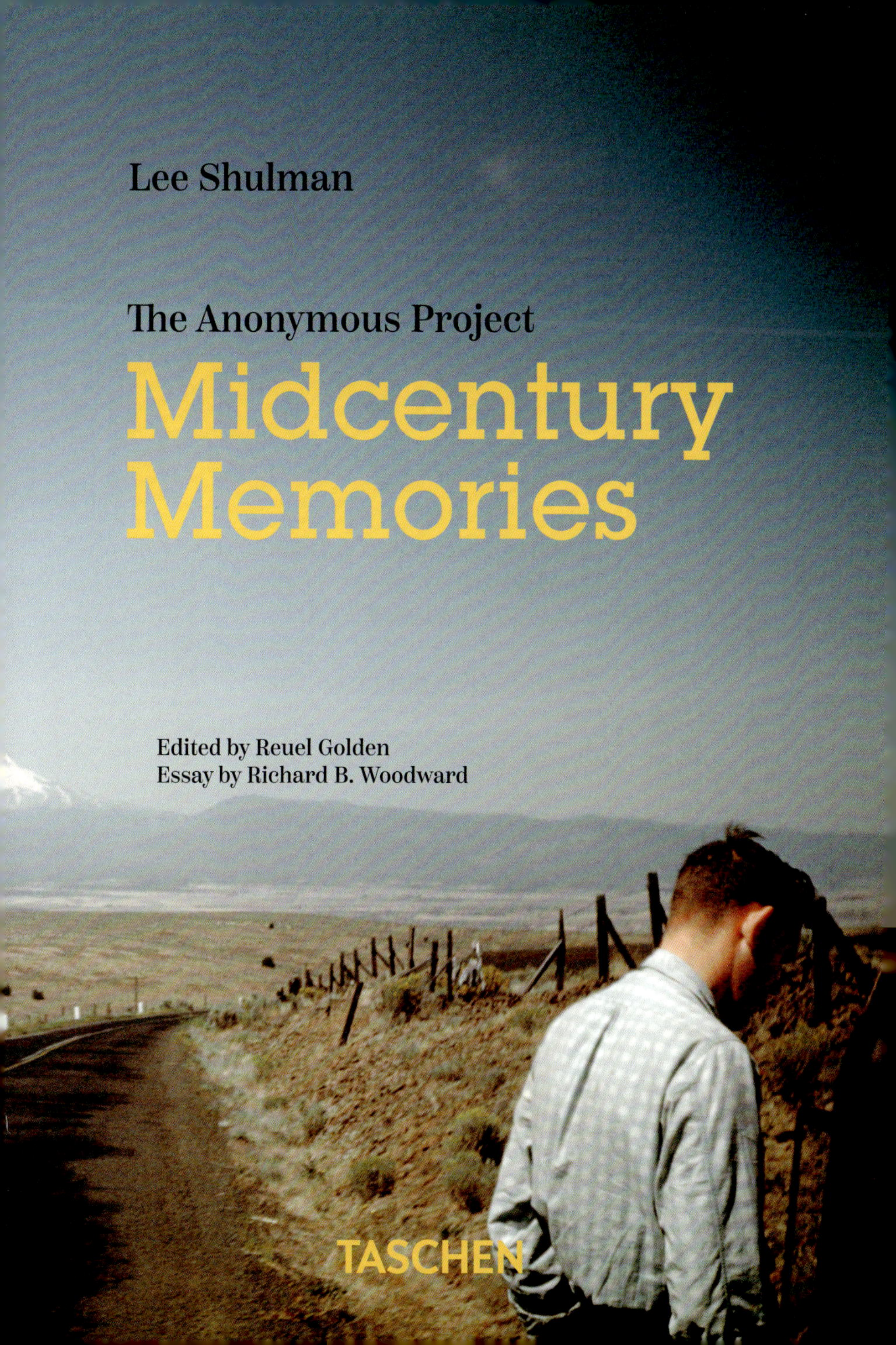

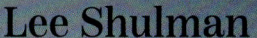

TASCHEN

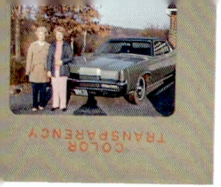
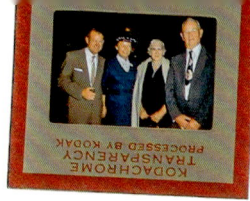
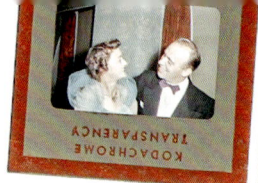
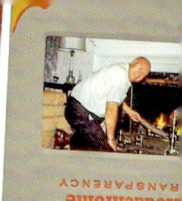
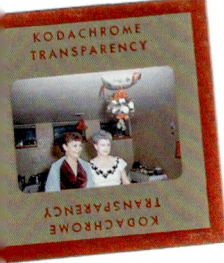
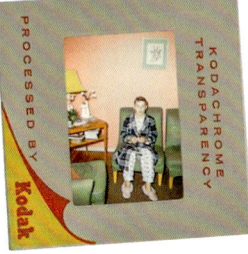
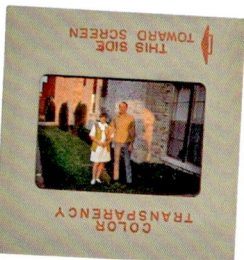
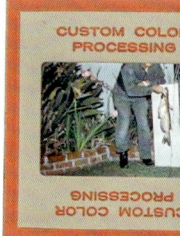
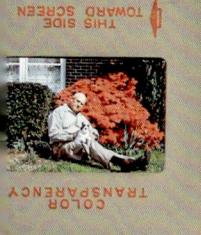
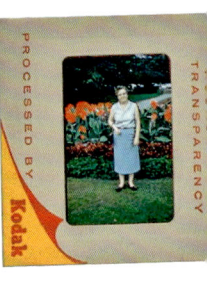
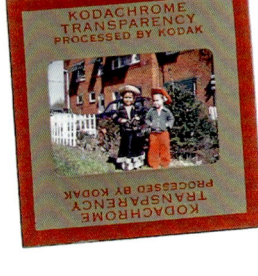
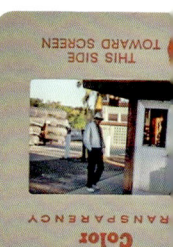

Collective Memories in Kodachrome 6

by Richard B. Woodward

The Photographs 14

Slide into the Past 184

Lee Shulman interviewed by
Reuel Golden

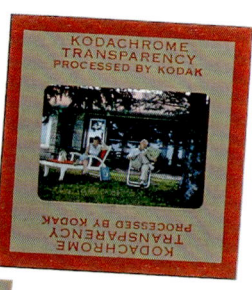
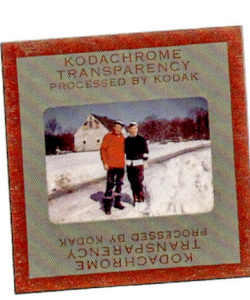
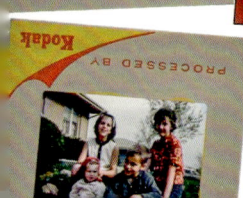
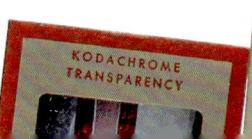
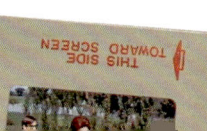
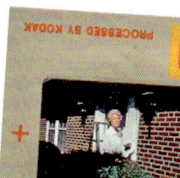

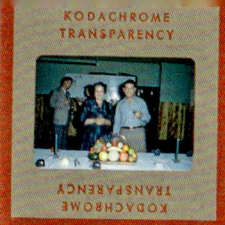

KODACHROME
TRANSPARENCY

KODACHROME
TRANSPARENCY

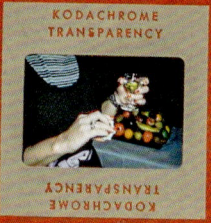

PROCESSED BY

Kodachrome

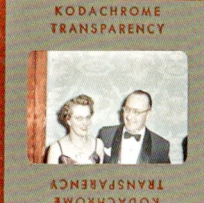

KODACHROME
TRANSPARENCY

KODACHROME
TRANSPARENCY

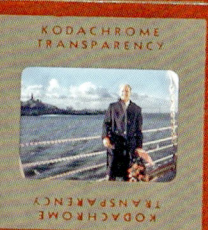

KODACHROME
TRANSPARENCY

KODACHROME
TRANSPARENCY

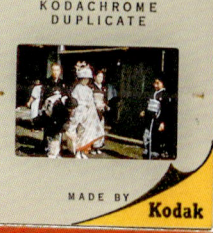

KODACHROME
DUPLICATE

MADE BY Kodak

KODACHROME
TRANSPARENCY

KODACHROME
TRANSPARENCY

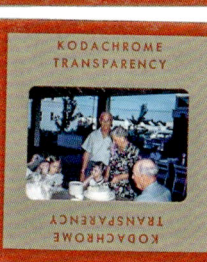

KODACHROME
TRANSPARENCY

KODACHROME
TRANSPARENCY

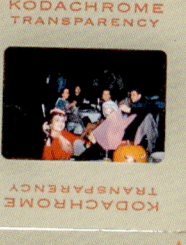

KODACHROME
TRANSPARENCY

KODACHROME
TRANSPARENCY

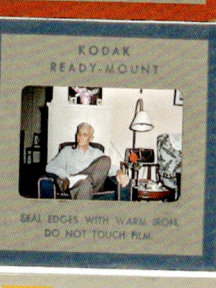

KODAK
READY-MOUNT

SEAL EDGES WITH WARM IRON.
DO NOT TOUCH FILM.

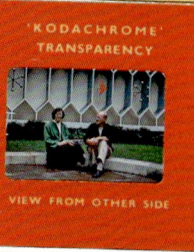

'KODACHROME'
TRANSPARENCY

VIEW FROM OTHER SIDE

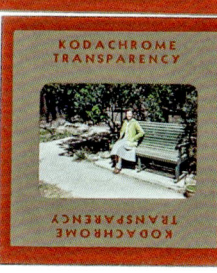

KODACHROME
TRANSPARENCY

KODACHROME
TRANSPARENCY

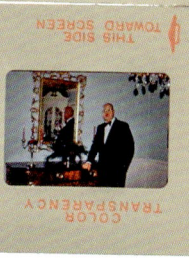

THIS SIDE TOWARD SCREEN

COLOR
TRANSPARENCY

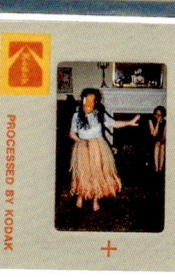

PROCESSED BY KODAK

Kodachrome
SLIDE

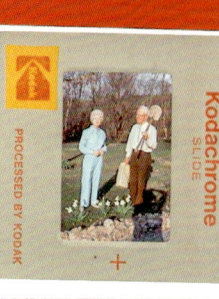

PROCESSED BY KODAK

Kodachrome
SLIDE

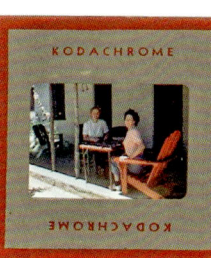

KODACHROME

KODACHROME

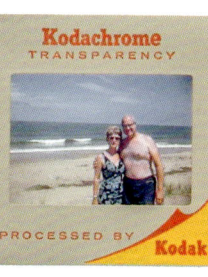

Kodachrome
TRANSPARENCY

PROCESSED BY Kodak

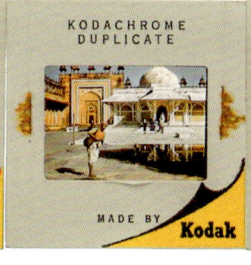

KODACHROME
DUPLICATE

MADE BY Kodak

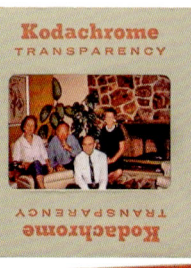

Kodachrome
TRANSPARENCY

TRANSPARENCY
Kodachrome

1961 NFAA

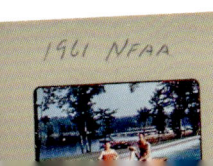

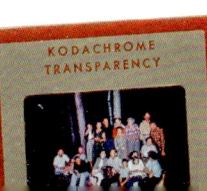

KODACHROME
TRANSPARENCY

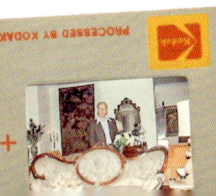

PROCESSED BY KODAK

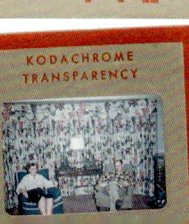

KODACHROME
TRANSPARENCY

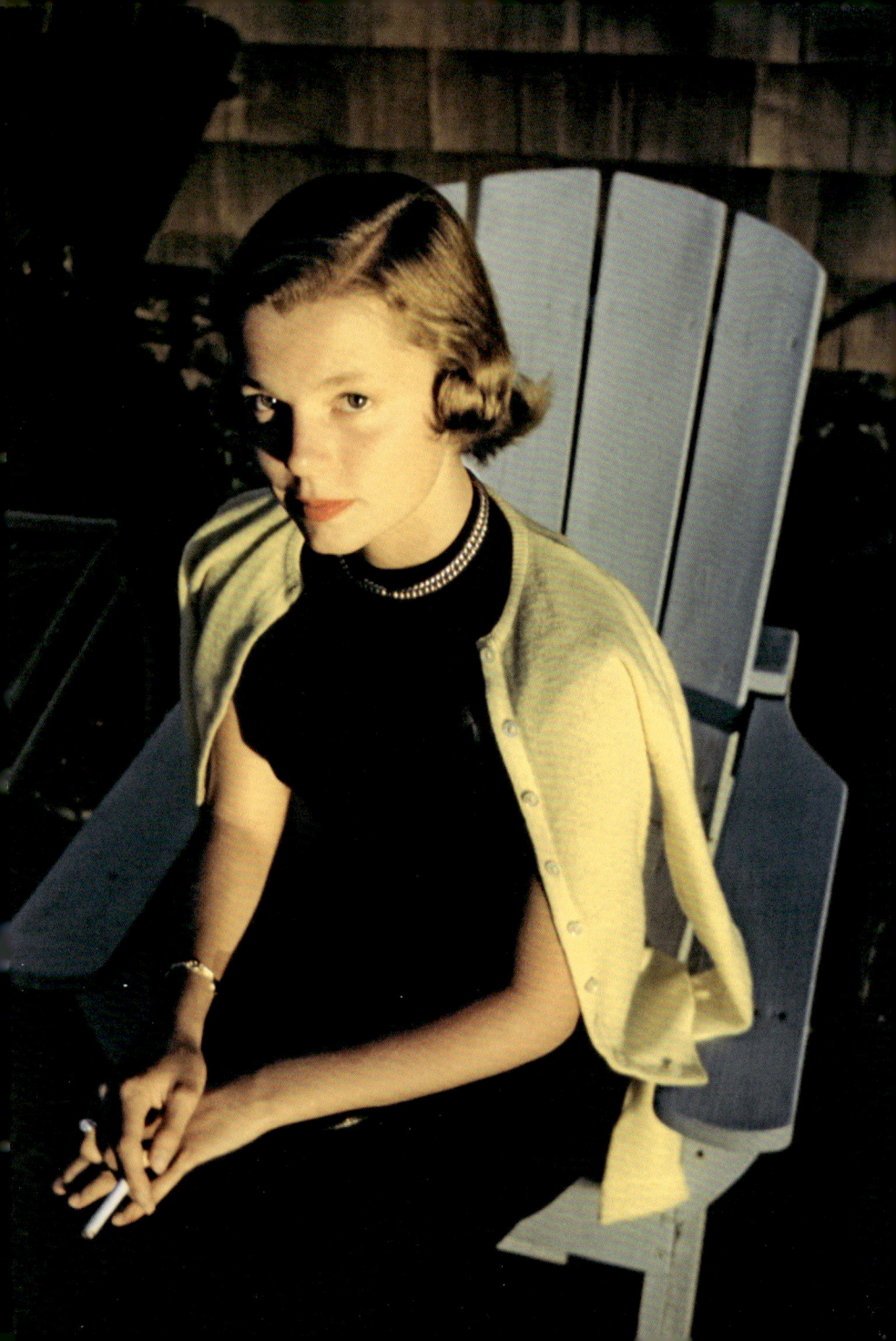

Collective Memories in Kodachrome

by Richard B. Woodward

A young woman is seated on the edge of a blue Adirondack chair. A thin and expensive yellow sweater draped over her shoulders and bare arms, she wears a high-necked black dress and holds an unlit cigarette in her right hand. Her icy hauteur might have caught the eye of Alfred Hitchcock, who could have cast her as the threatened heroine's younger sister. The Anonymous Project is a collection of similar scenes—the sweet, awkward, random moments that no one recalls now unless someone had recorded them in a photograph.

As can be seen in these pages, people behaved with 35 mm cameras and Instamatics 50 years ago much as they do today with smartphones in the age of Instagram and Snapchat. They took pictures of what they ate and drank, where they vacationed, how they celebrated. They memorialized the births of babies; a child's pride in a new bicycle or a color television set; leisurely days by a swimming pool, lake, or ocean; sightseeing in national parks; fishing trips; weddings; office parties; family reunions; couples drinking, holding hands, kissing, or dancing, sometimes with lampshades on their heads.

These occasions were meaningful only to the participants, and perhaps not even to them. Imagining what those meanings might be, the buried emotions or motives that prompted someone decades ago to press the shutter as an old man sat sleeping in a chair, is the larger purpose behind The Anonymous Project.

To aid in this recovery effort, neither the photographers nor any of the people photographed are named. Nor are any of the mundane specifics (dates and places) normally used to identify photographs disclosed.

These redactions are intentional. In editing his collection, English filmmaker Lee Shulman, the founder and creative director of the project, decided to exclude all background information, even in rare cases when he was able to provide it. Captions would only distort the interpretative experience he wants the viewer to share.

The project has been designed to widen the typical responses to a book of photographs and isn't offered as fine art or as historical documents from a particular year, country, family, or individual. Instead, think of each image as akin to the first line in a short story or a freeze-frame from a home movie—as floating, authorless, kaleidoscopic pieces from the late 20th century's collective memory.

Shulman and his assistant, photo publisher Emmanuelle Halkin, have amassed more than 700,000 color slides and pared those down to a collection of about 10,000, of which a sample can be found here. The earliest examples date from the late 1930s, while the majority is from the 1950s through the 1970s—the years of the first baby boom. Most of the images depict Americans, but the people and rituals of England and Europe are also well represented, along with a smattering from Japan and Africa. Many of these images were purchased on various websites, some in flea markets. Many more were donated by people who heard about the project and wanted to participate in its operative philosophy.

Other exhibitions and books have recognized the snapshot's unique value. Over the last 50 years, curators and collectors have taught us to appreciate photographic "accidents" and "mistakes"—unforeseen intrusions into the frame, monstrous reflections from obliterating blasts of flash—for their artless charm or as evidence of a body language that "correct" photographs sometimes don't capture. Museums have begun to buy and display historical collections of photographs by unknown amateurs.

Shulman shares an affectionate regard for this formerly disrespected style but has chosen to poke around in an even more neglected area of the photographic past. Few have bothered to collect en masse color slides from the late 20th century before. The Anonymous Project is singular for what it reveals about how we have chosen to portray ourselves across years and cultures—a secret history of unpredictable diversity and remarkable similarities that has been lying in plain sight for 75 years.

Unlike the daguerreotype or black-and-white photographic prints, the color transparency is not a widely cherished object. The Autochrome Lumière, an early direct-positive color process on glass that drew the attention of Alfred Stieglitz and others during the early 20th century, was too expensive and fragile for mass public acceptance. Not until the color slide was produced on celluloid-reversal films in the 1930s did it gain popularity.

The most beloved and purchased of these by the middle class around the world was Kodachrome. Introduced in 1935, and steadily improved upon for more than half a century, it needed lots of light for details to register. Under the right conditions though, skies were never bluer and trees never greener than they were in the saturated hues of Kodachrome, as old copies of *National Geographic* and the chorus of Paul Simon's anthem to nostalgia attest.

The downside was that slides were much easier to make than to look at. Once they came back from development by Kodak or Agfa or Ilford or Fuji, it wasn't clear what to do with them. You couldn't paste transparencies in a photo album or put them on your desk at the office. Professional photo editors could study details in a 35 mm slide with a magnifying hand viewer or loupe. But the only chance most people had to review how well (or poorly) they had photographed something in Kodachrome or Ektachrome was by setting up a slide projector. The invention of these machines predated photography by several centuries. The Dutch physicist and astronomer Christiaan Huygens (1629–1695) is usually credited as the first to describe and build a magic lantern, which used a light source to project glass slides against a flat surface. Because these illuminated images occupy space in a room, which needs to be dark for the slides to be legible, and because they require an operator, the technology of the magic lantern has close affinities with theater and cinema.

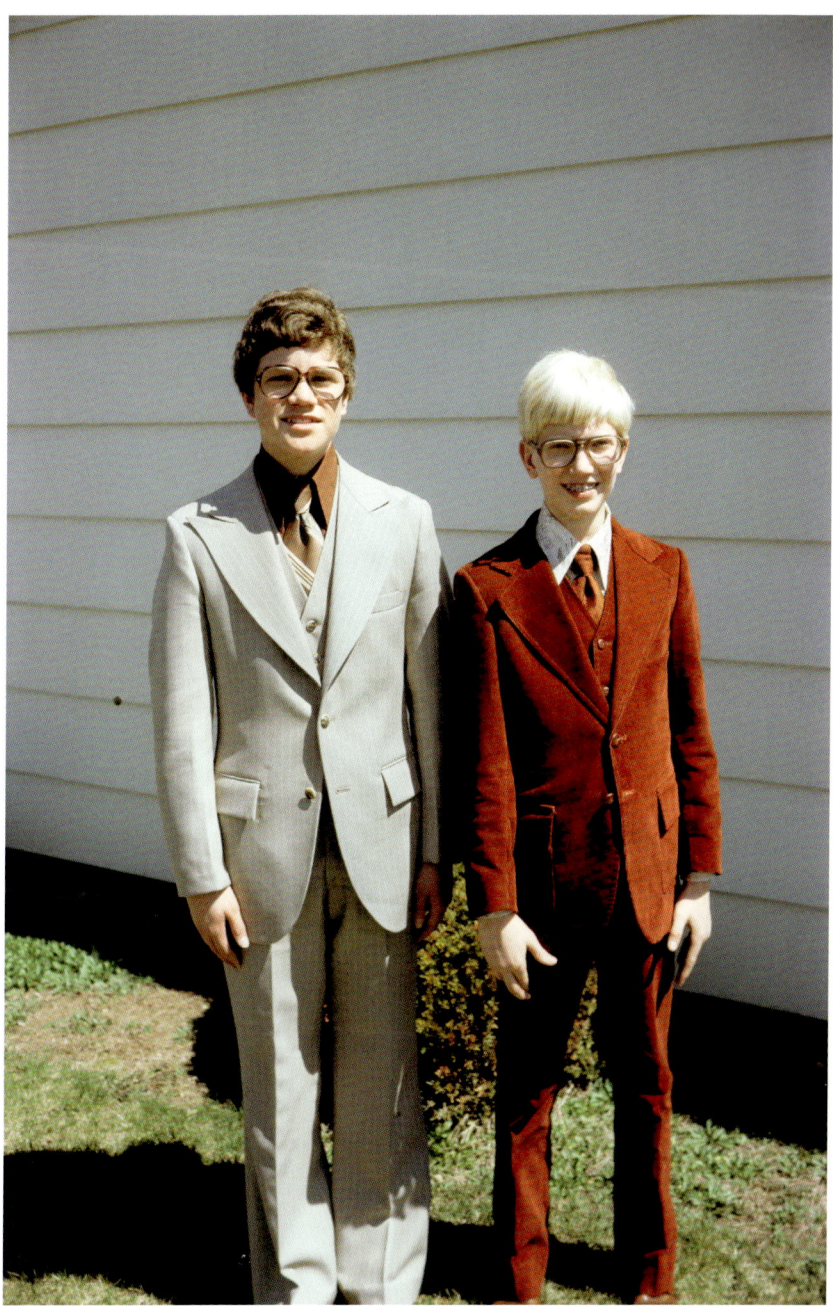

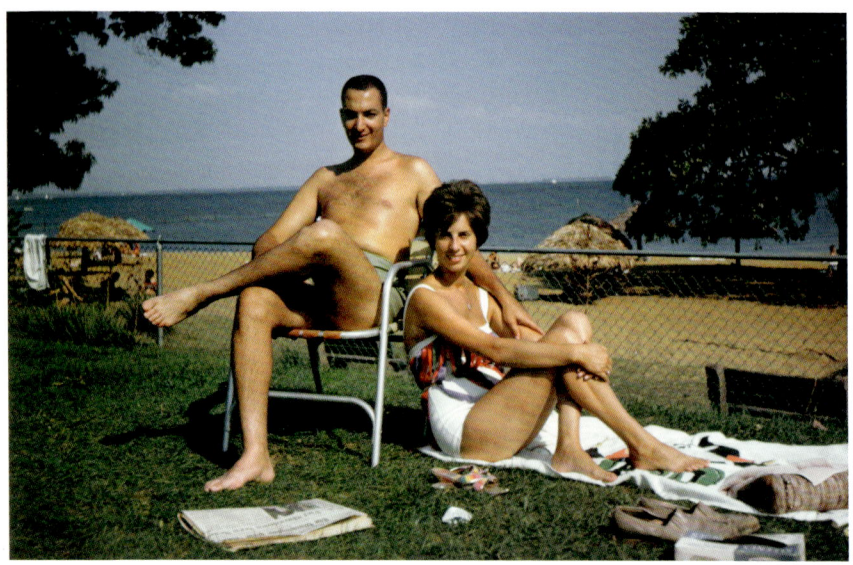

In the first chapter of *In Search of Lost Time*, Marcel Proust recalls his melancholy attempts as a boy to entertain himself before dinner by projecting magic lantern scenes from the medieval legend of Geneviève de Brabant in his bedroom. Ingmar Bergman also grew up with one of these devices and staged operas with them in his home. His autobiography is titled *The Magic Lantern*.

While looking at slides on a wall was a private, theatrical experience for Proust and Bergman, for most of us born later in the 20th century the experience was much less dramatic and solitary. In the 1950s and '60s, as projectors entered middle-class American and European homes and school classrooms, the slide show became a group activity, and more often than not a coerced one under the dictatorship of a parent or teacher.

The person in the family hierarchy who organized the trays or held the remote control—the role of photographer in chief was usually the father's—would set the order and the pace, which was often agonizingly slow with long pauses for commentary. The slides themselves had no afterlife beyond their one-night-only appearance in a living room or den. Most disappeared back into their cardboard boxes and never saw daylight again. Shulman estimates that many of the images in his book have not been viewed by anyone, even by those to whom they once belonged, for 60 years.

The Anonymous Project has liberated these fragments of history from their consigned darkness and the tyranny of the linear slide show, allowing the rituals of family outings in the 1950s and '60s to stimulate our imaginations, much as Proust's was by medieval legends.

Almost all the memories assembled in this book are pleasant ones. Family dissension has been largely suppressed. Is the widespread contentment on the faces of the people here a mask worn for the camera? Or was much of the world genuinely less anxious and unhappy, even at the height of the Cold War, than we seem to be now? It is significant—and fascinating—that in virtually every image here, photographer and subject seem to know one another. In this embracing album of humanity, no one exists in isolation. There are no strangers here.

The world depicted, it must be said, is overwhelmingly white and middle class. The higher cost of color transparencies and the expense of having to own a slide projector perhaps discouraged large sectors of the population, who chose to photograph their daily lives not using slide film.

Even if other ethnicities were better represented, it's doubtful their facial expressions would differ much from those seen here. Amateur photographers have always tended to portray their friends and families as smiling rather than in distress, at rest instead of busy at work. Being photographed used to necessitate presenting one's best self as well as wearing one's finest clothes. In turning these pages and meeting for the first time a group of unknown characters, each reader may develop attachments to a few favorites. One of mine is of a youngish, white, middle-class American couple standing in a parking lot eating ice cream. Their clothes and eyeglasses and the cars behind them suggest it's the late 1950s or early '60s. He wears a white shirt, a tie with a bar clip, a pocket protector, cuff links, and no ring; she is attired in a

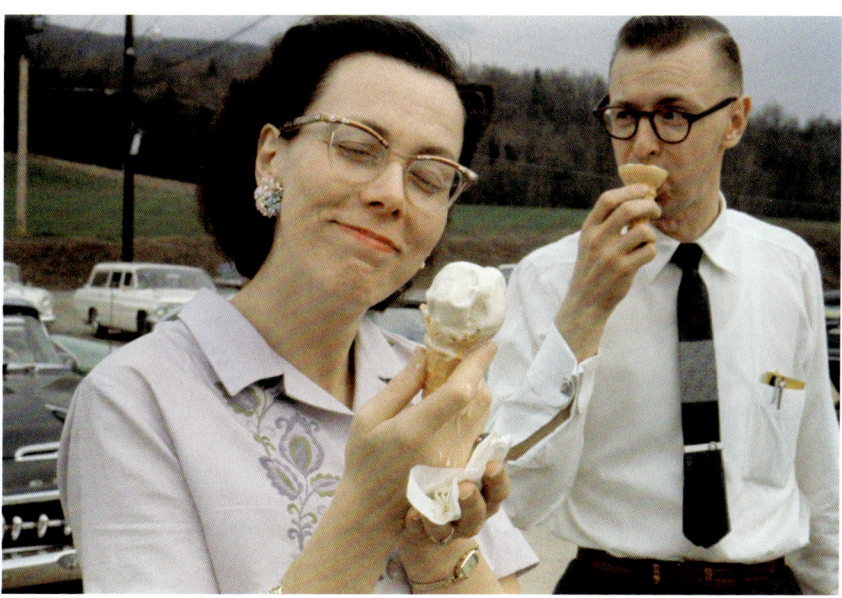

lavender dress and large earrings. Perhaps they are rewarding themselves after sitting through church on a steamy morning. He is about to start devouring his wafer cone, whereas she has been savoring the frozen milk and sugar on her tongue. The smile on her face tells the photographer that she's in no hurry to bring an end to this small pleasure.

Knowing nothing for sure about these people, viewers aren't confined too narrowly to the facts of a situation and can fantasize to their heart's content. Storytelling can be yet another act of restoration, which is the central mission of The Anonymous Project. The technology that created and animated these images is now defunct. Kodachrome 64 film was discontinued in 2009. The last Kodak slide projector was manufactured in 2004. The color in many of these slides has already begun to fade.

Unwanted or orphaned memories are being salvaged here as well. The first photographs thrown out by any family will be ones of people whom the living can no longer identify. Governments are equally merciless when it comes to the anonymous dead. Unidentified bodies that no one claims are buried without headstones in a potter's field.

The people and places recorded on slides were particularly susceptible to losing all connection to their origins. The cardboard or plastic sleeves that held 35 mm transparencies did not allow much room for annotation around the borders. (The flat white back of a paper photograph, on the contrary, seemed to invite the listing of names or even messages.)

The Anonymous Project therefore foretells all of our fates. Records of days at the beach or sitting in the kitchen or riding in a car will eventually become untethered from our biographies. In a shorter time than many of us would like to think, our names will begin to disappear even if the images of our anonymous selves endure.

This isn't as dire or uncommon as it sounds. In the long history of pictures, it's only recently that we have been able to identify the authors. In the thousands of cave drawings from the Paleolithic or Holocene periods, we know neither the artists nor the people whose bodies those imprinted hands belonged to. Their anonymity has only piqued our interest or admiration.

Anonymity is provisional too. These photographs aren't fake news; they're documents from the lives of real people. Should someone pick up this book and recognize the face of a relative or a friend, their anonymity would vanish. The history of clothing, hairstyles, automobiles, signage, architecture, interior design, food, and gestures help to indicate when and where a photograph was taken. The grain of the film and the palette of painted things in the industrial landscape are additional clues about time and place.

This book is then both a reminder of the impending amnesia that awaits images of almost everyone and an invitation to enter into the lives of people we don't know, such as they were or might have been. It's an enduring wonder of photography that the examples here, each capturing only a fraction of a second, collectively illuminate millions of lifetimes.

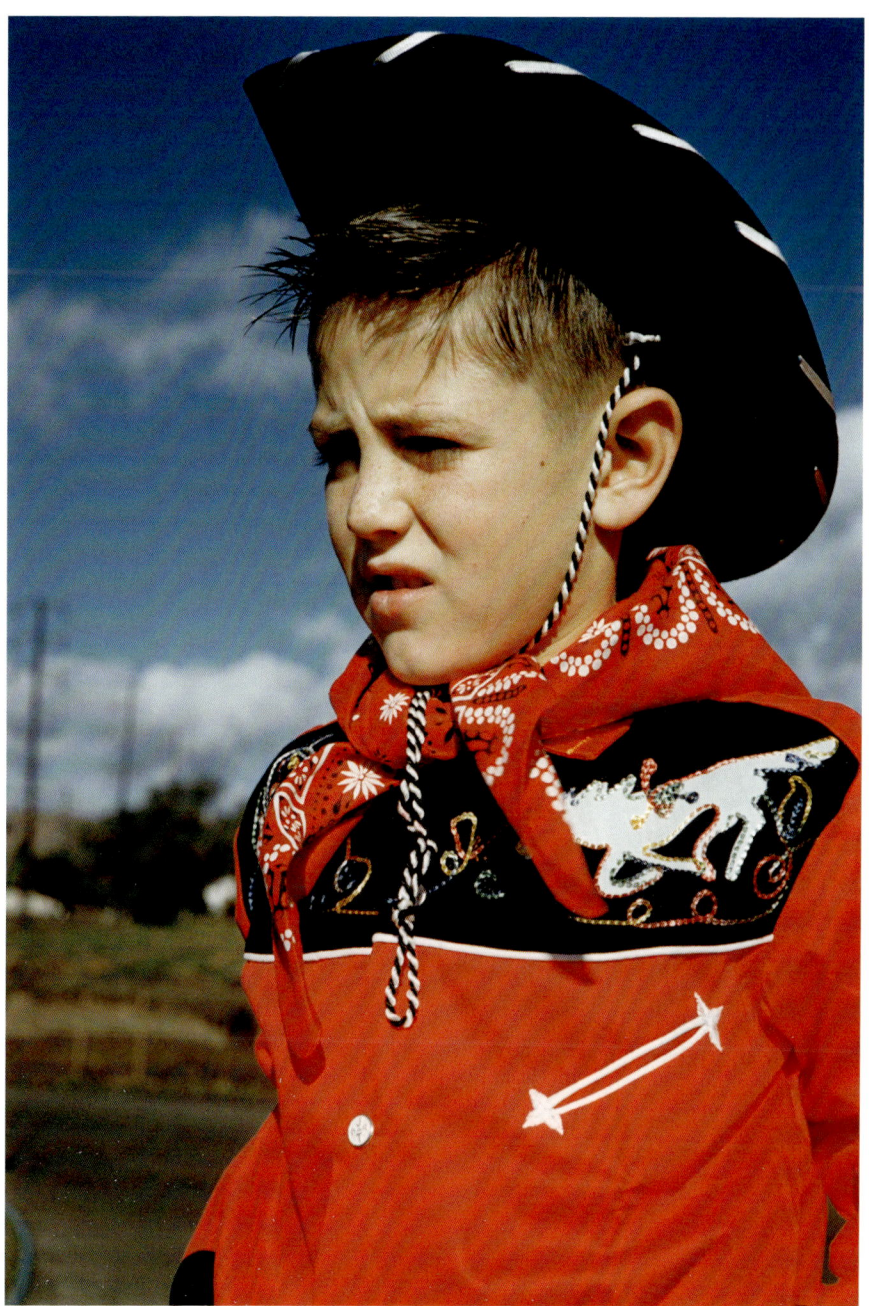

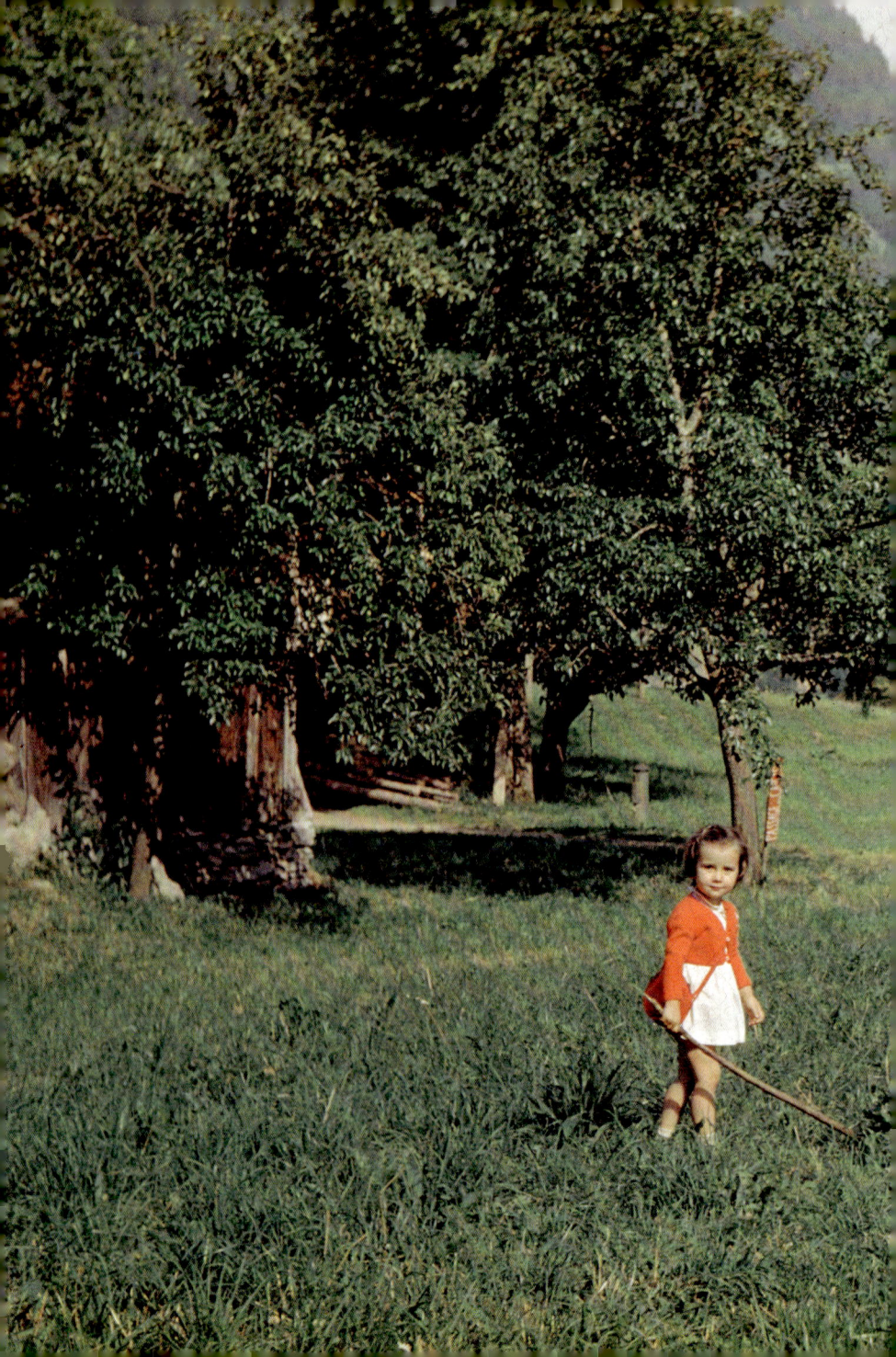

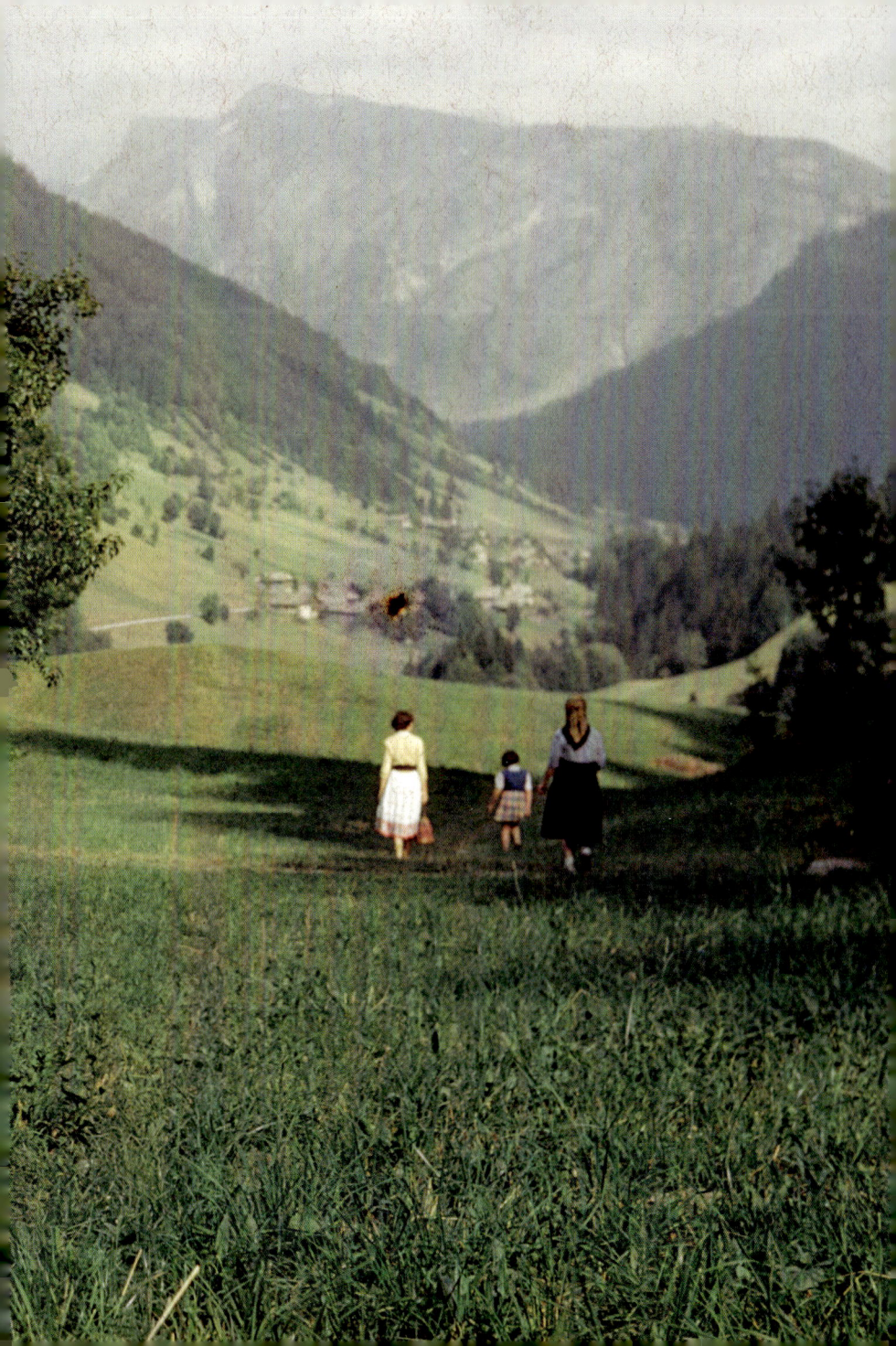

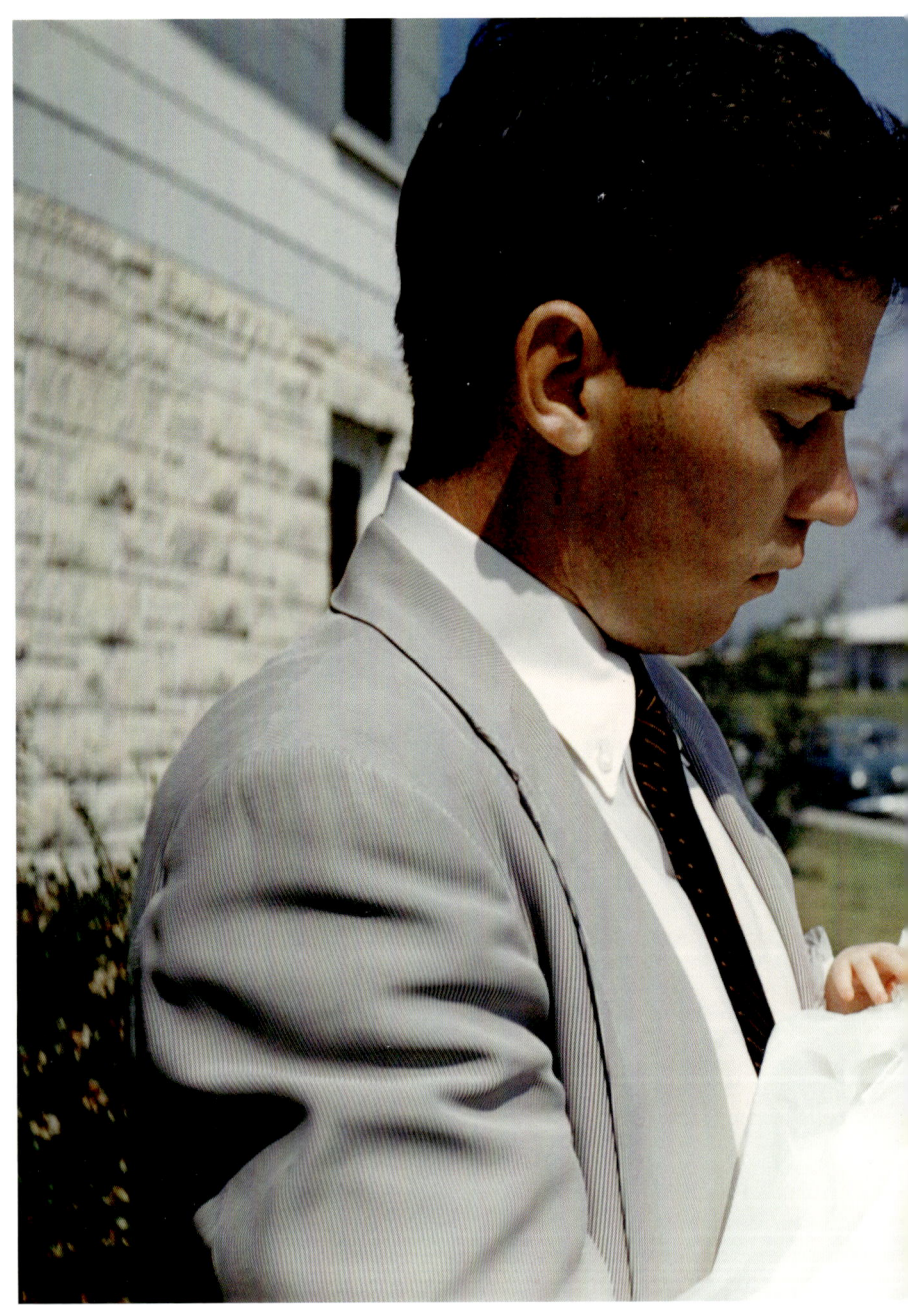

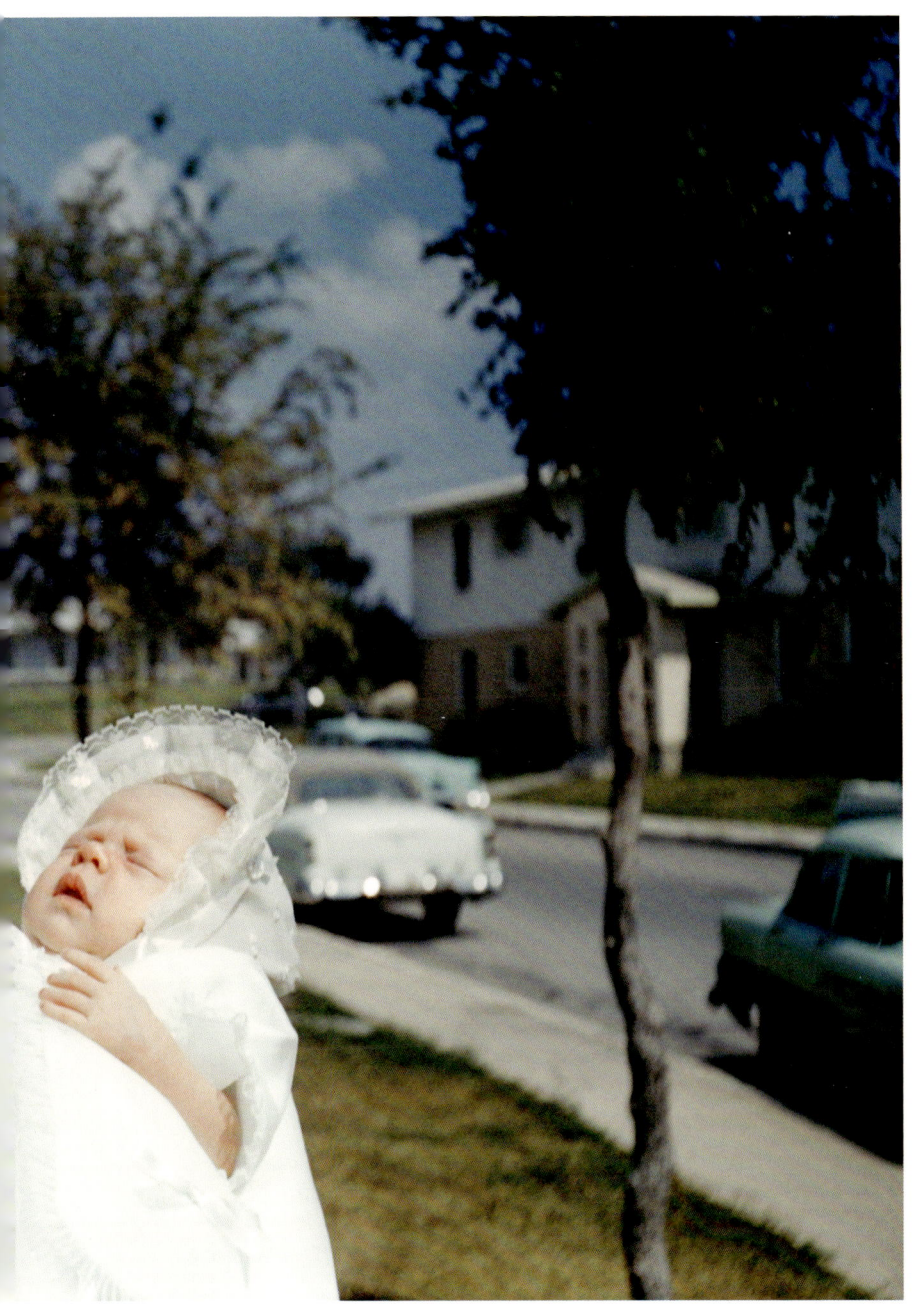

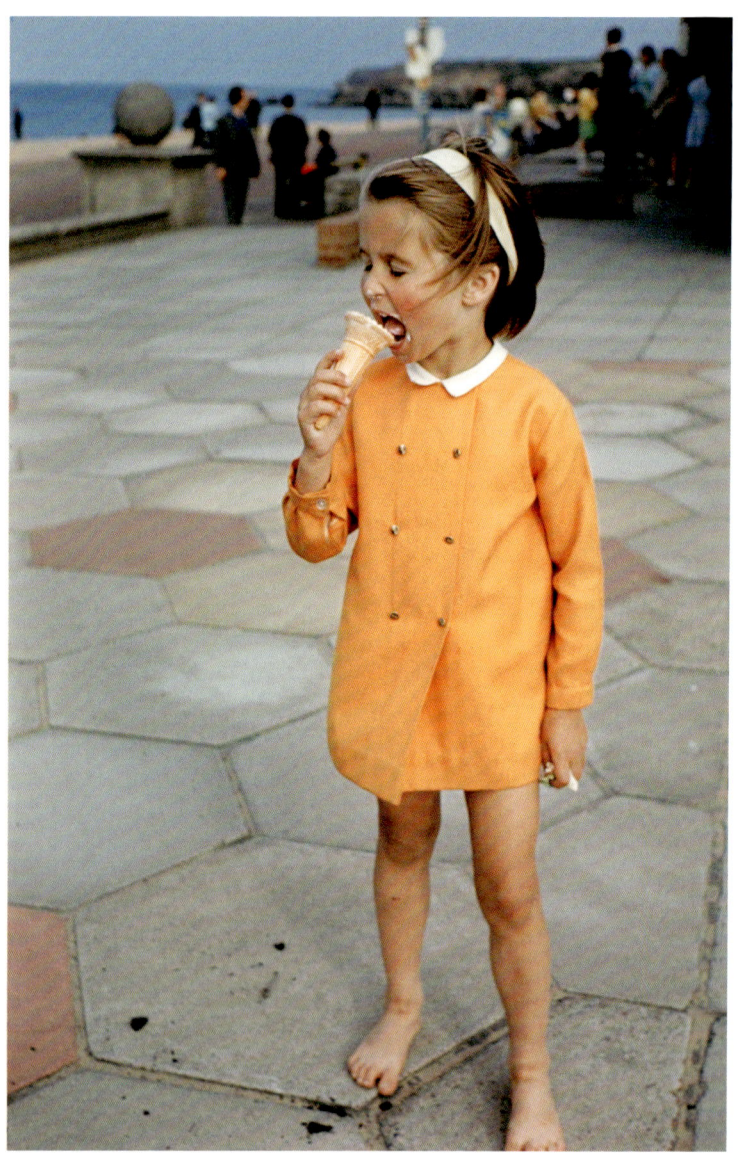

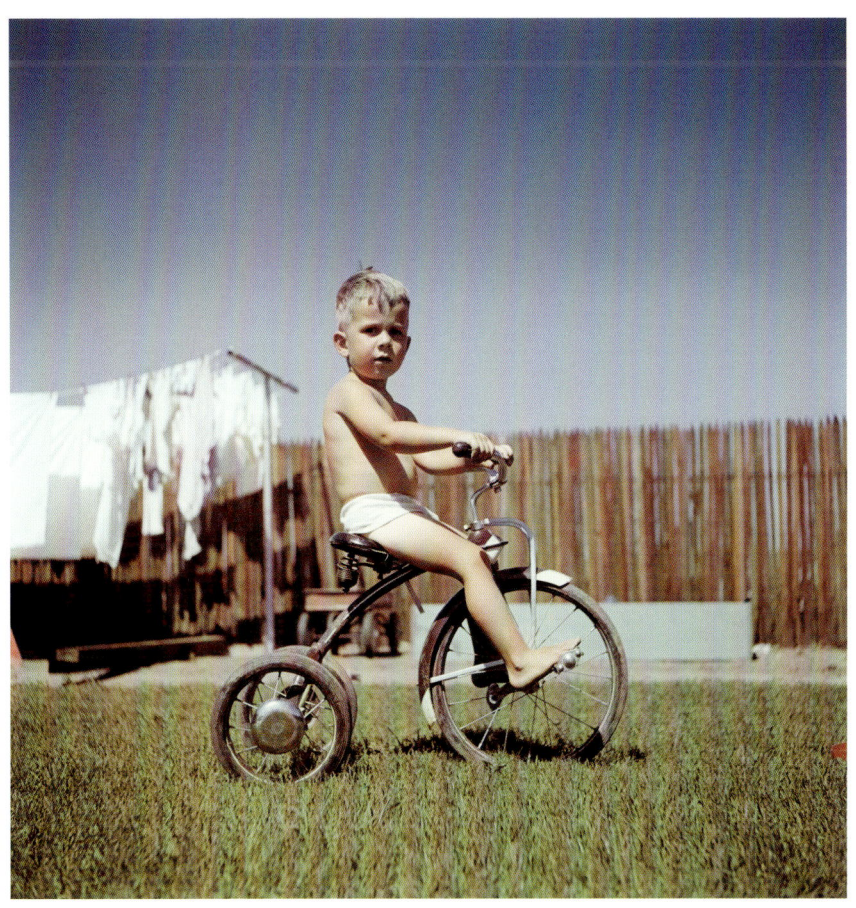

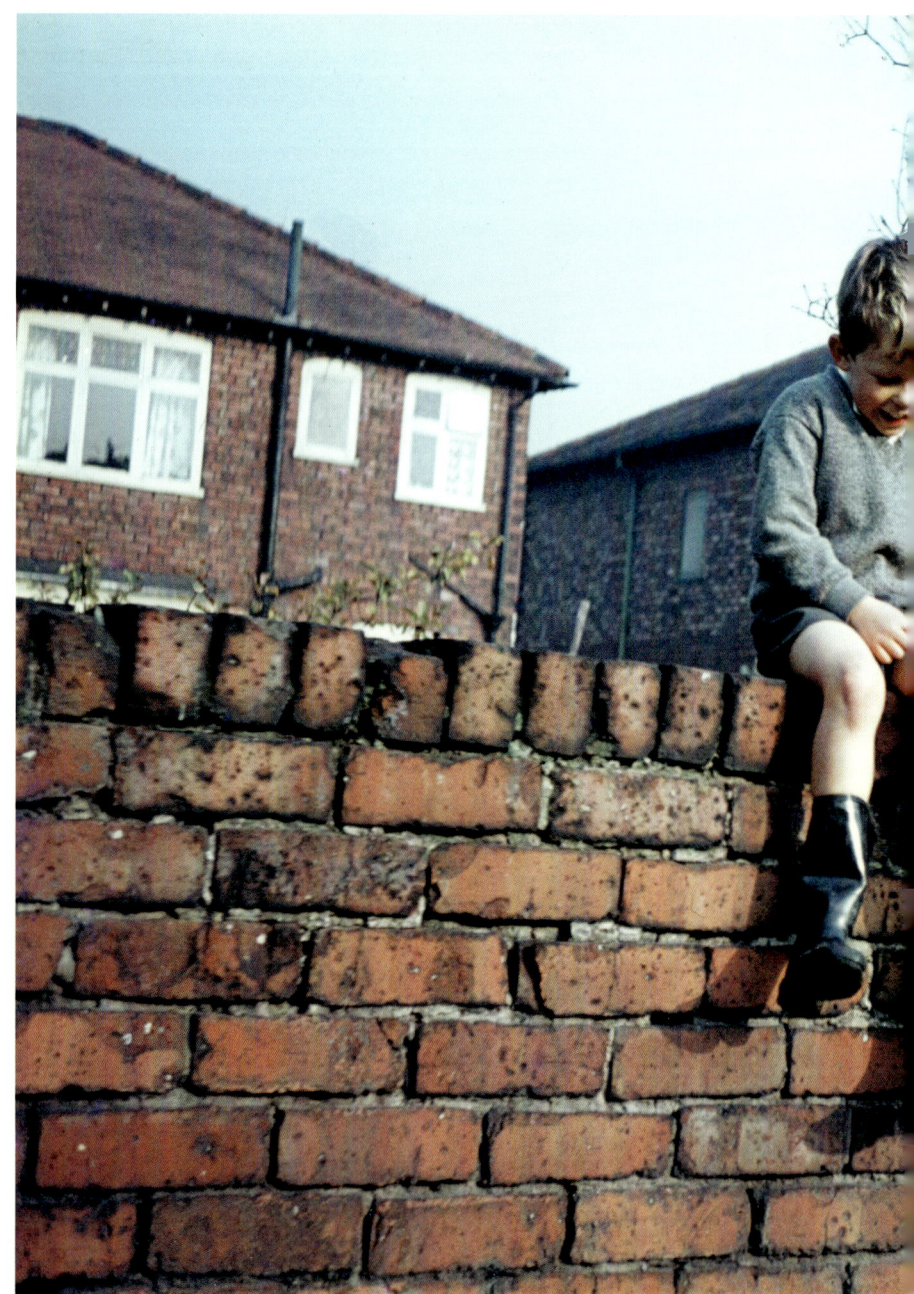

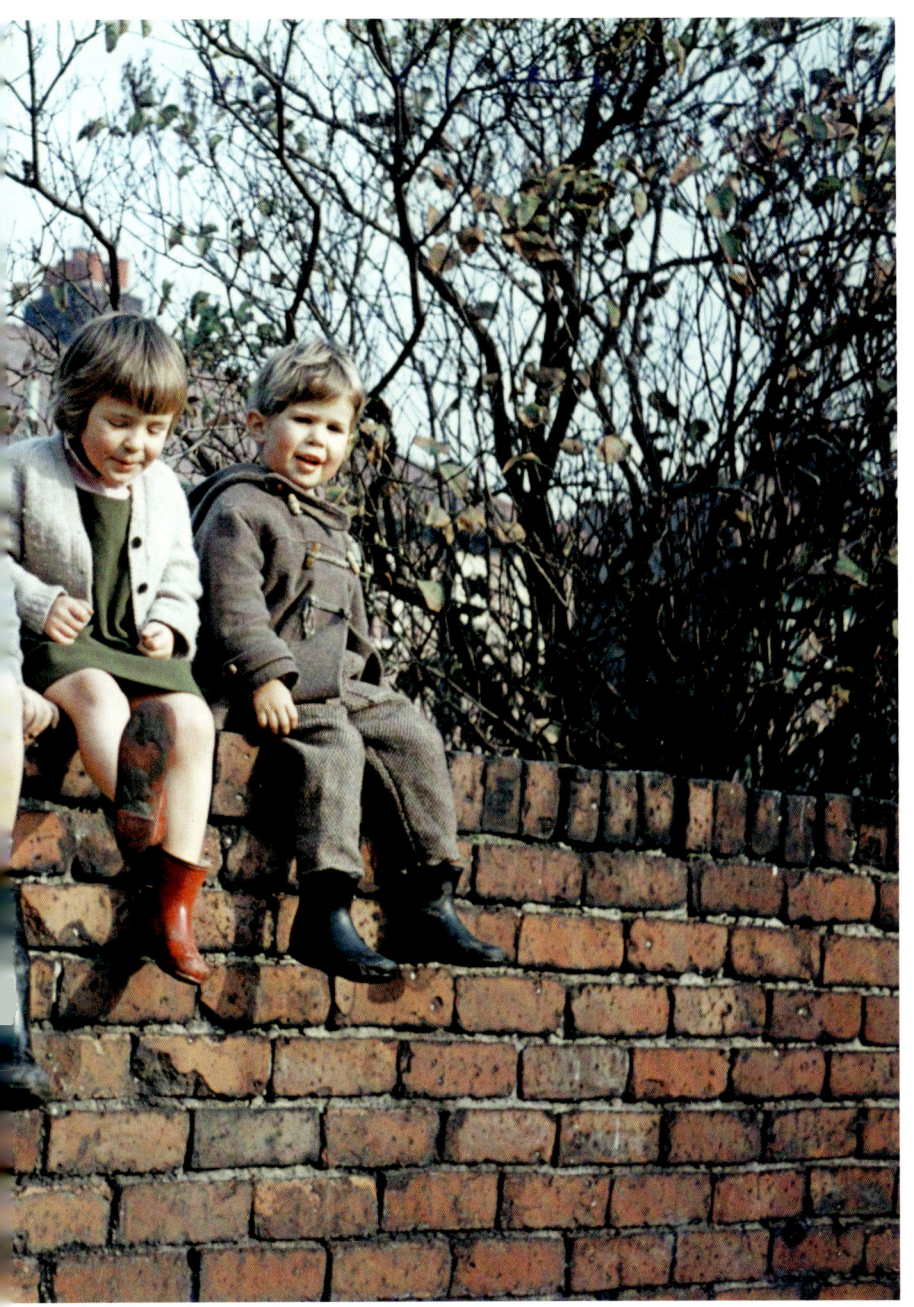

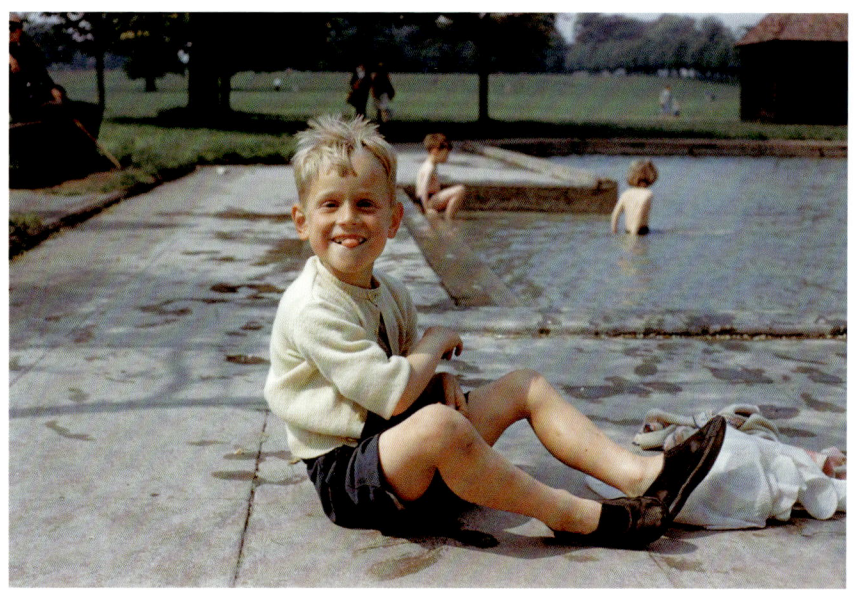

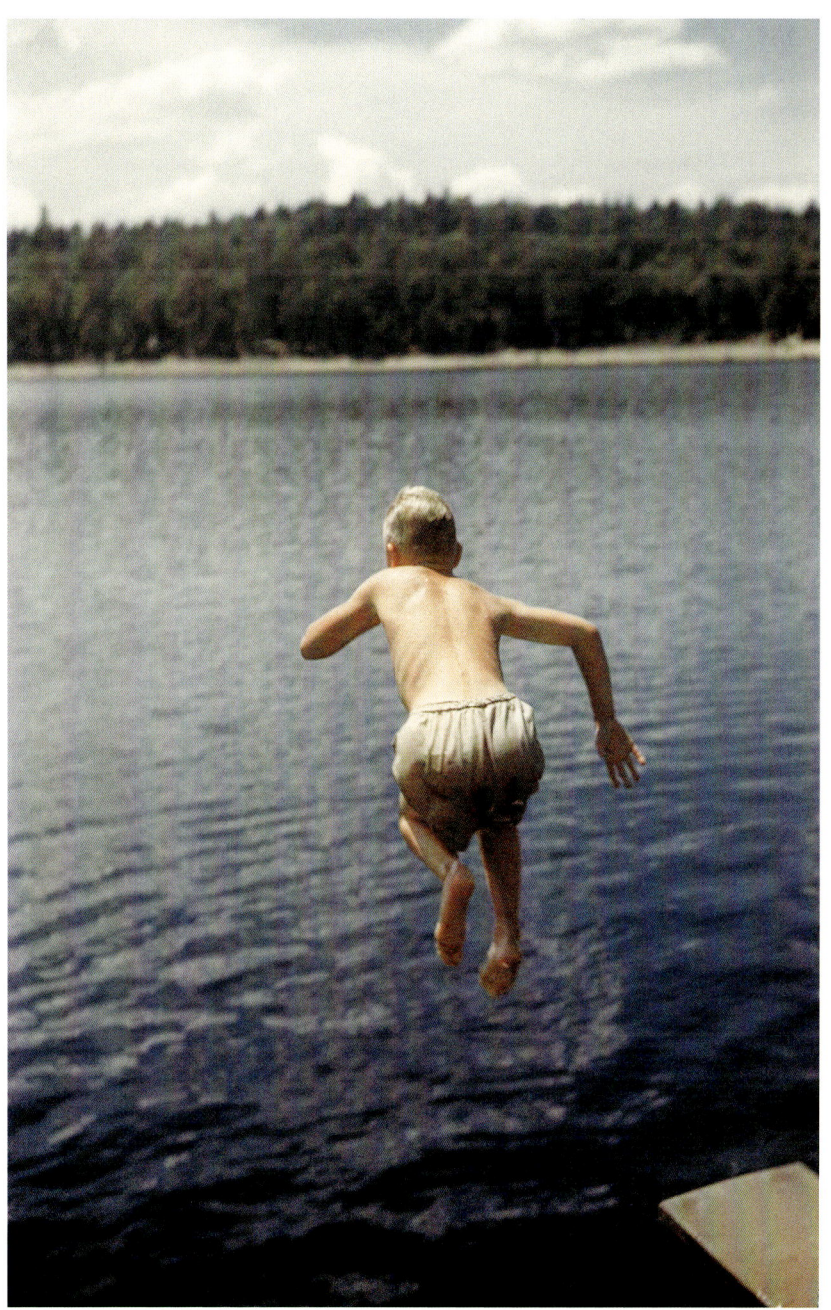

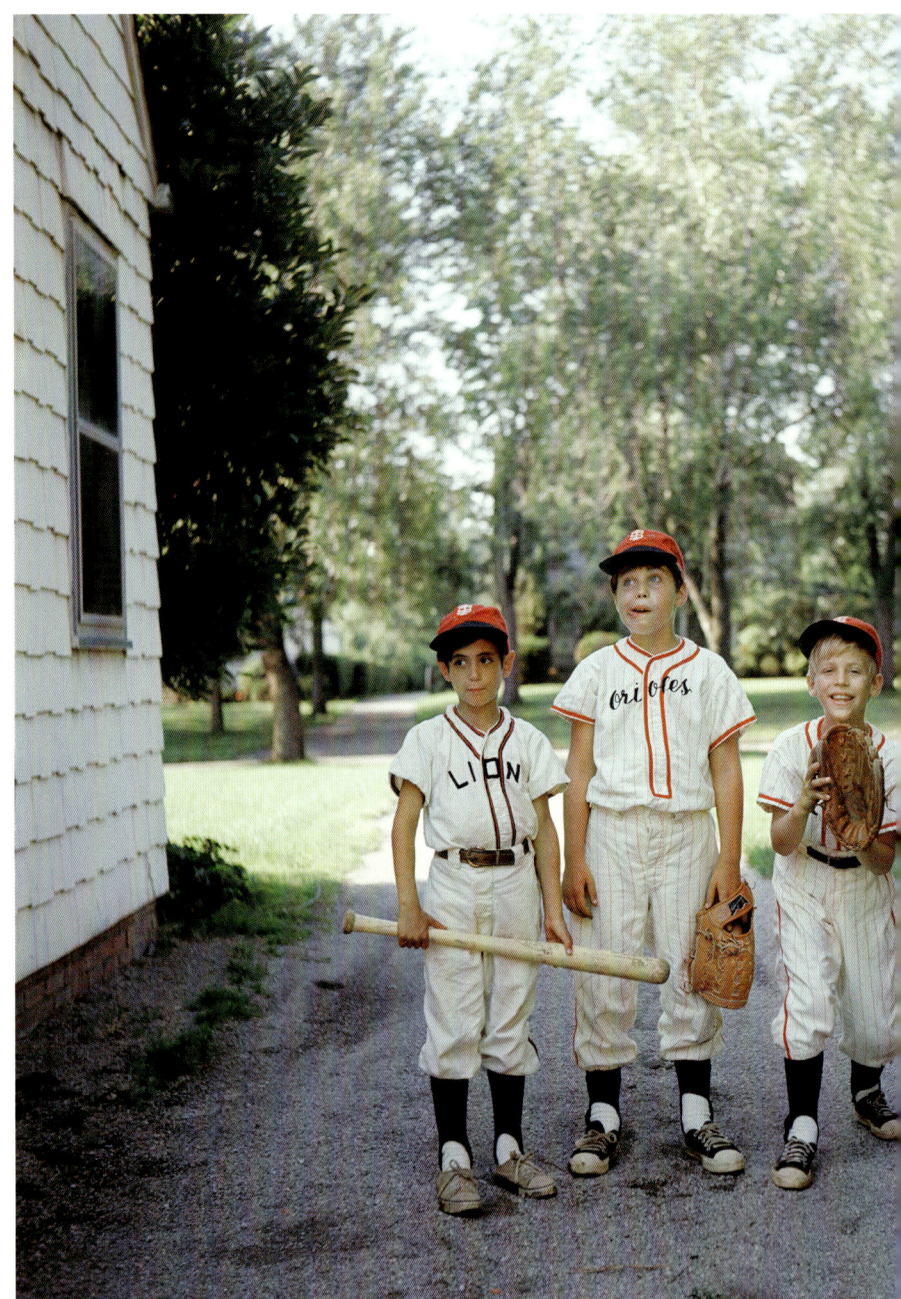

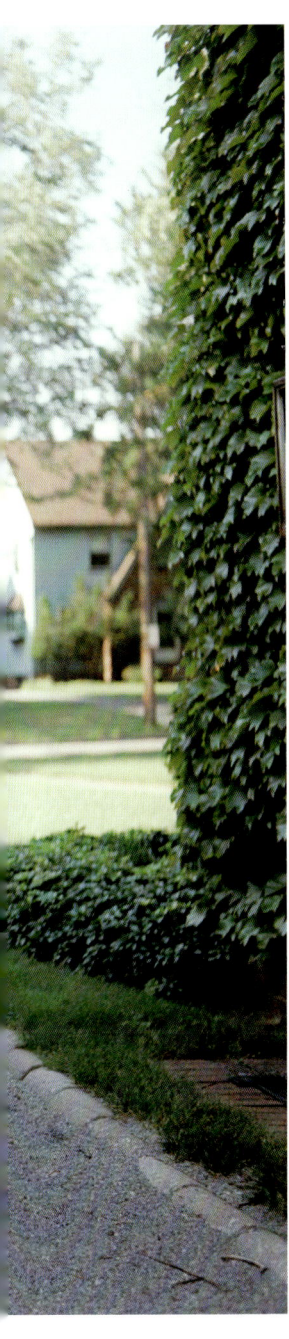

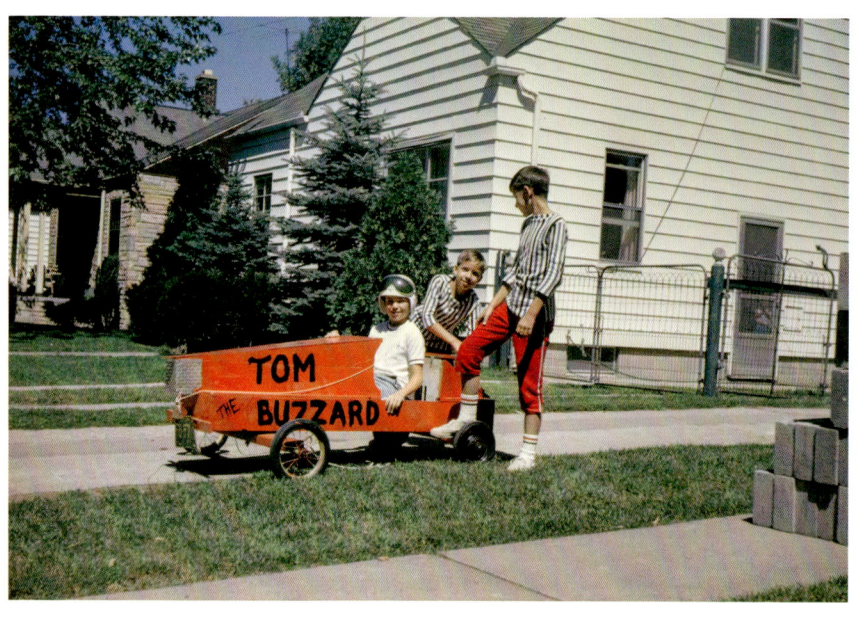

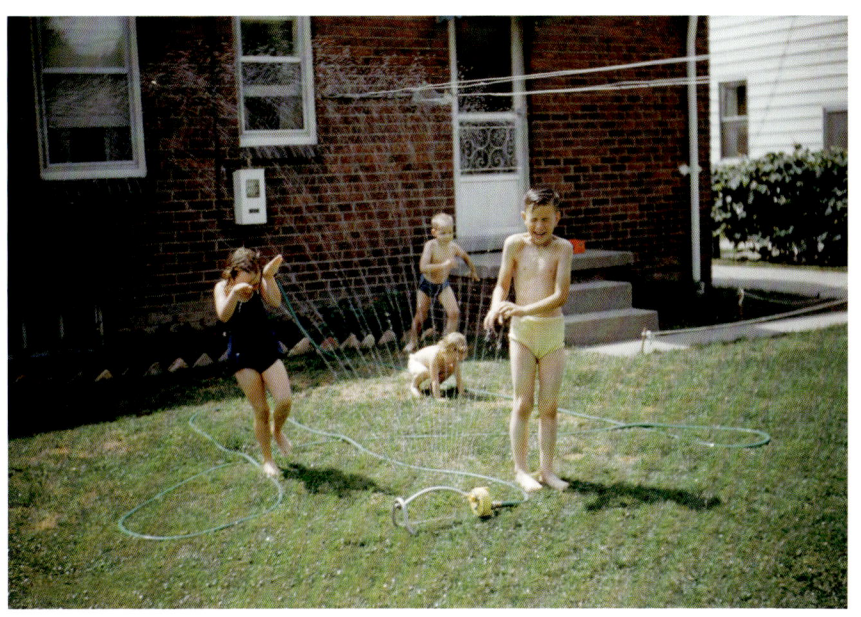

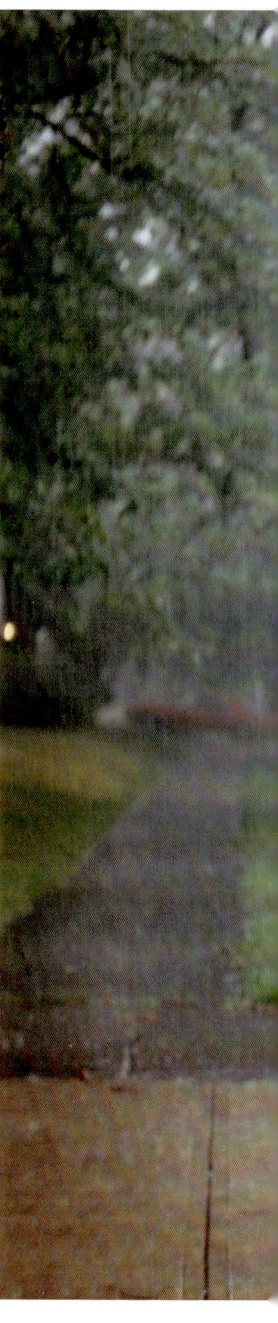

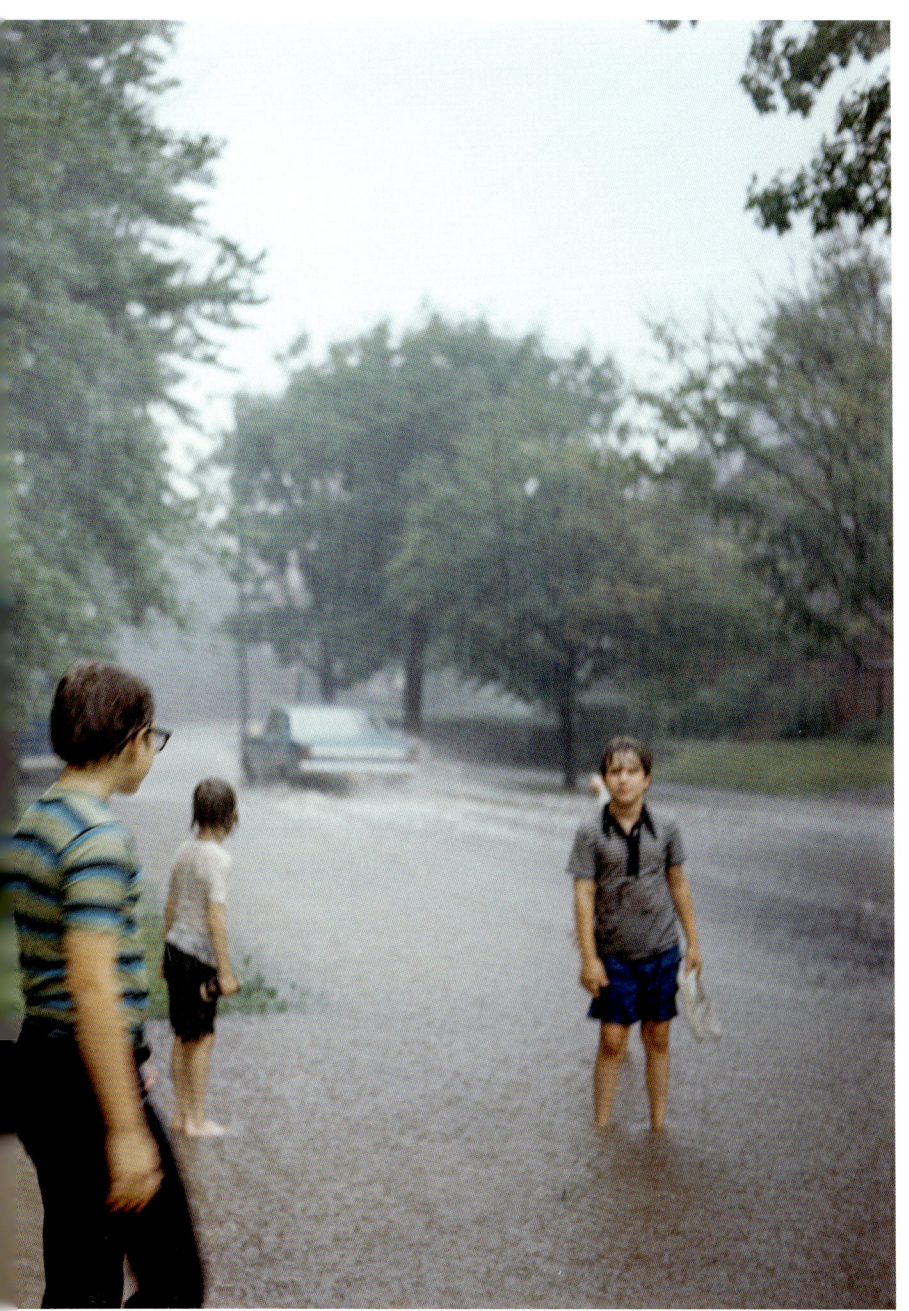

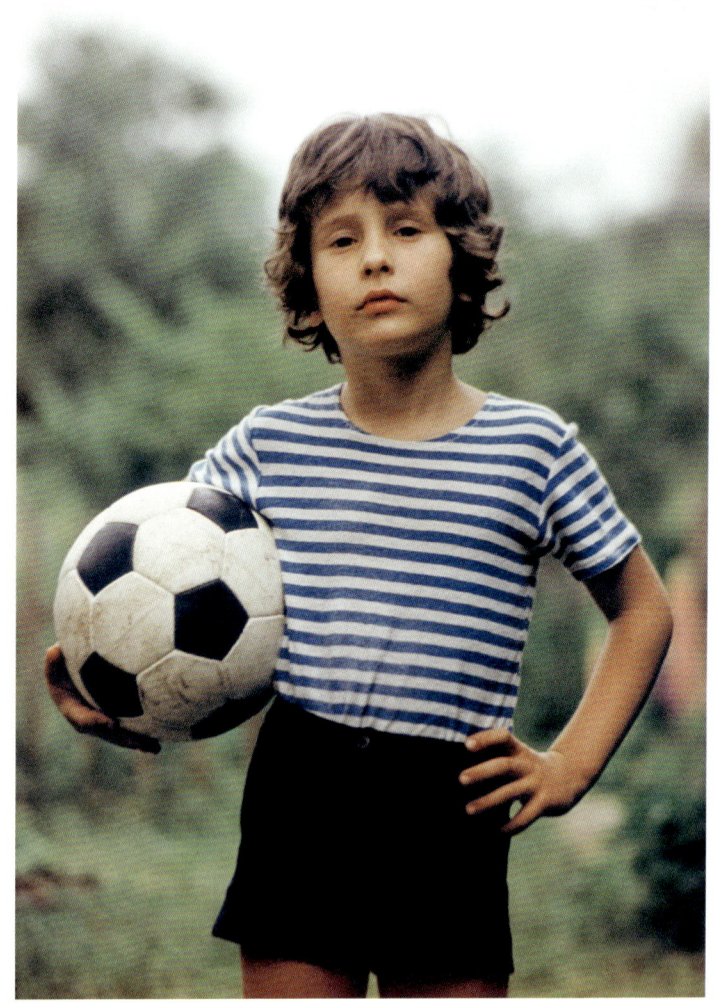

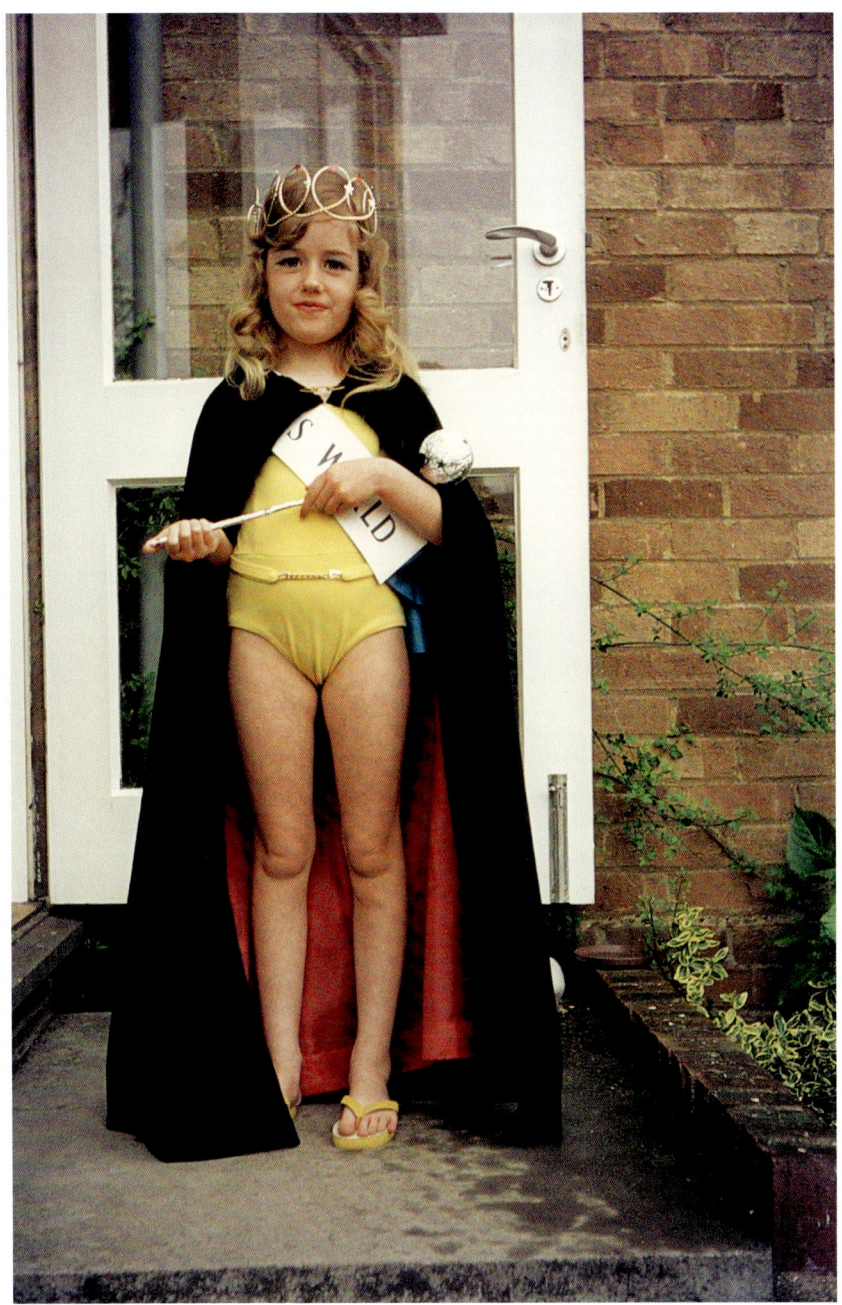

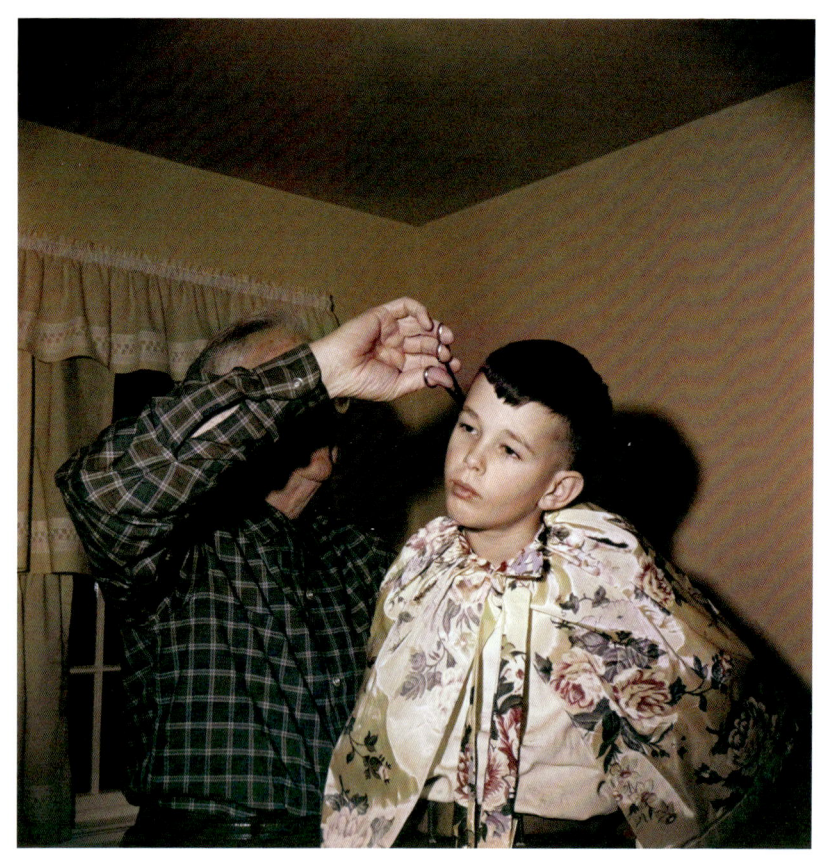

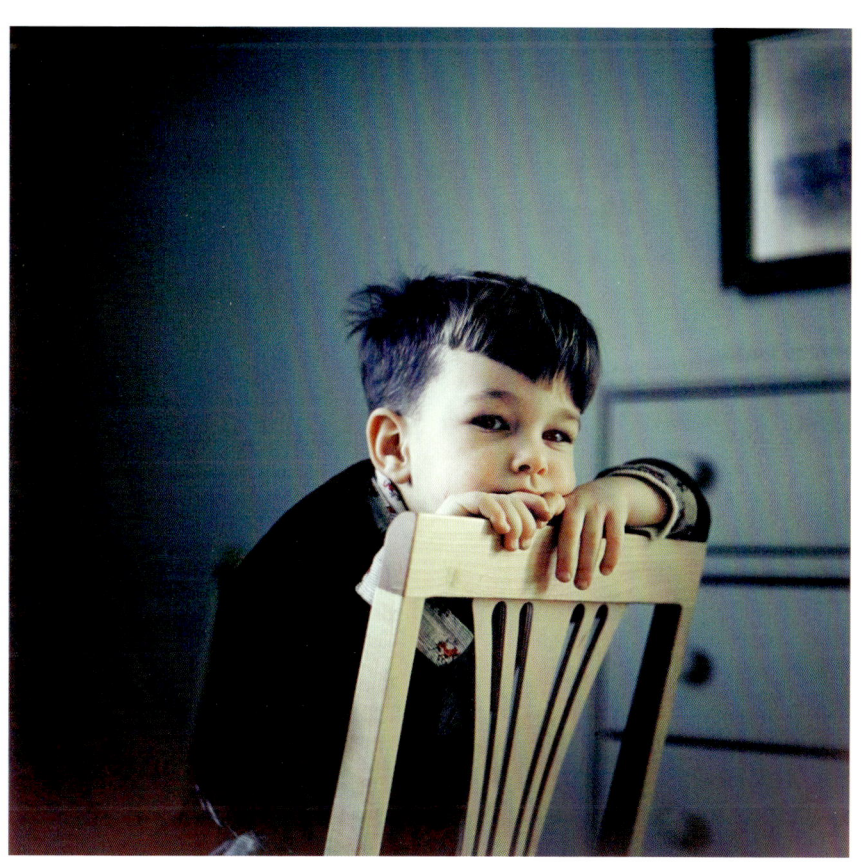

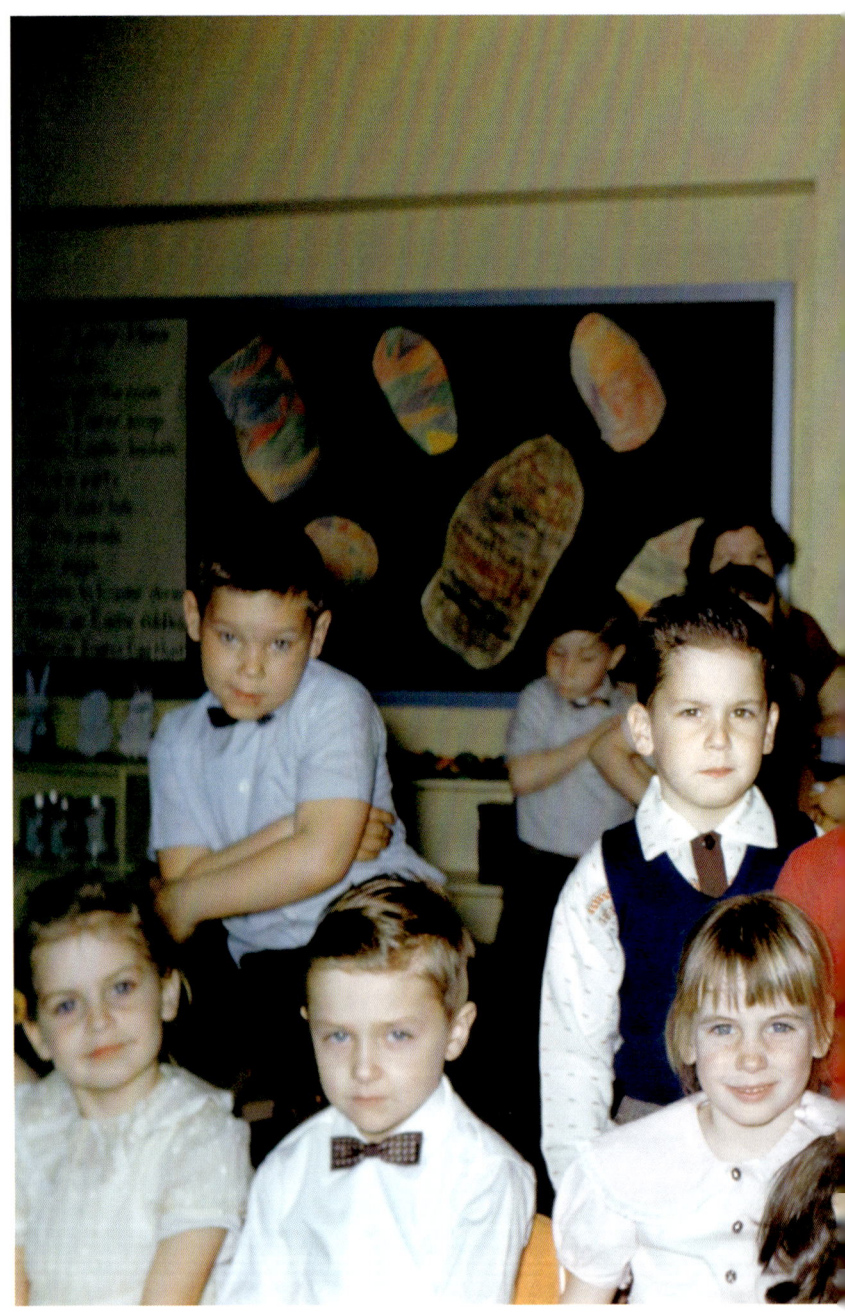

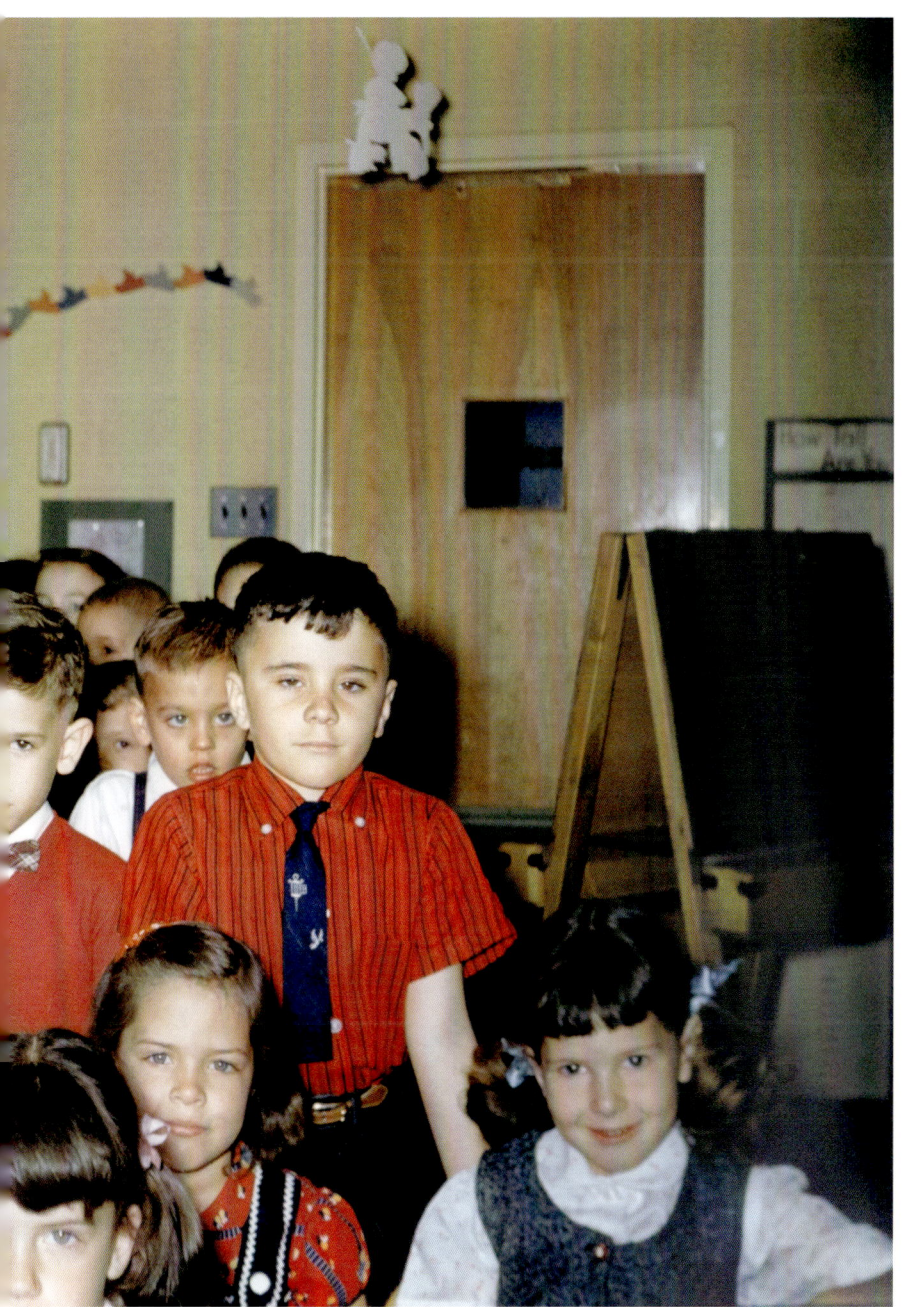

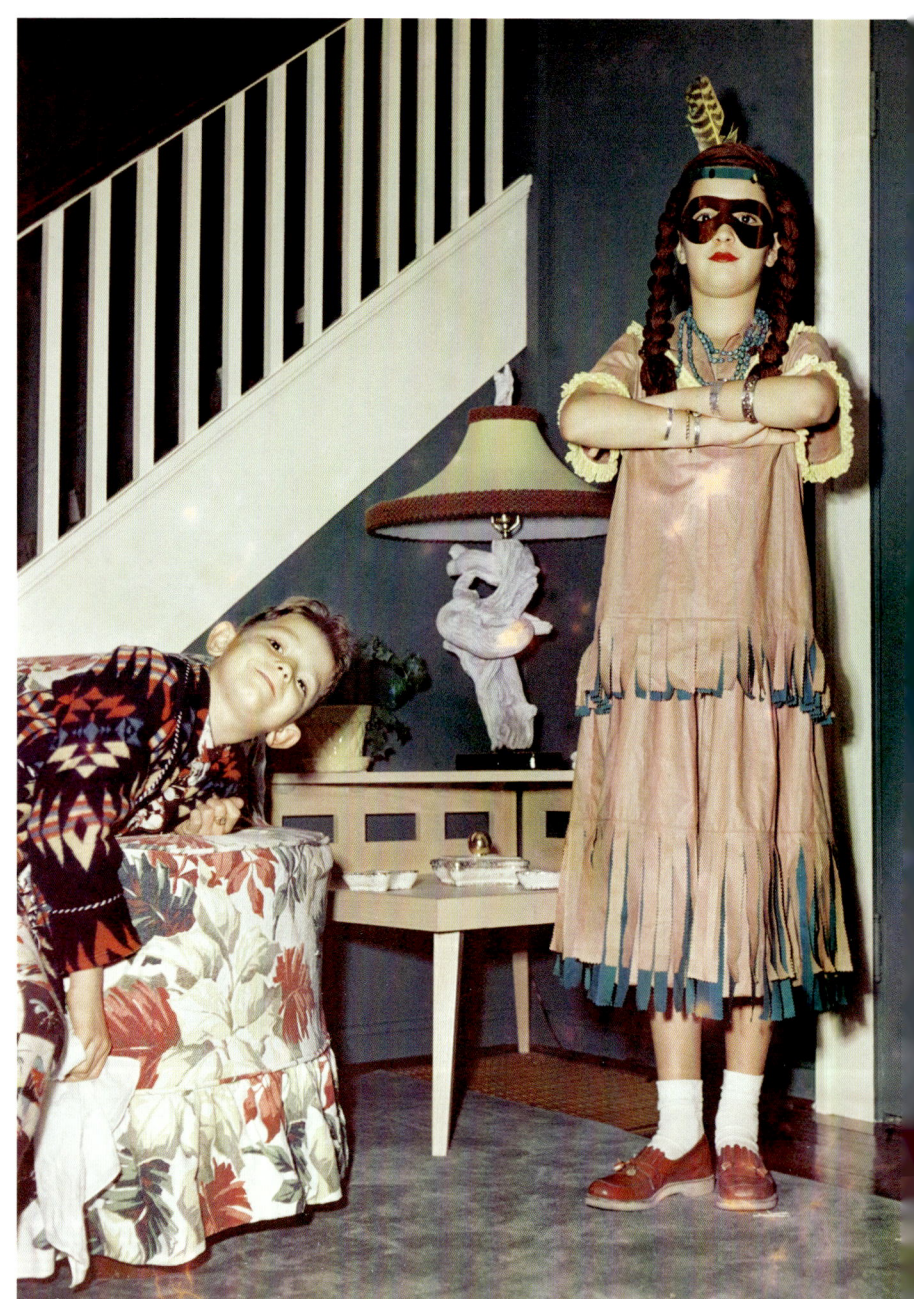

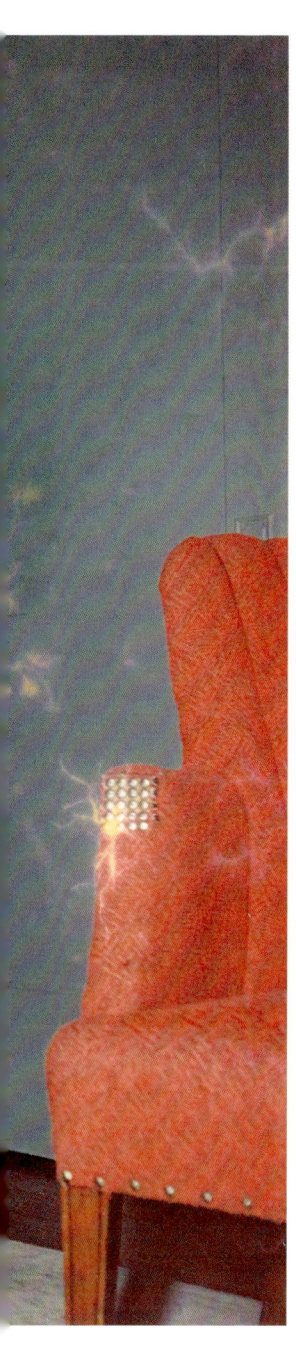

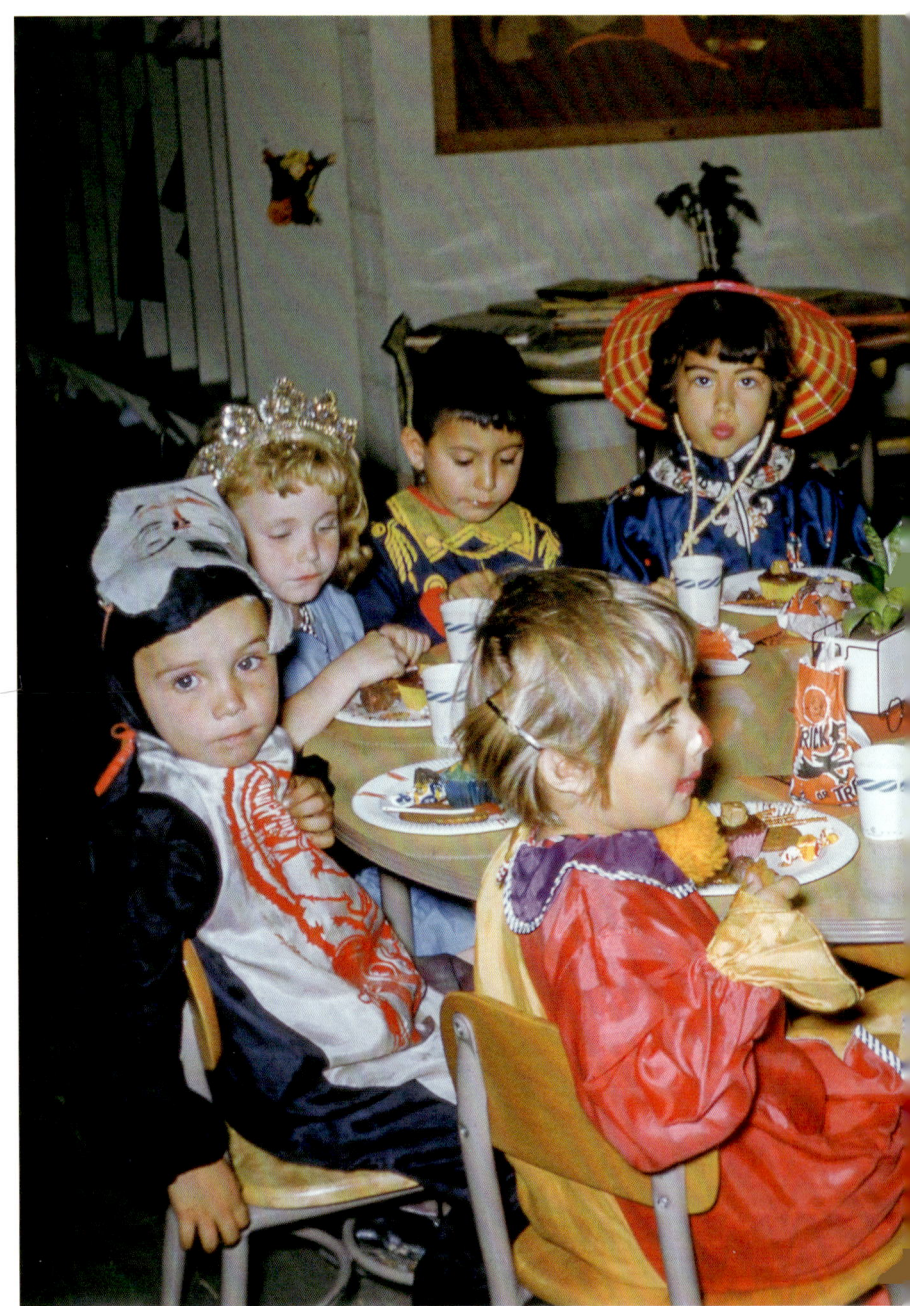

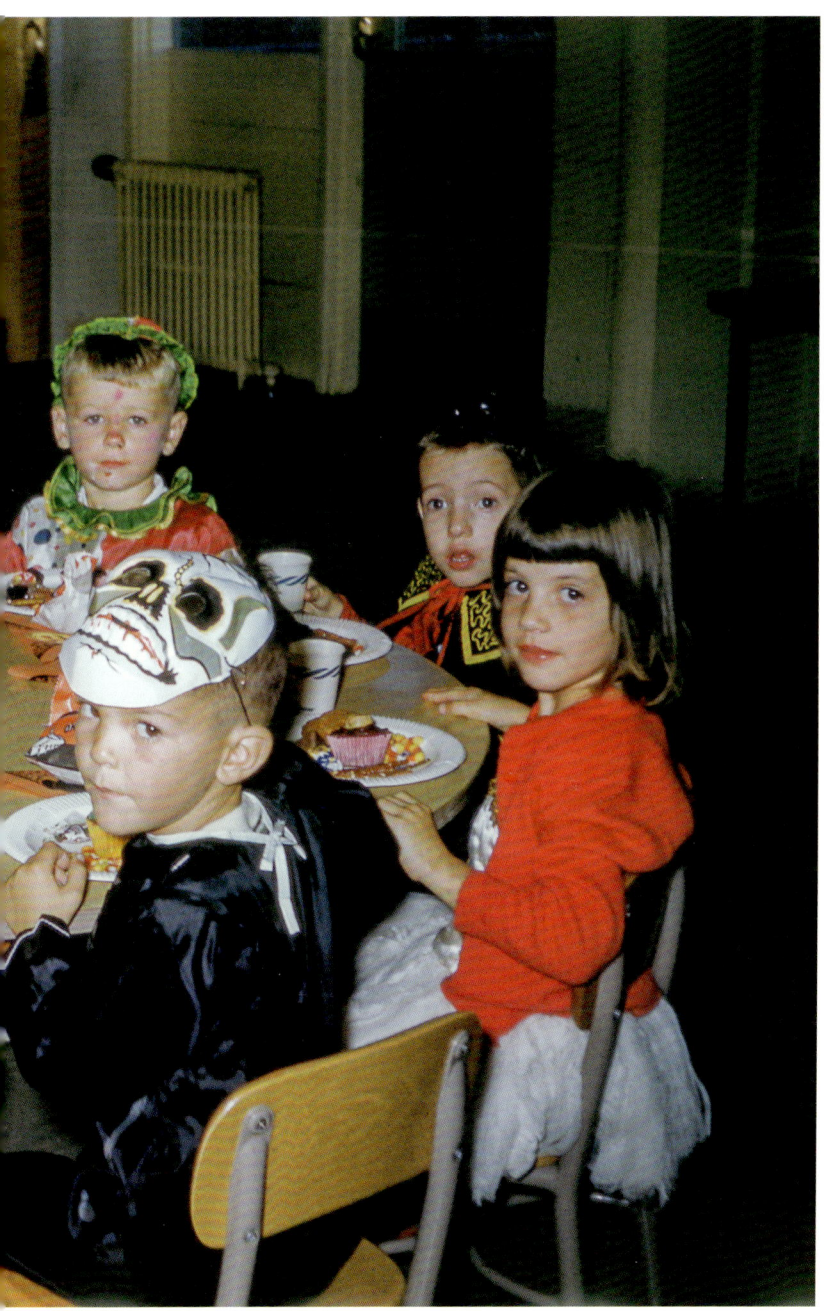

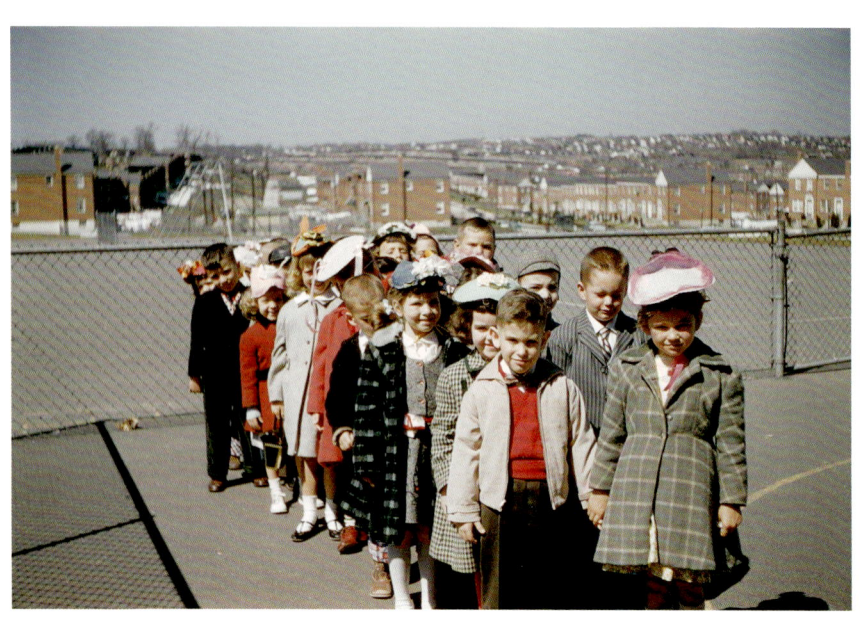

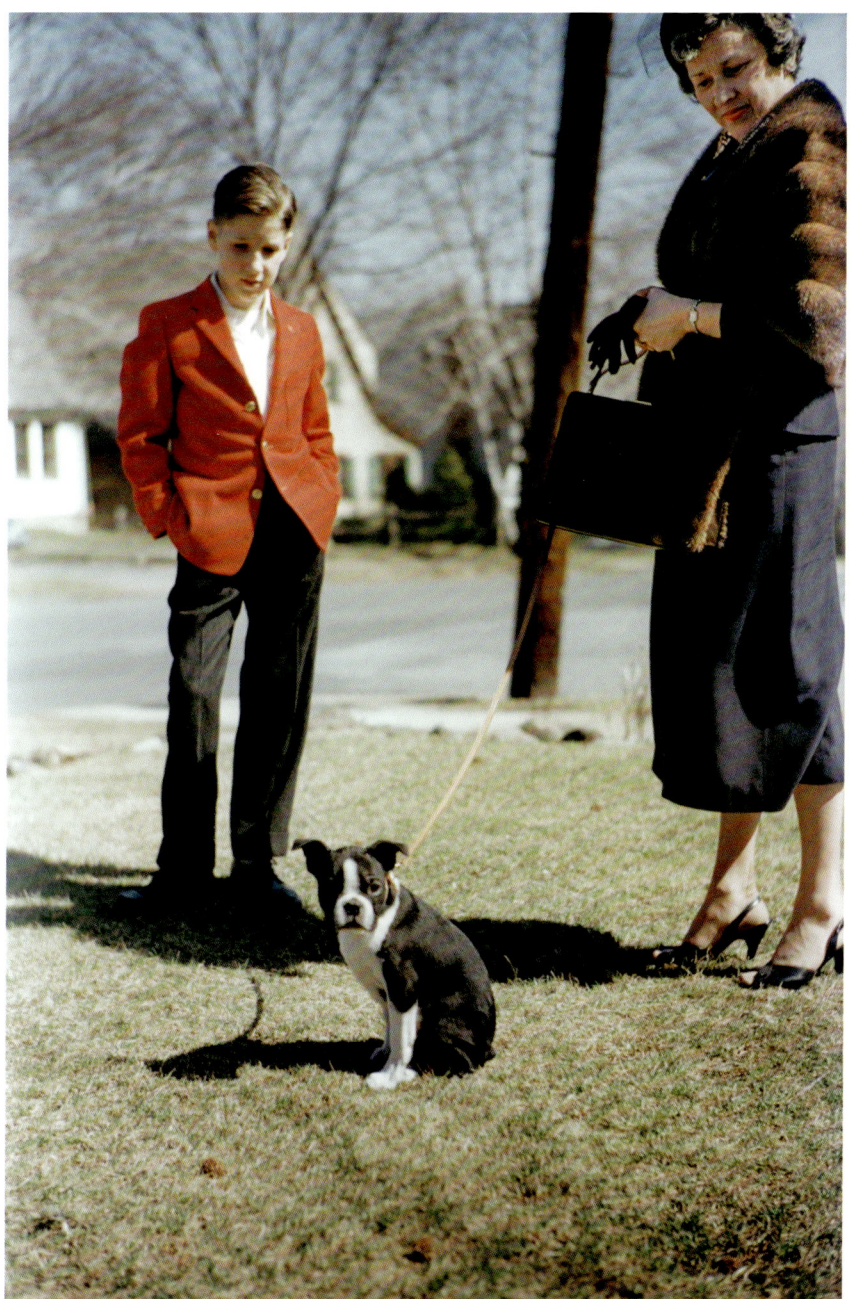

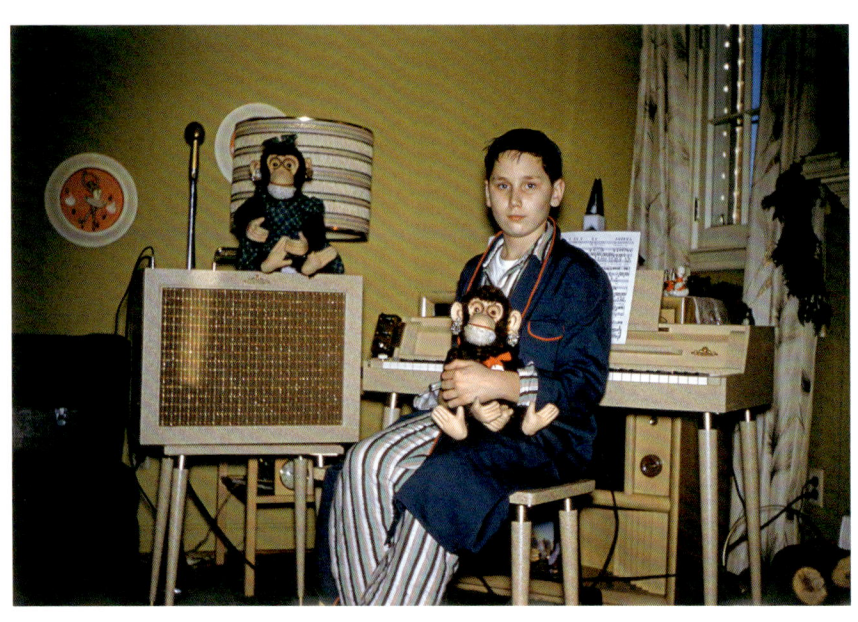

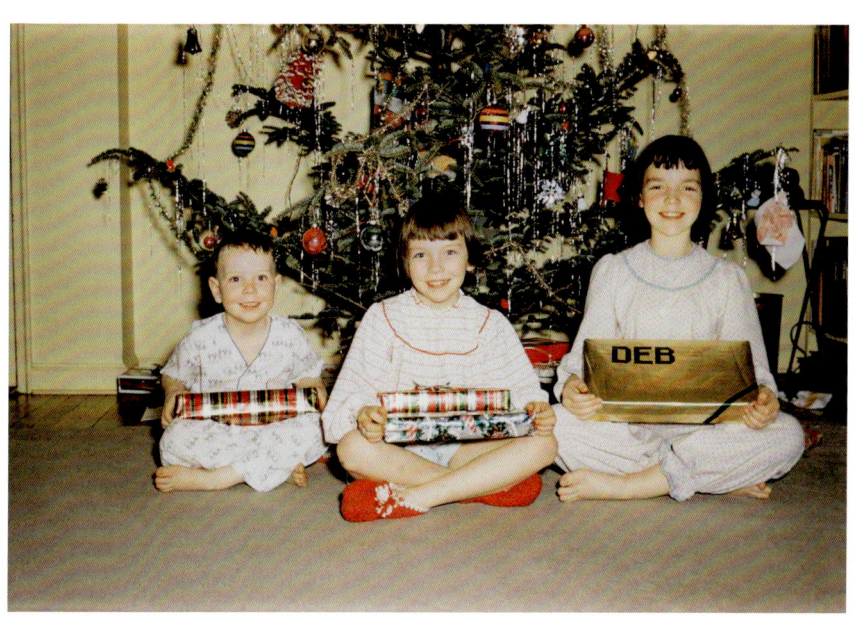

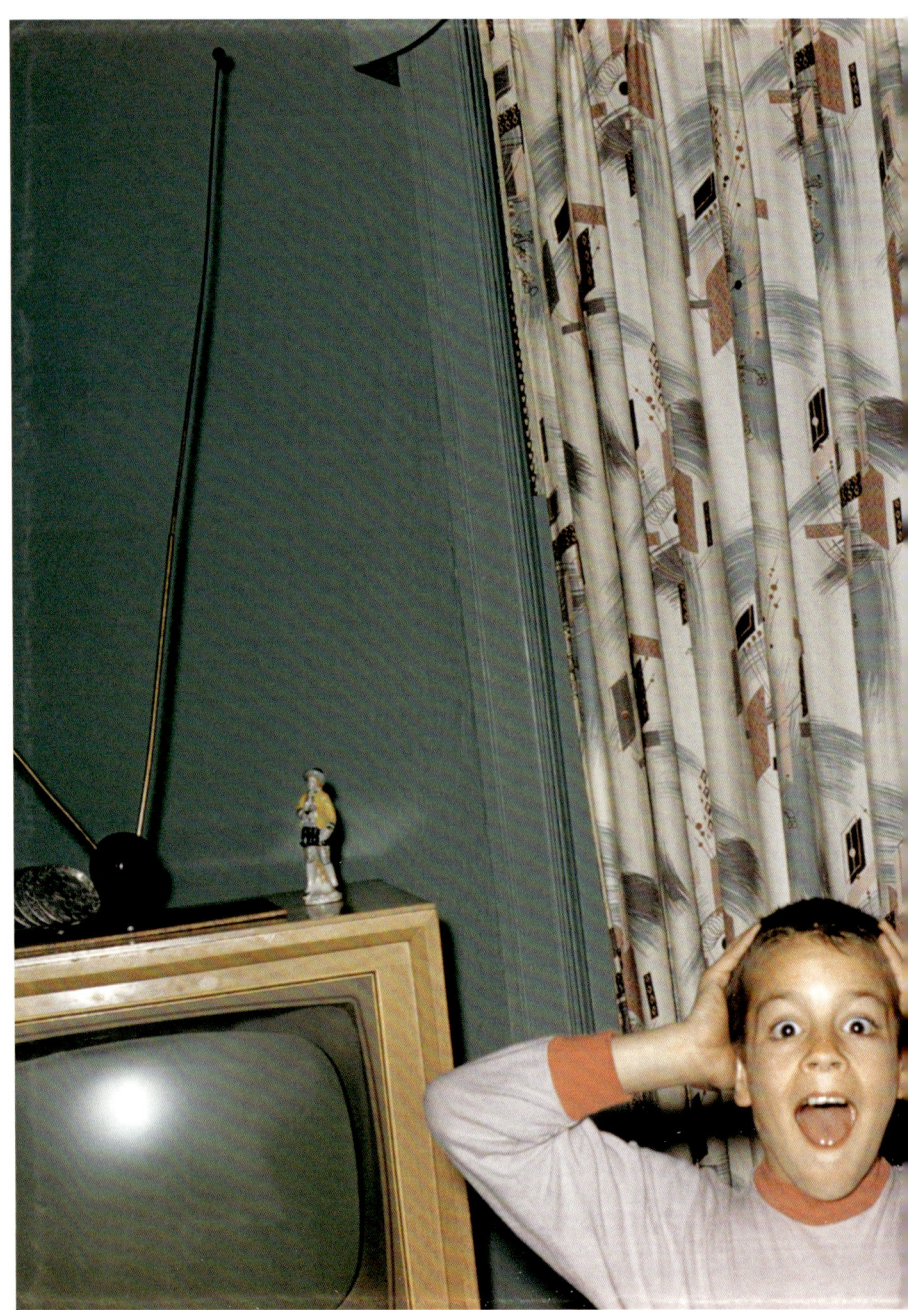

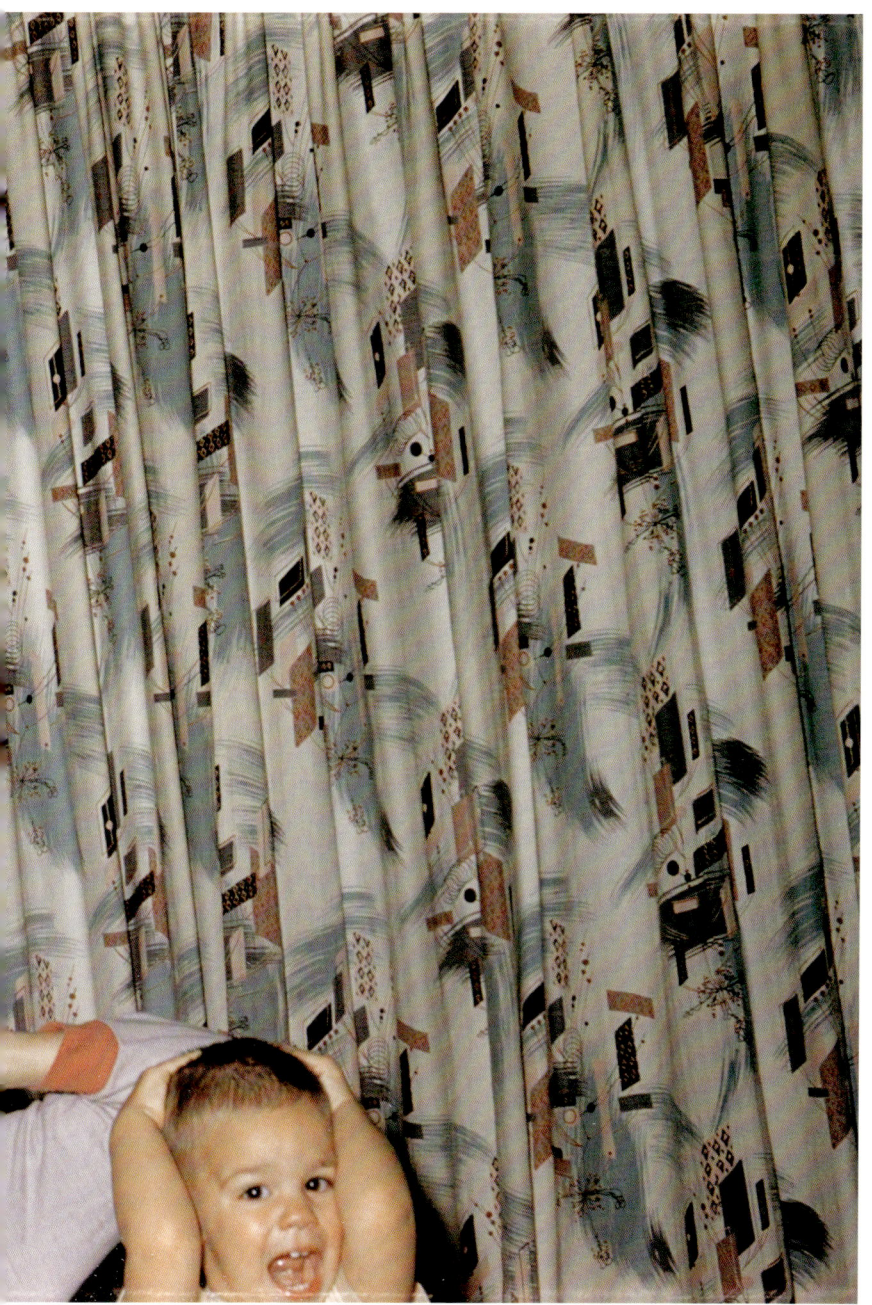

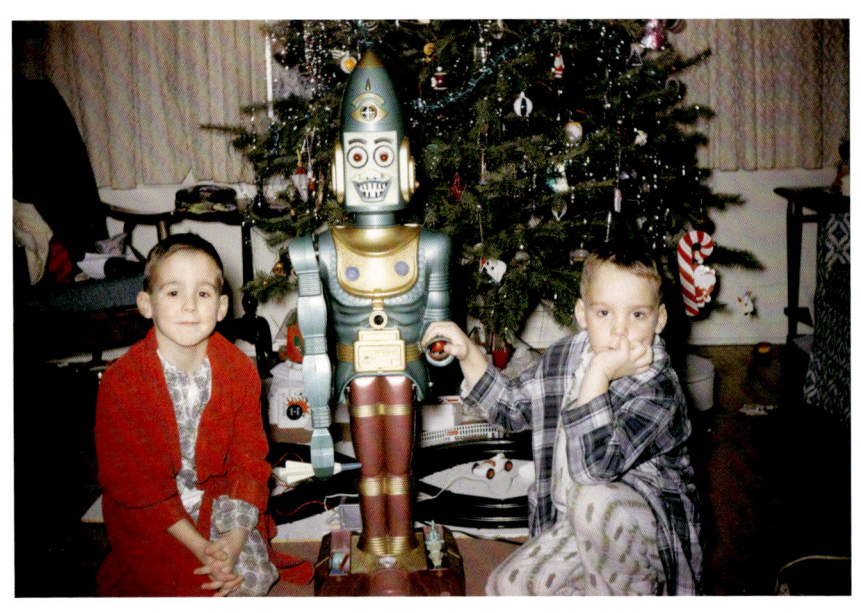

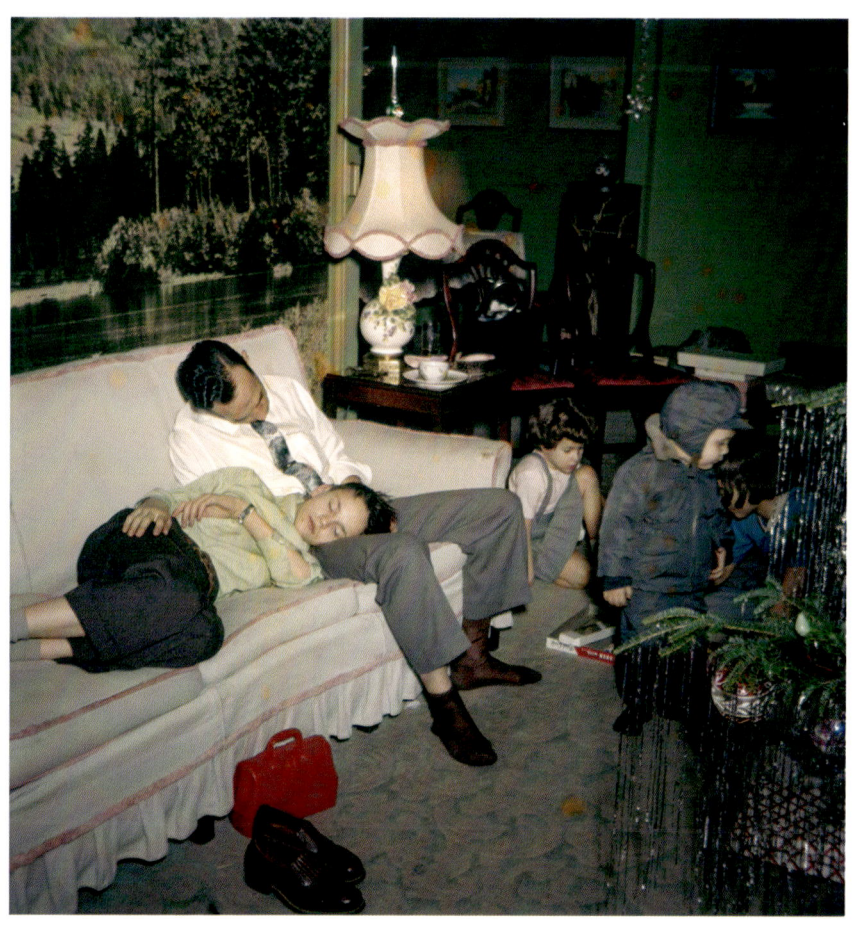

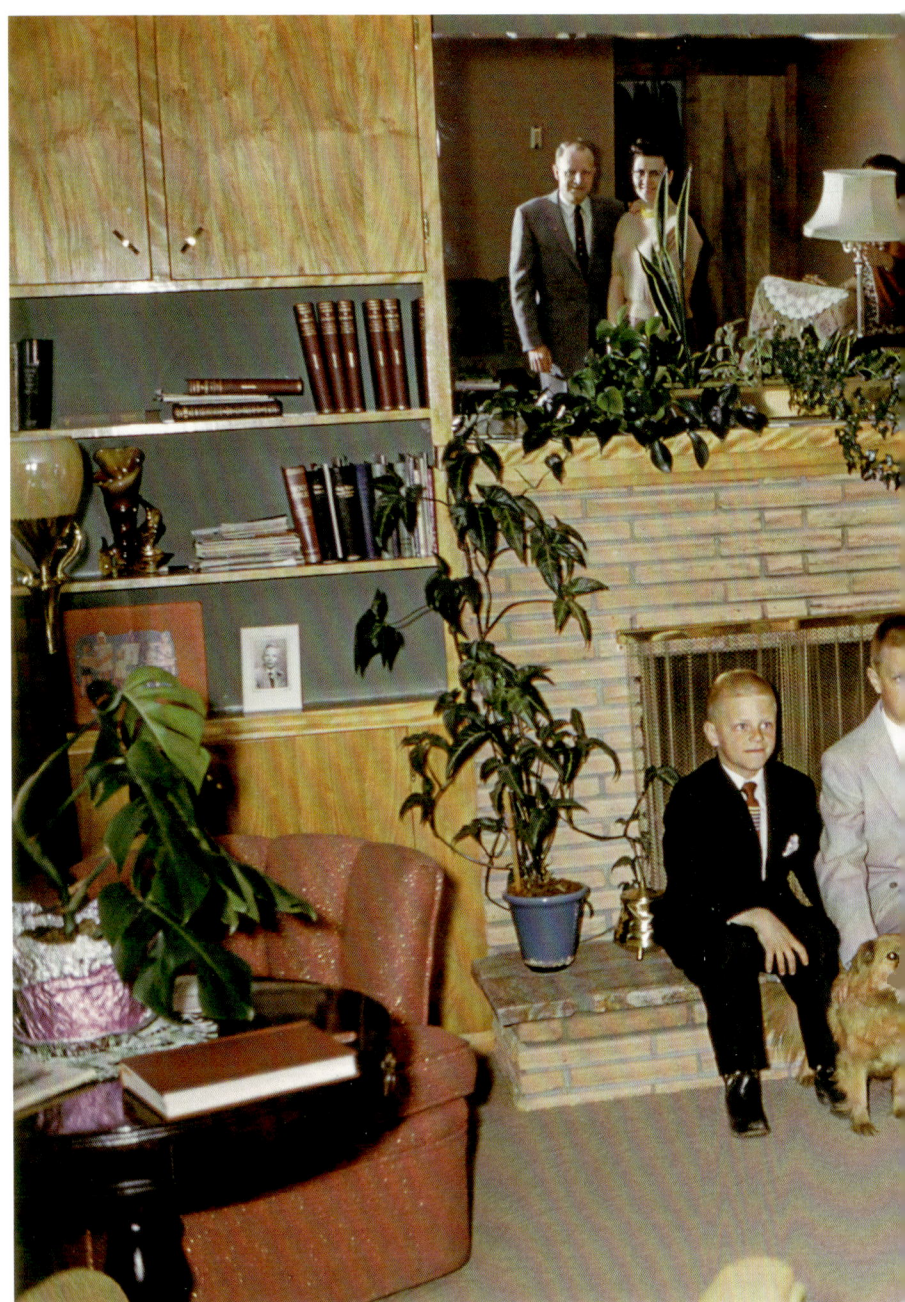

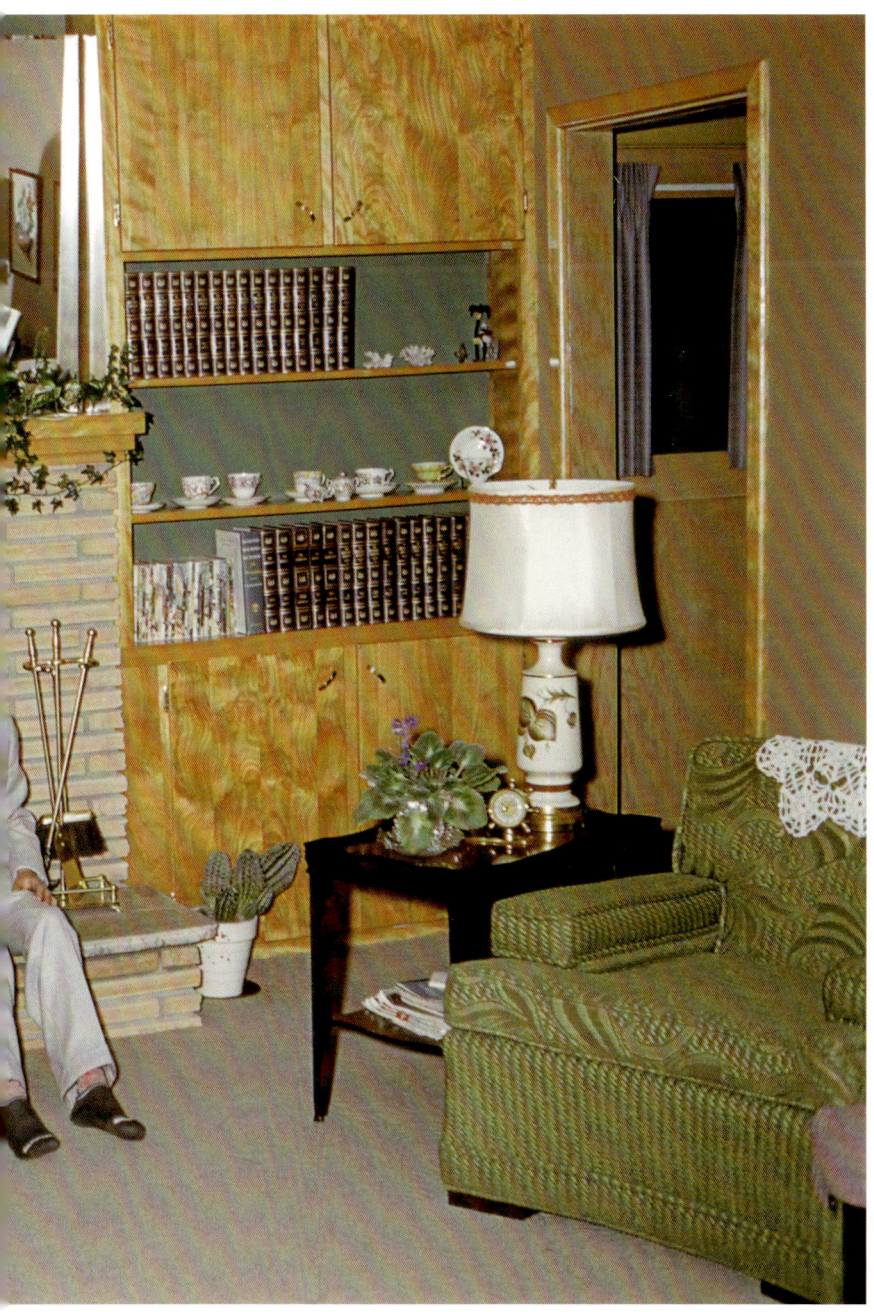

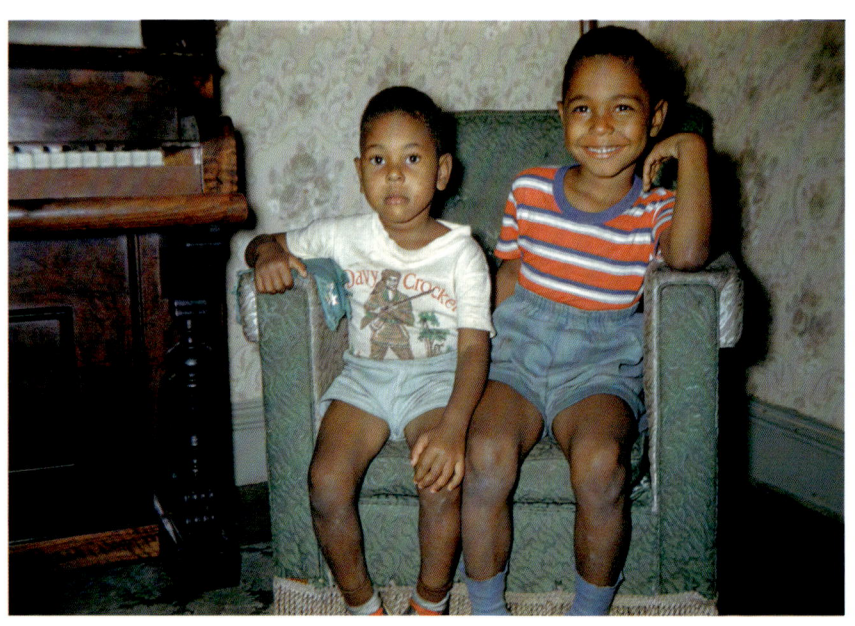

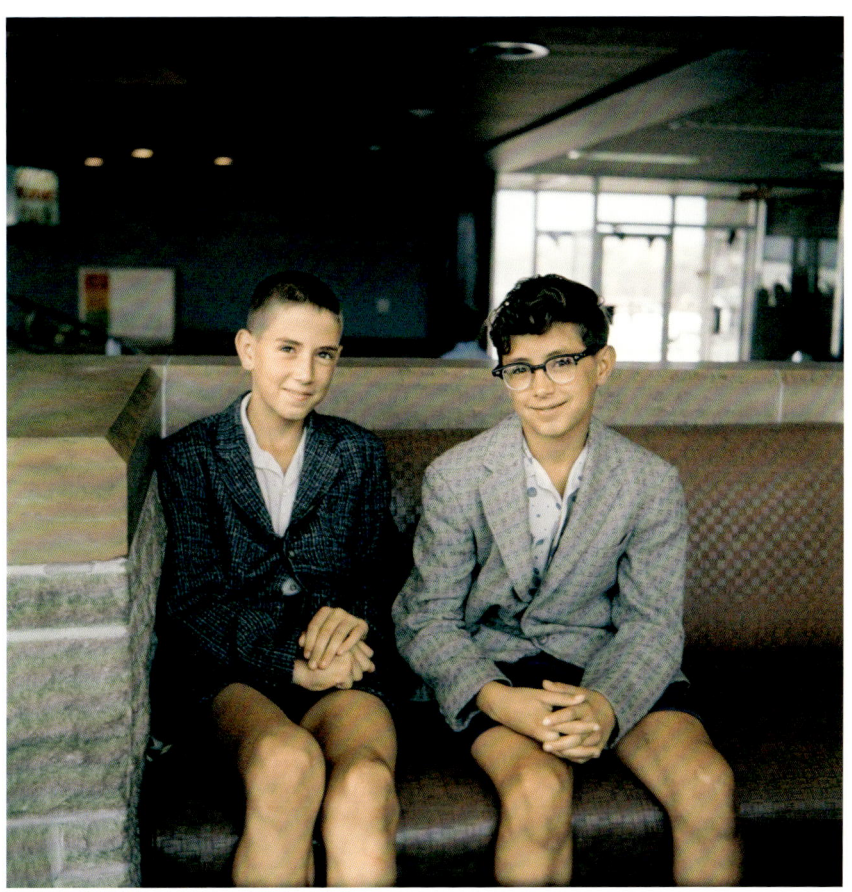

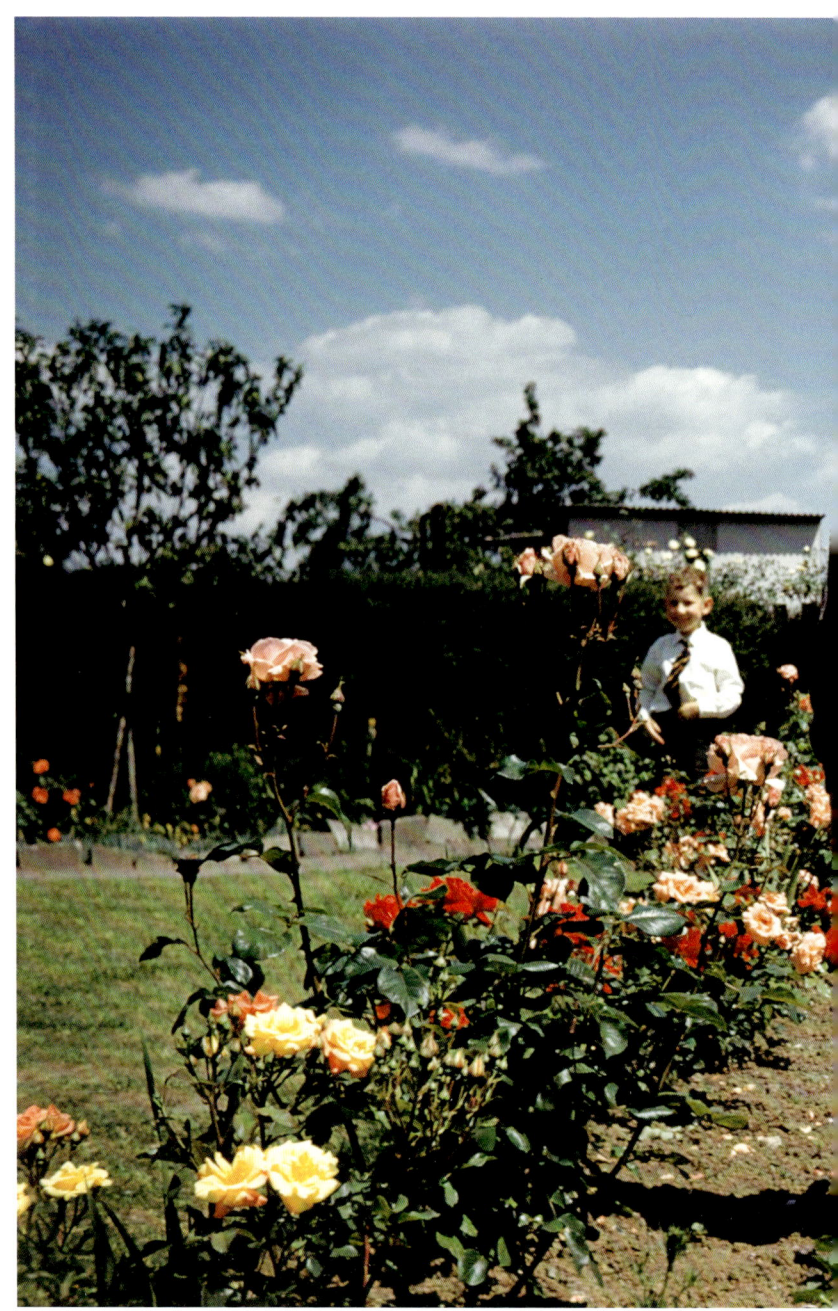

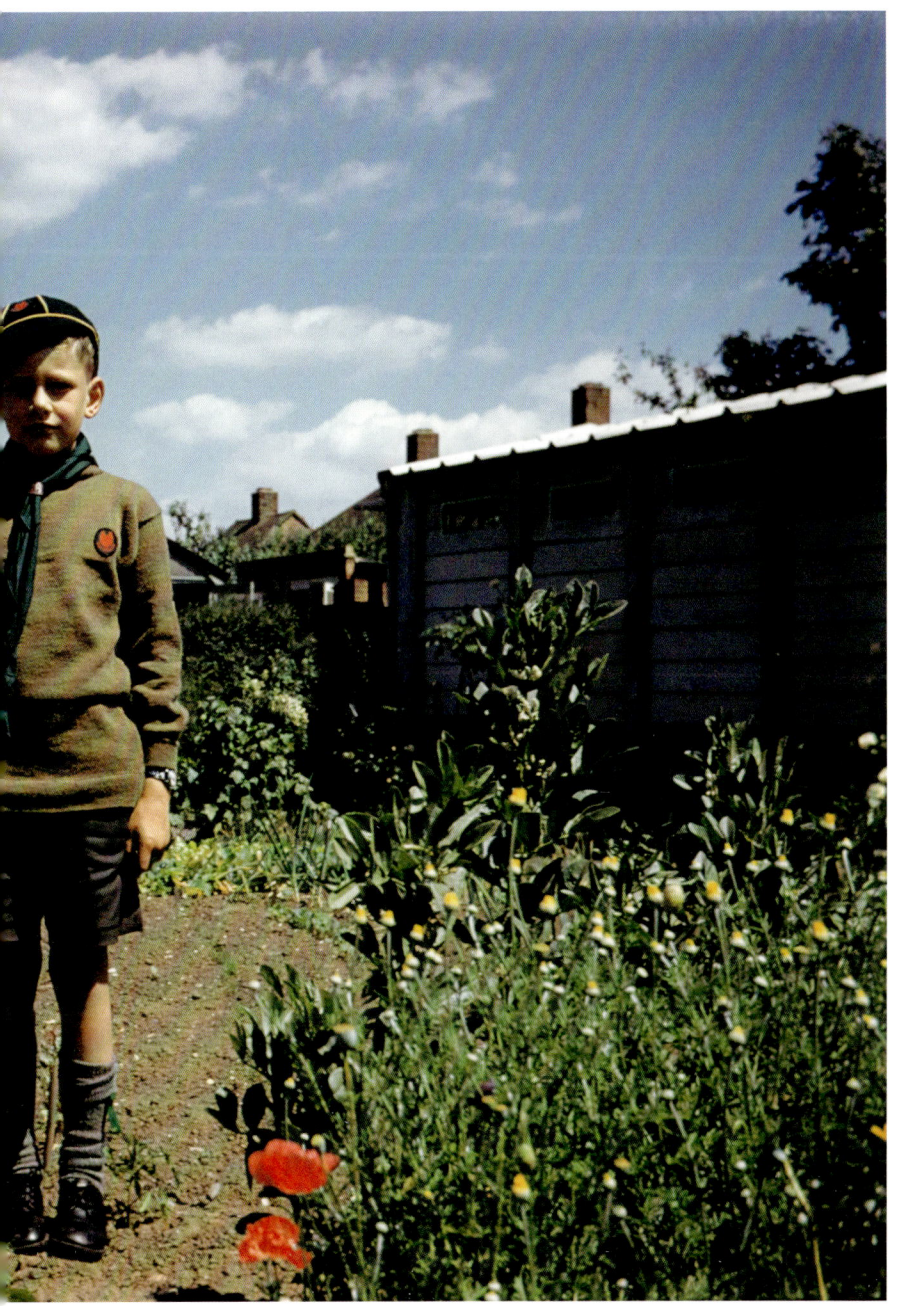

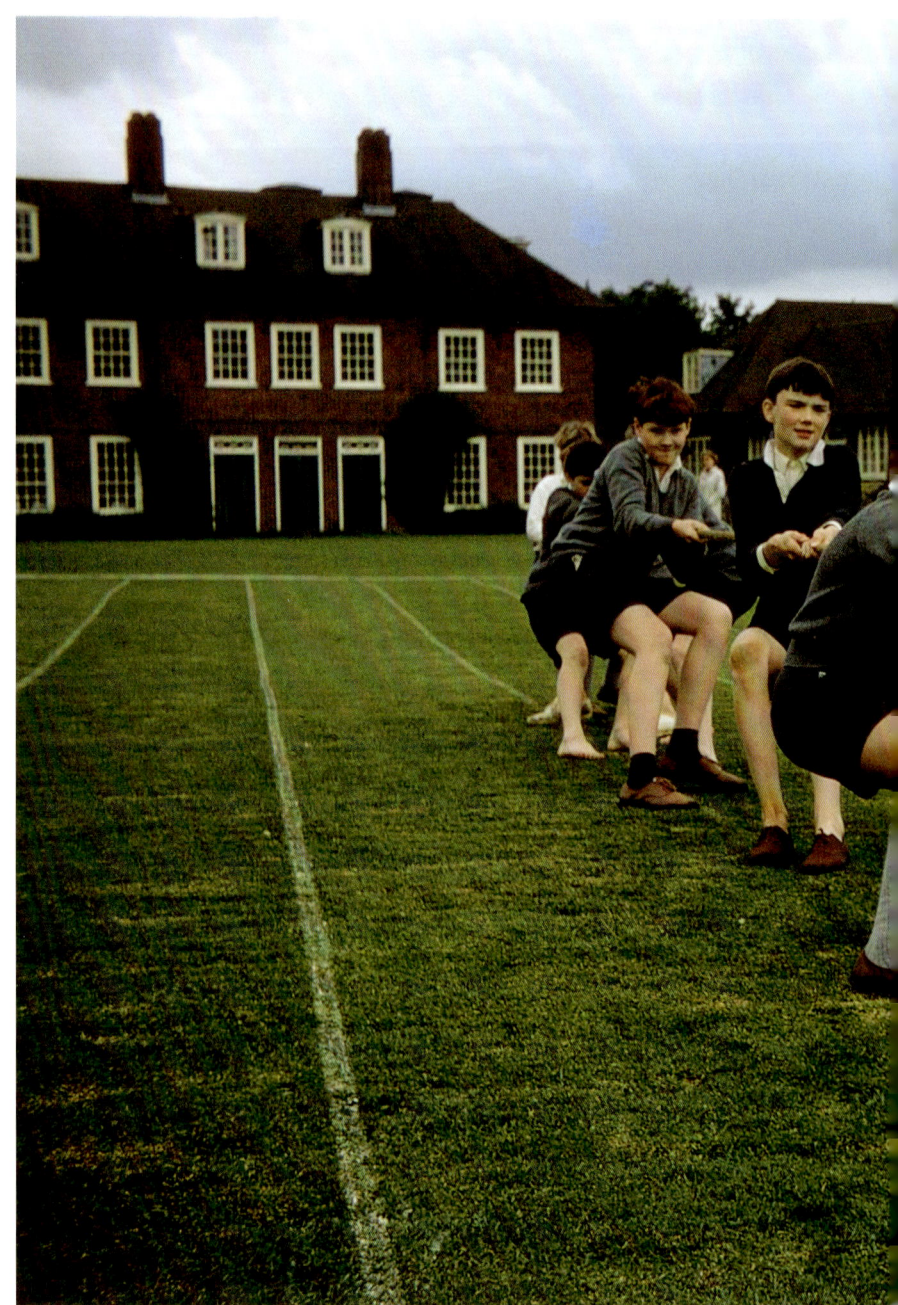

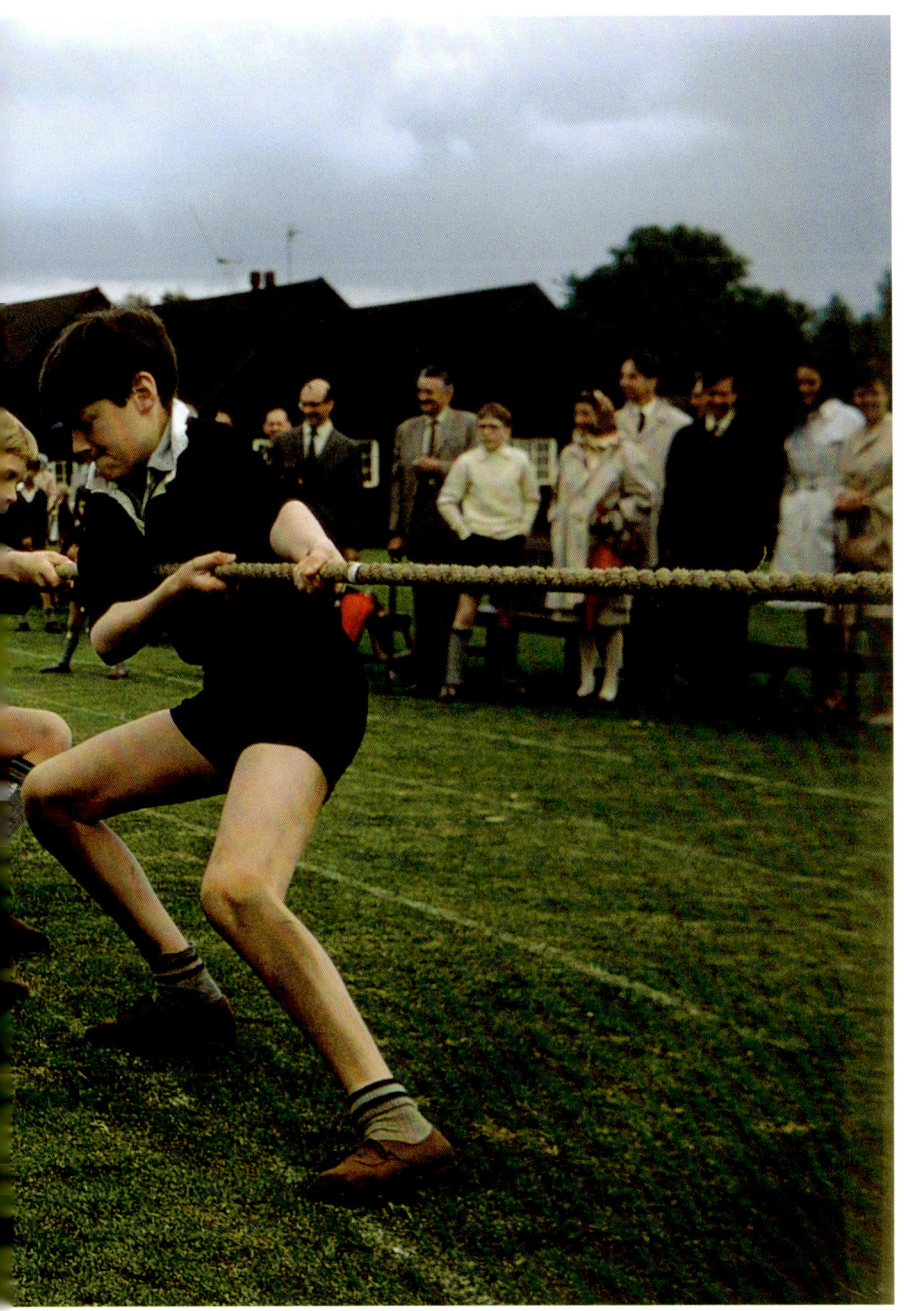

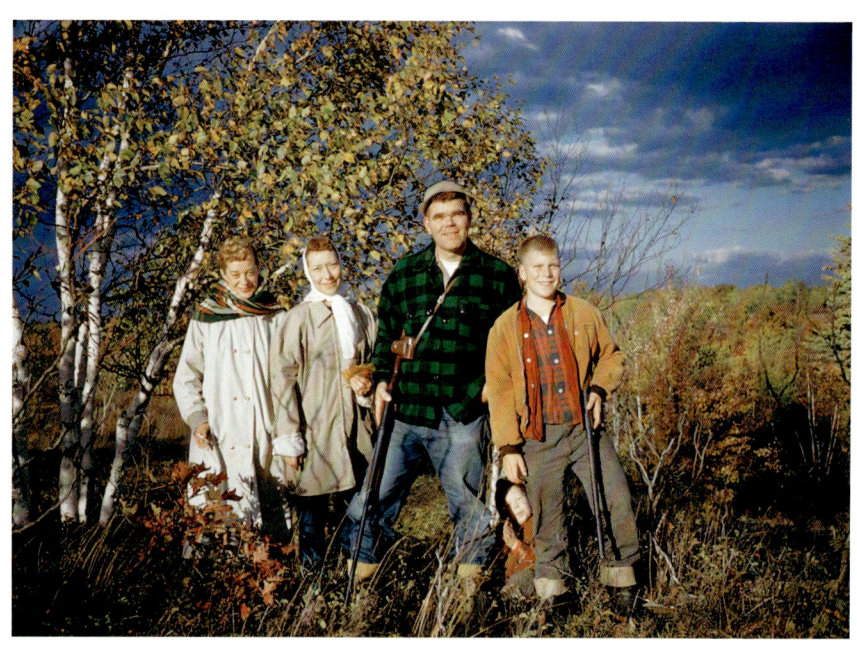

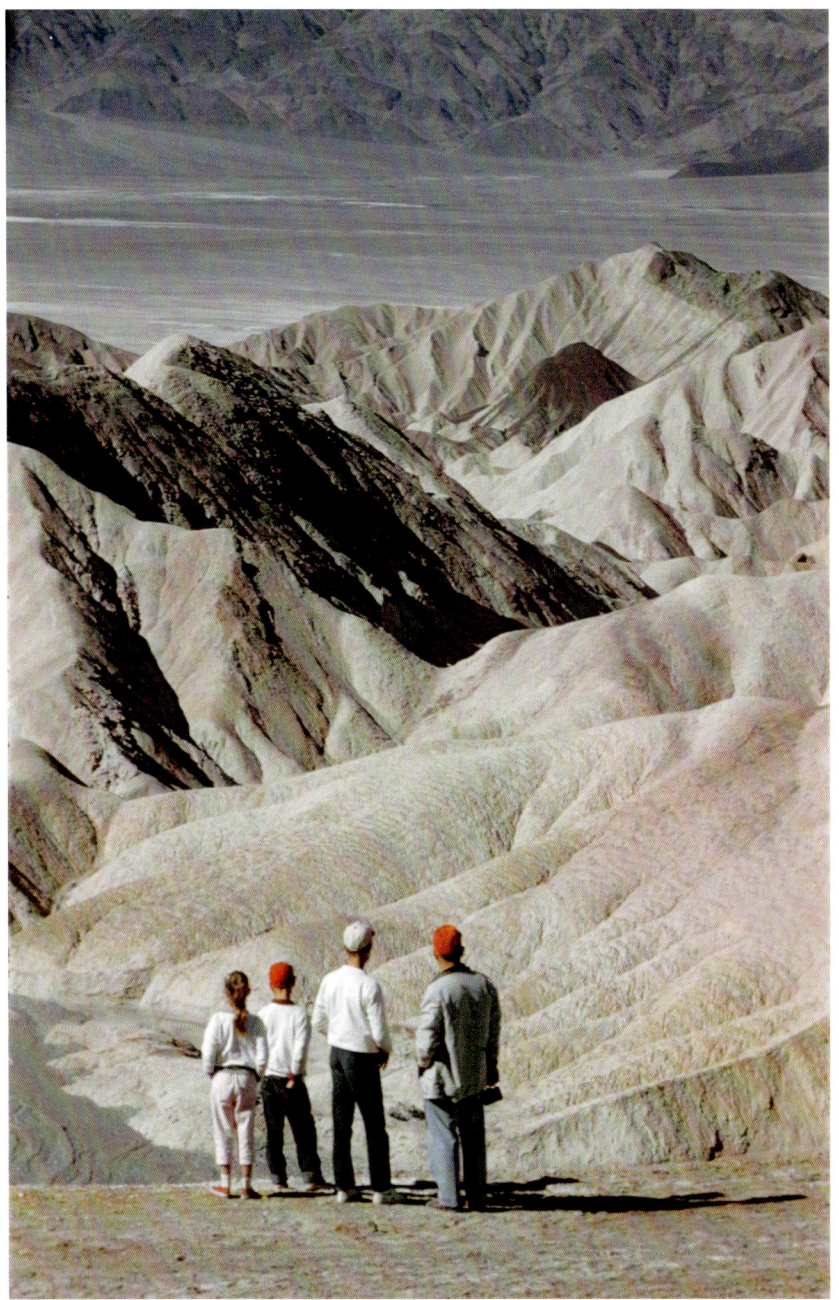

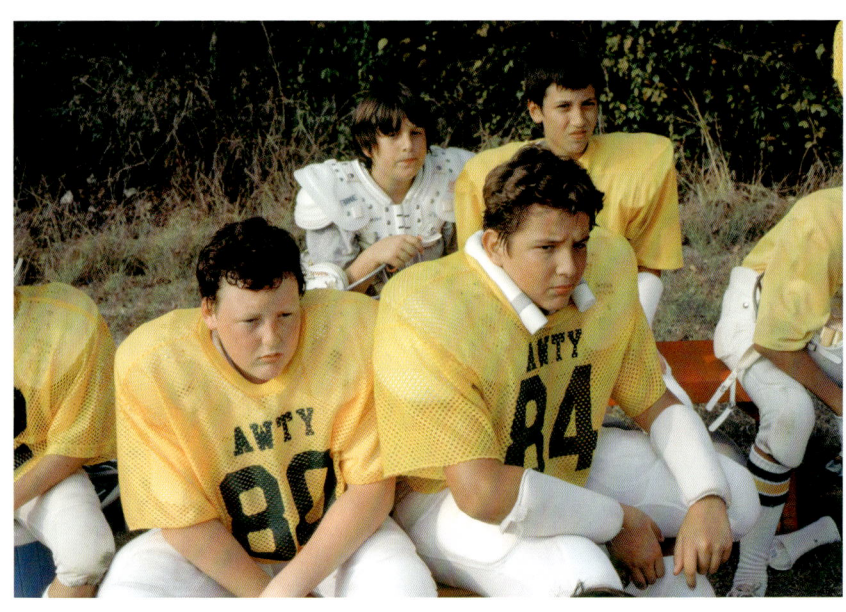

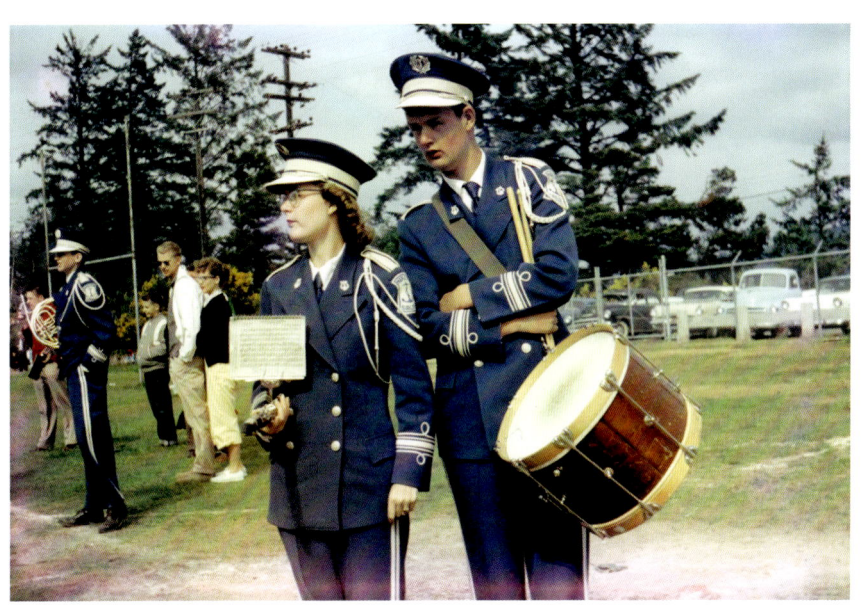

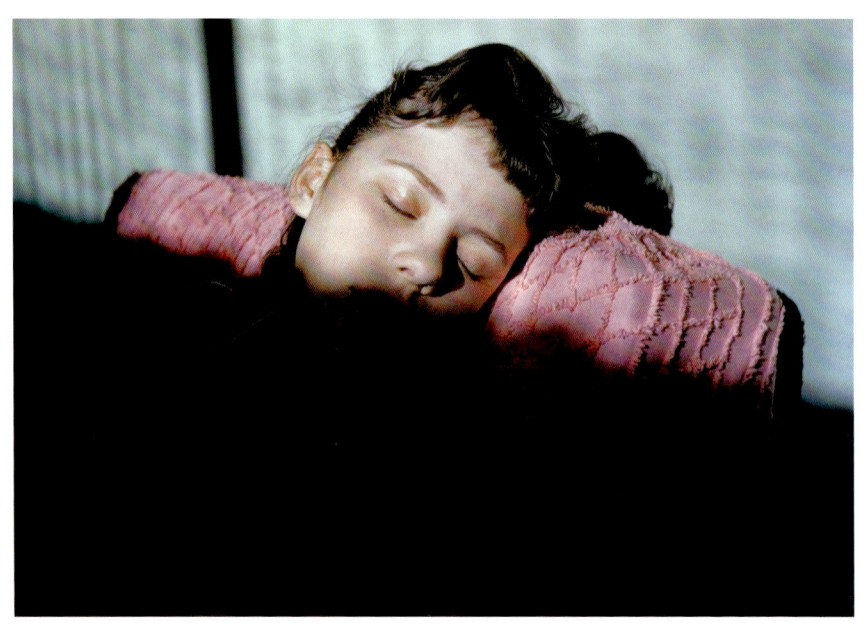

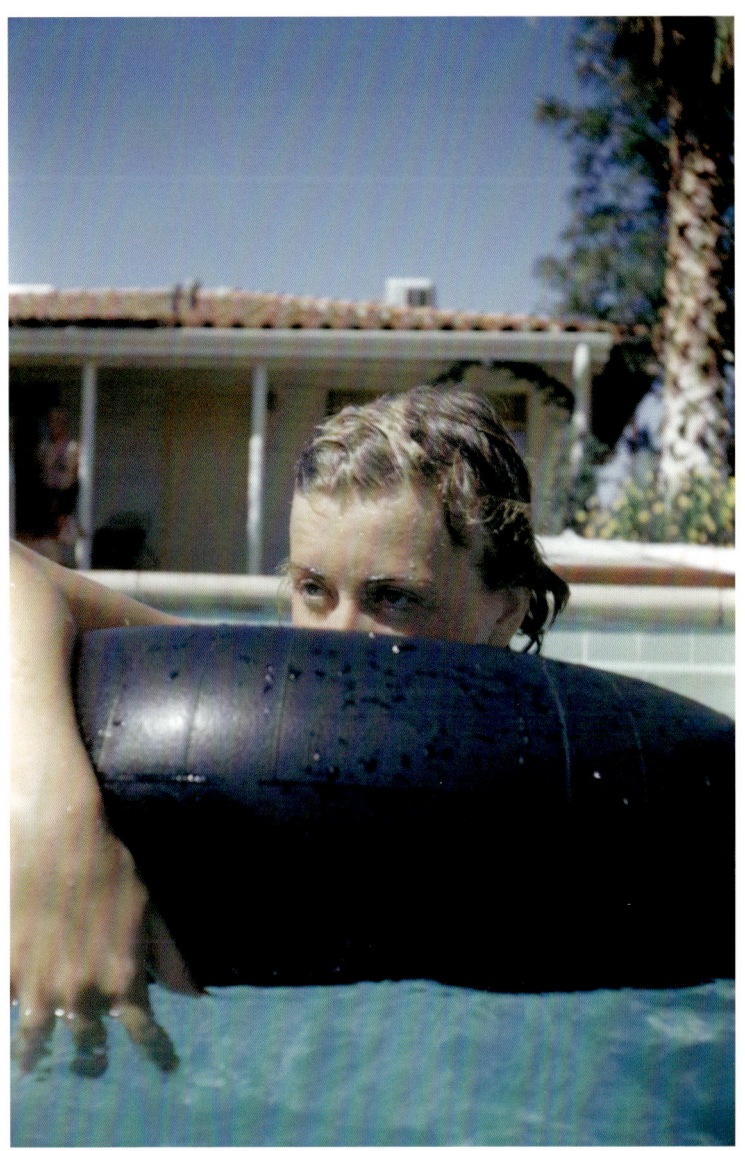

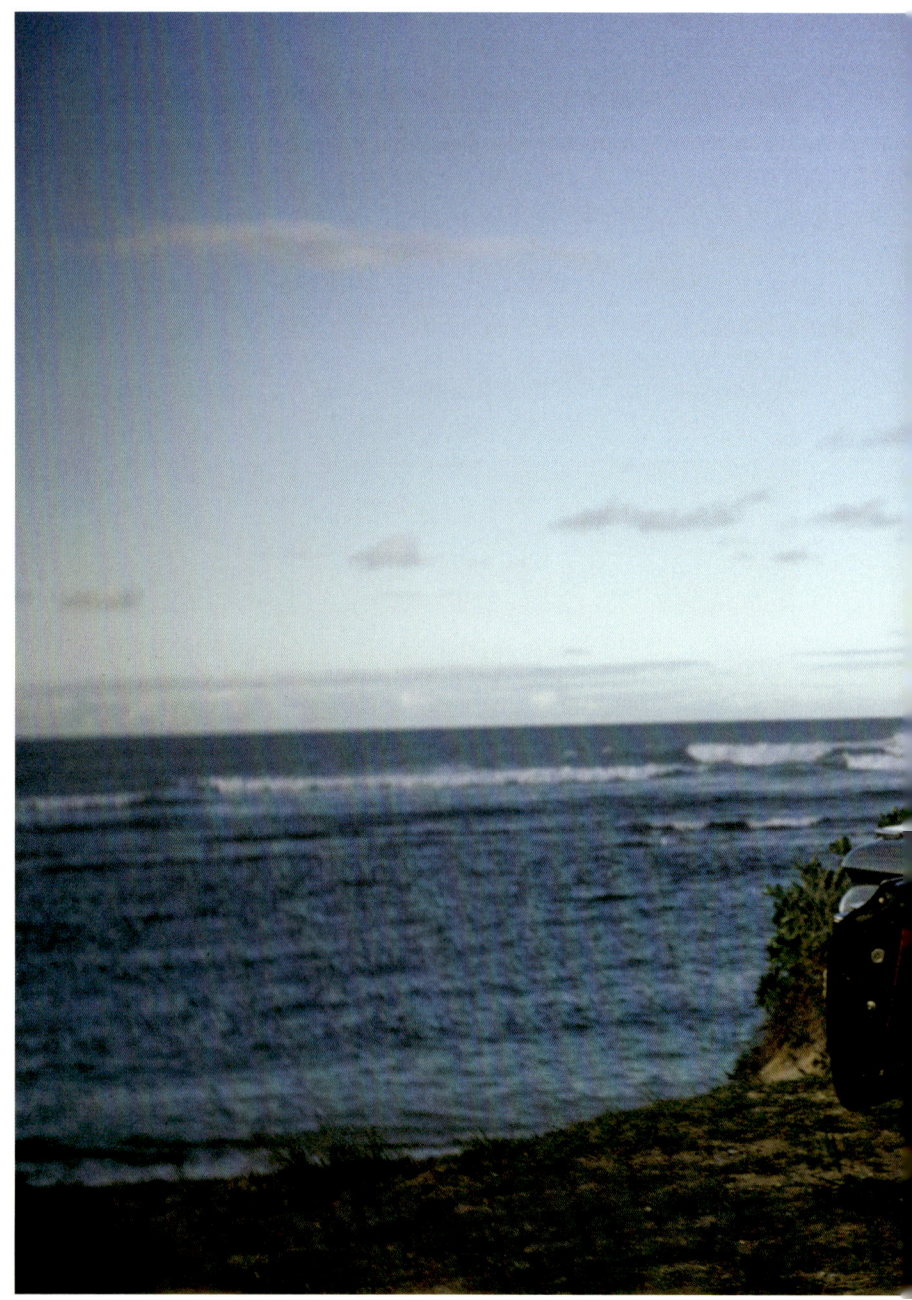

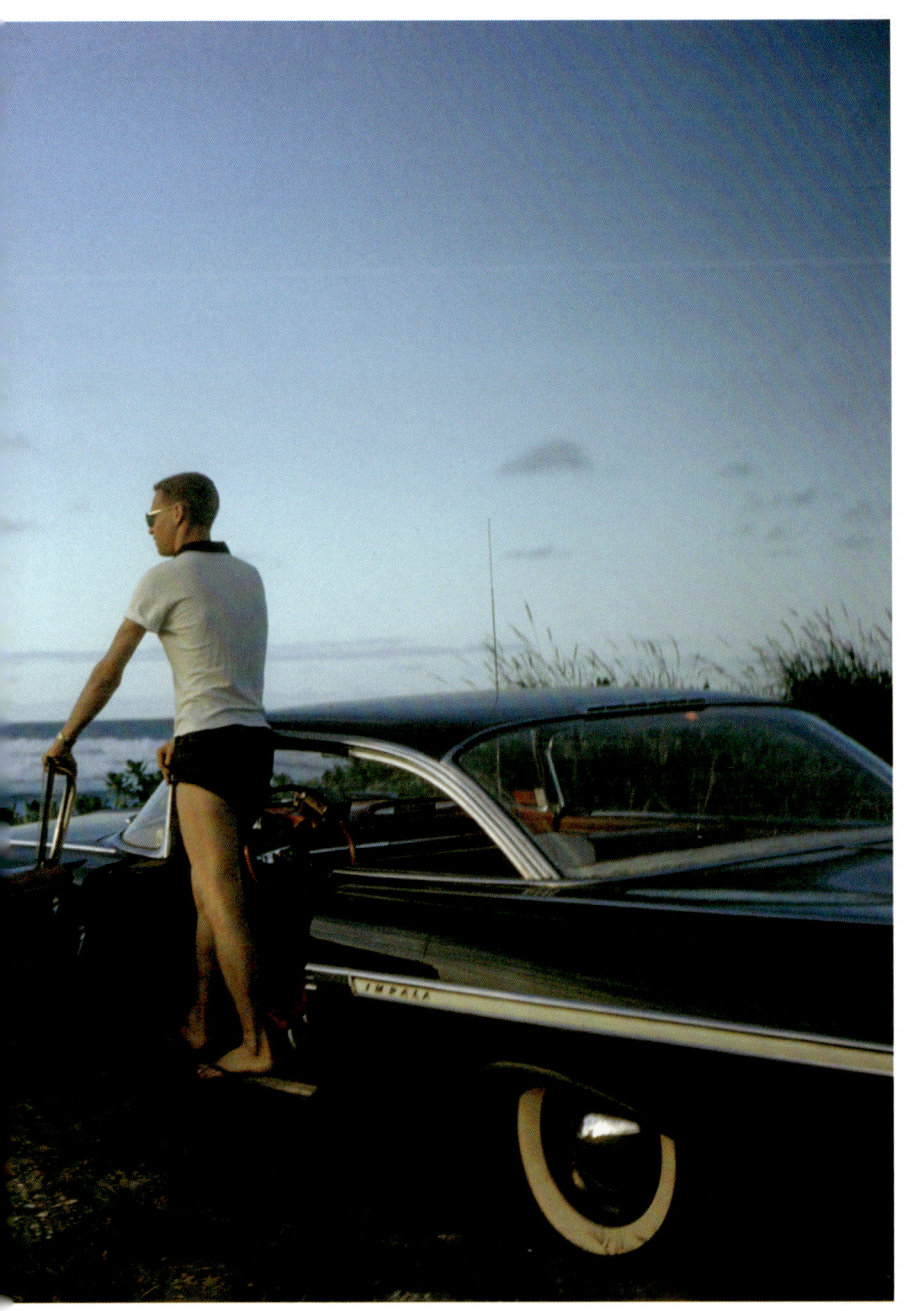

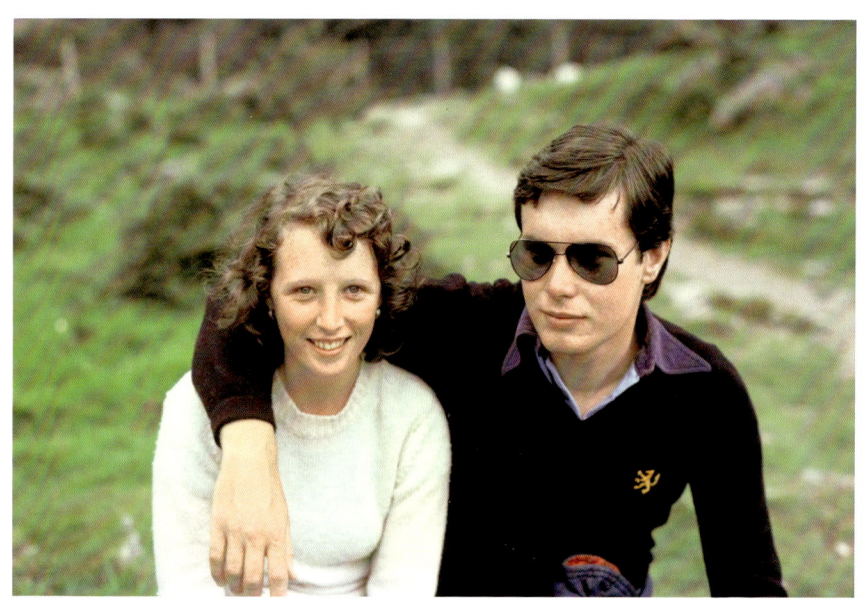

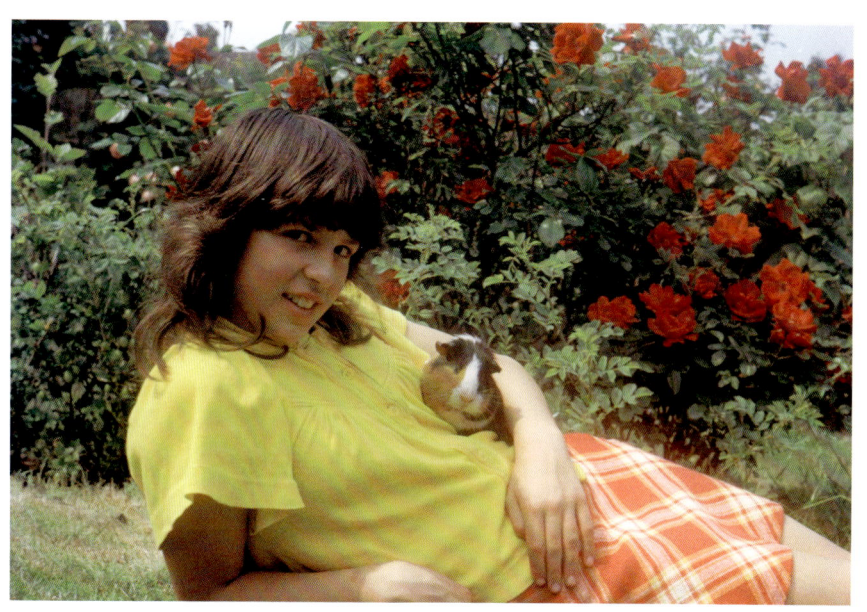

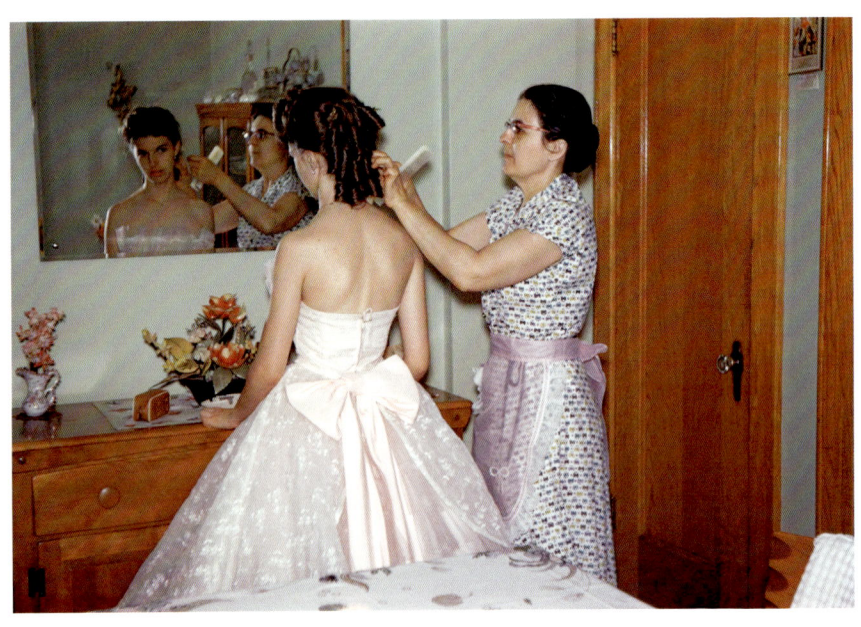

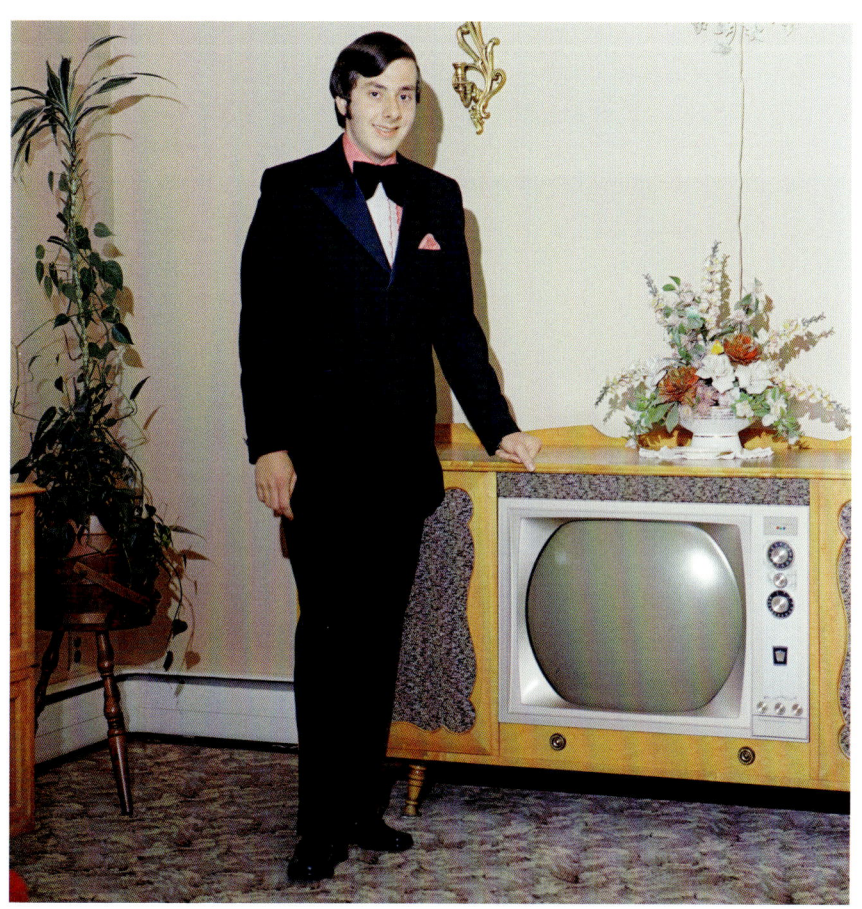

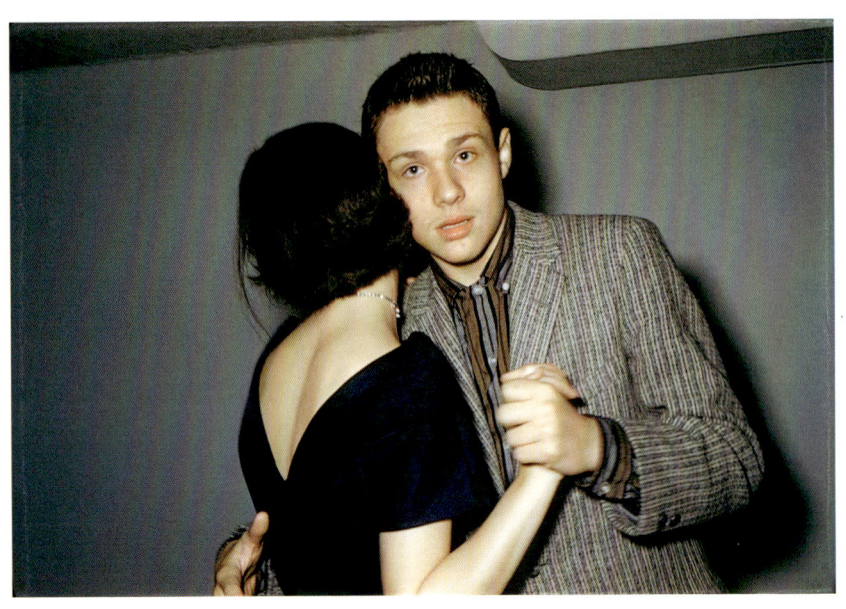

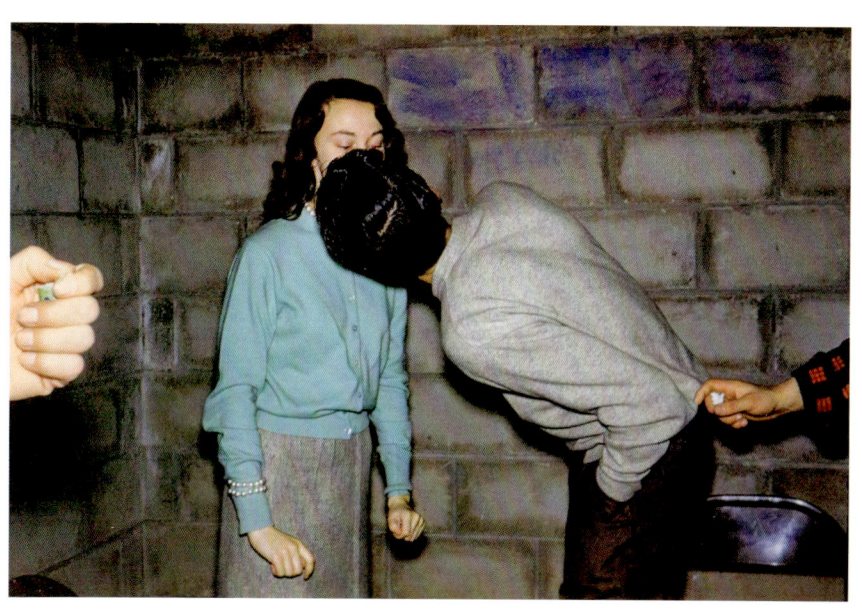

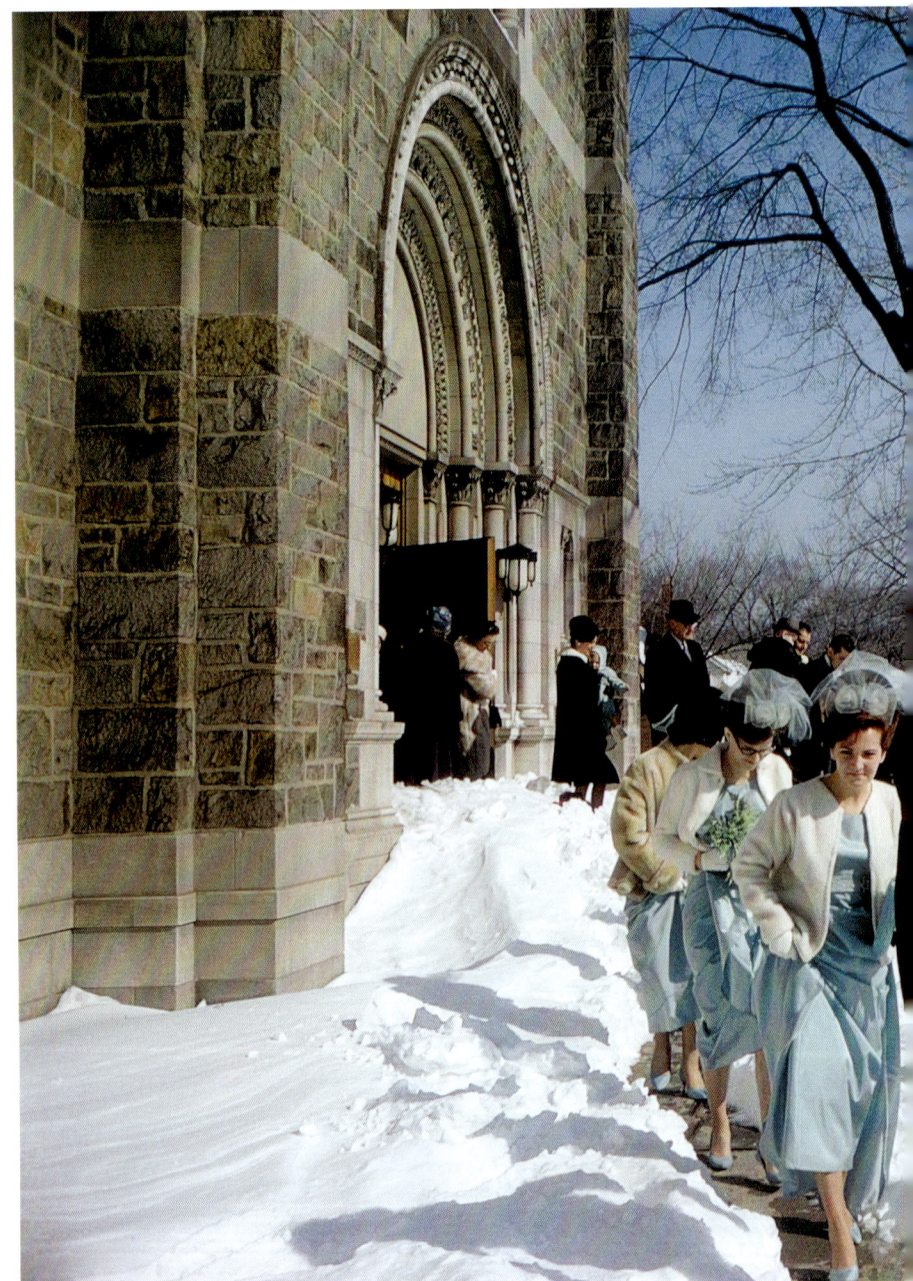

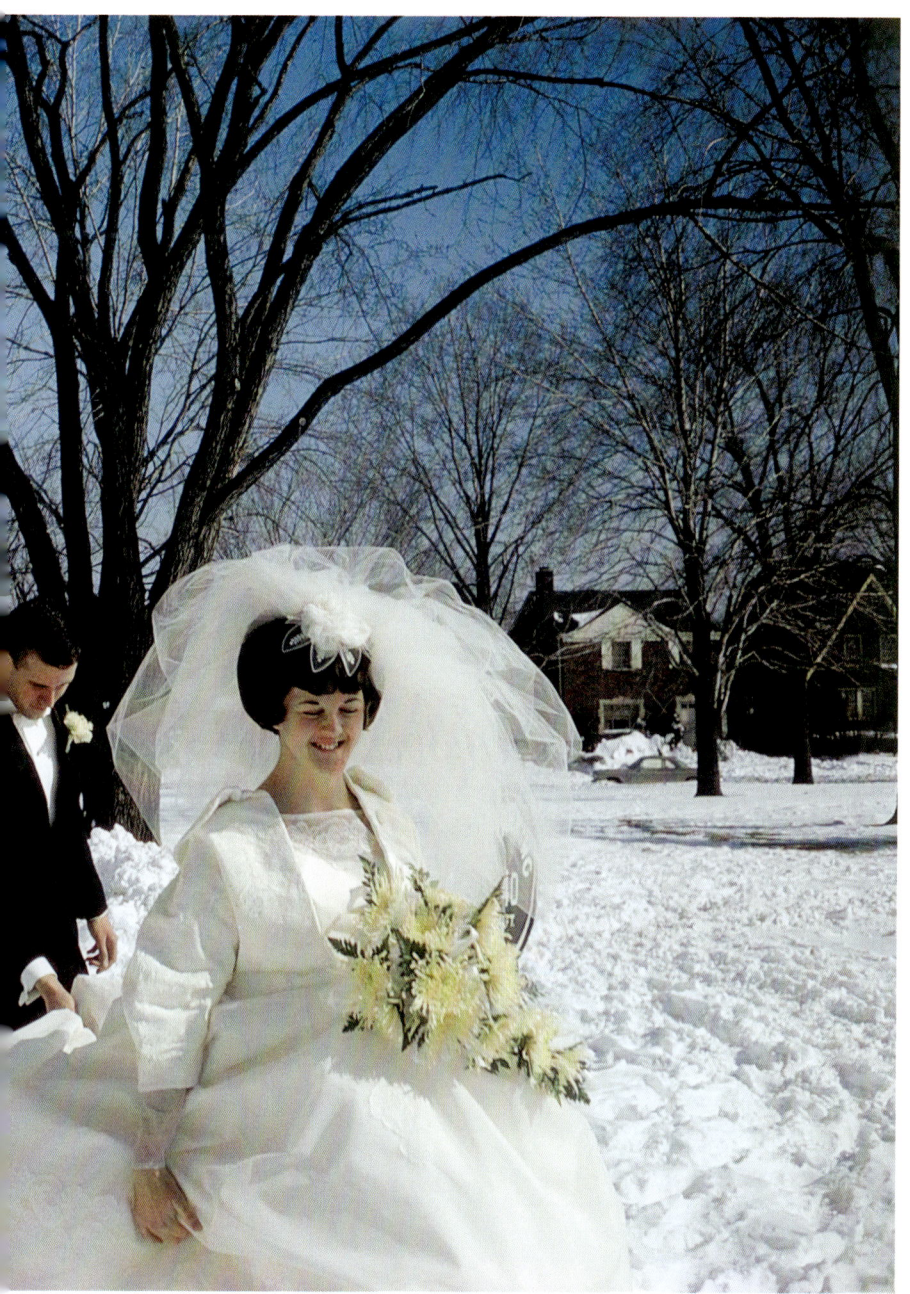

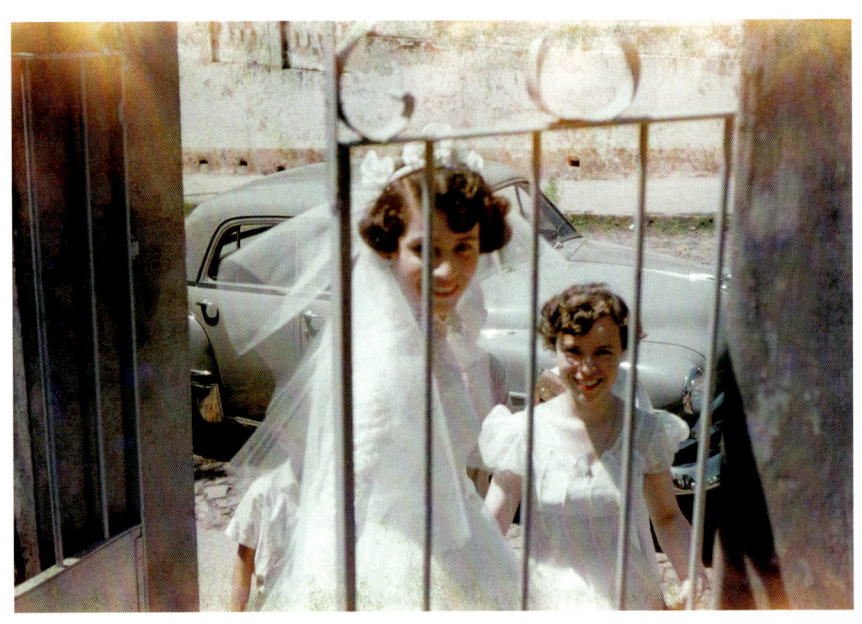

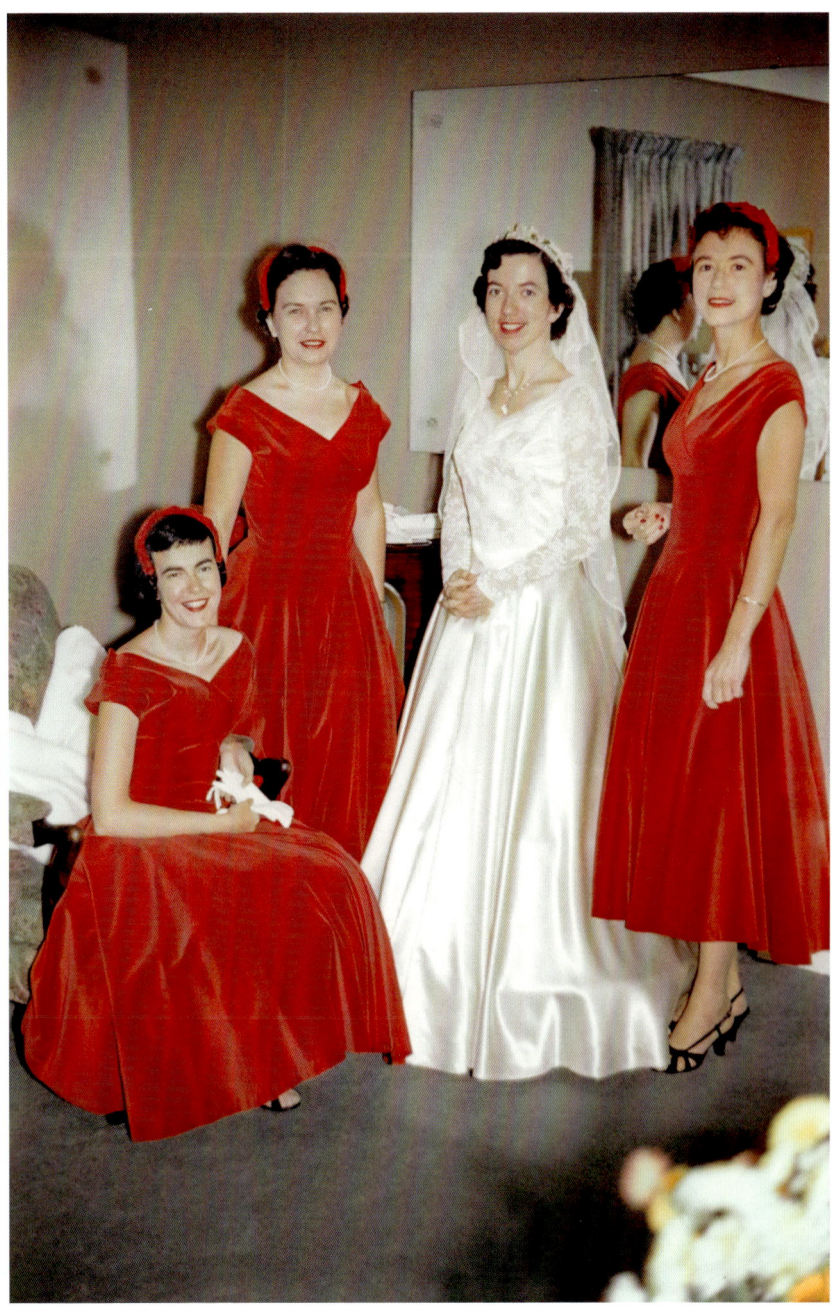

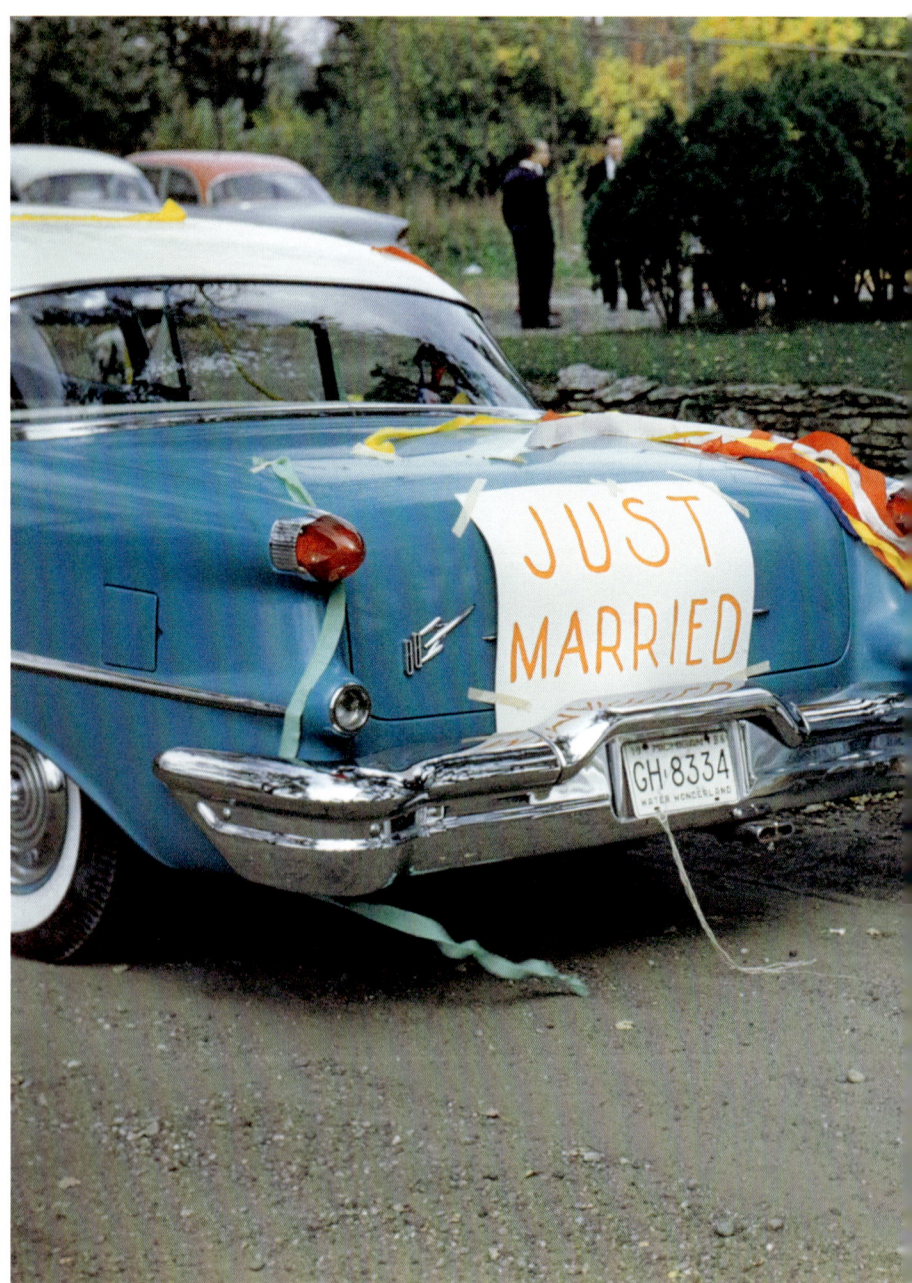

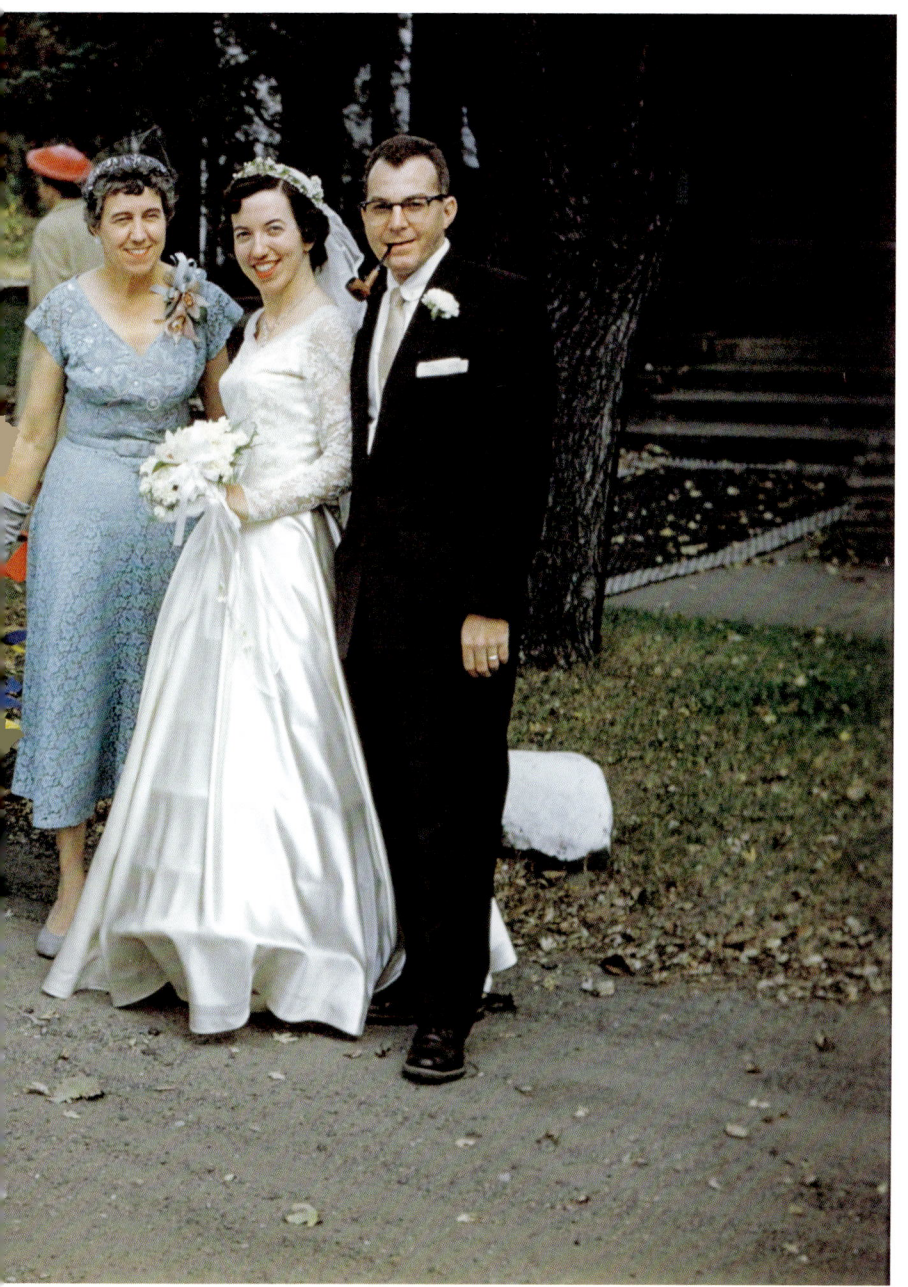

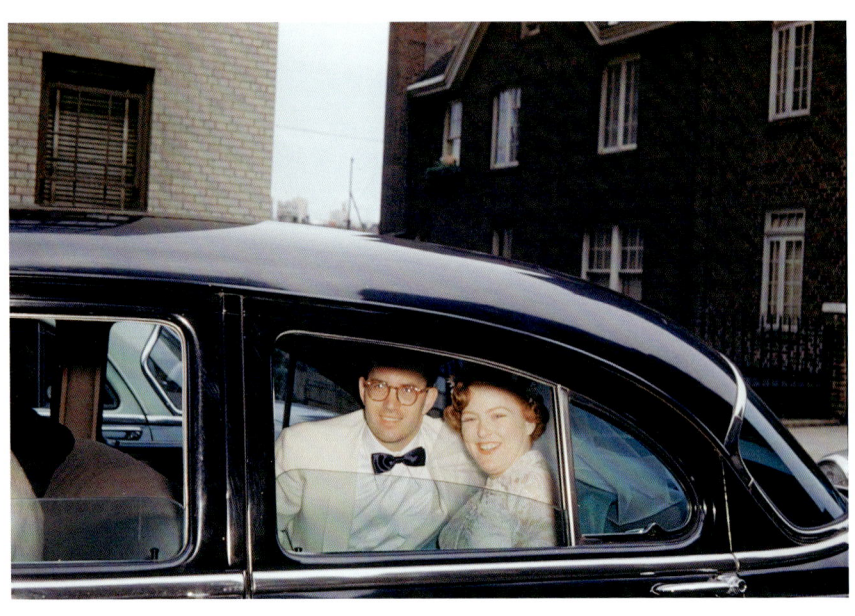

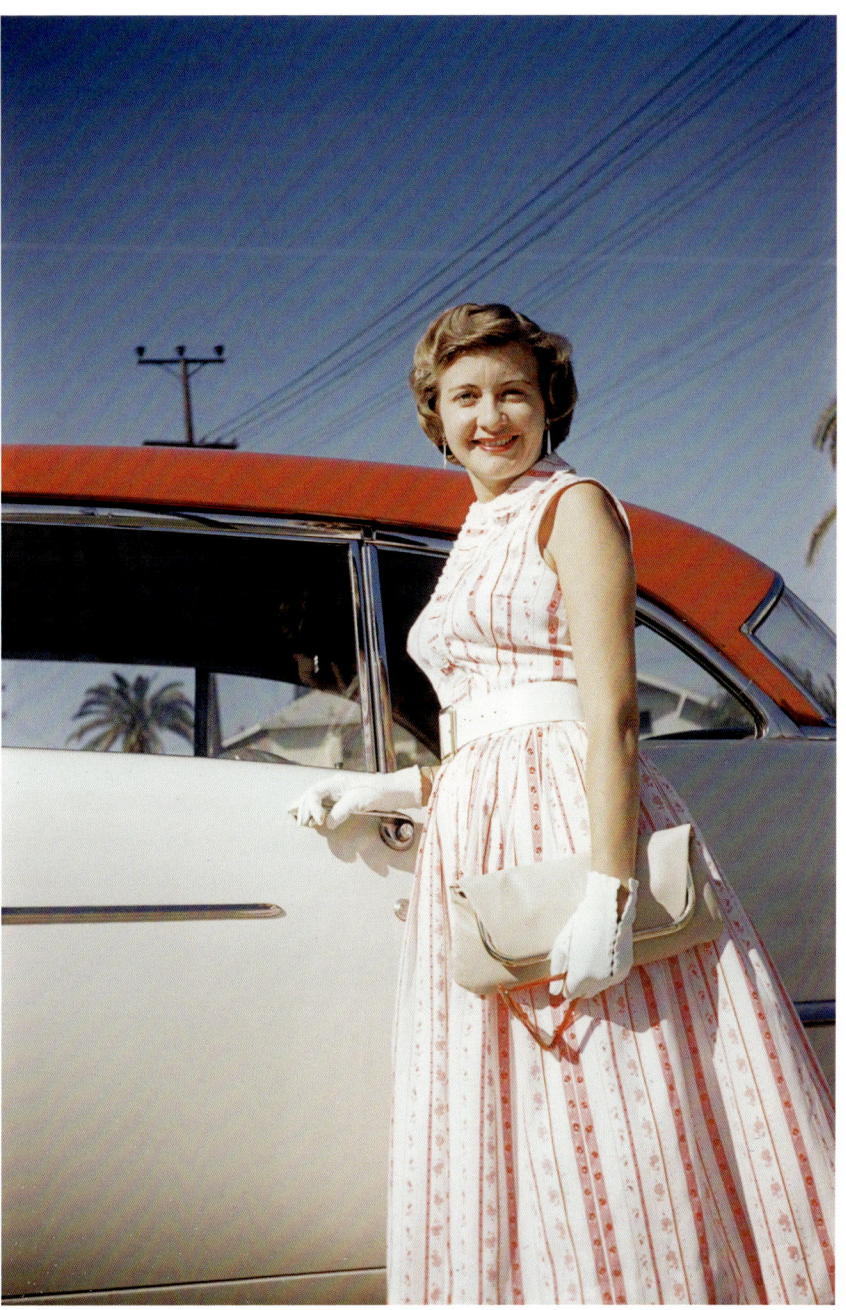

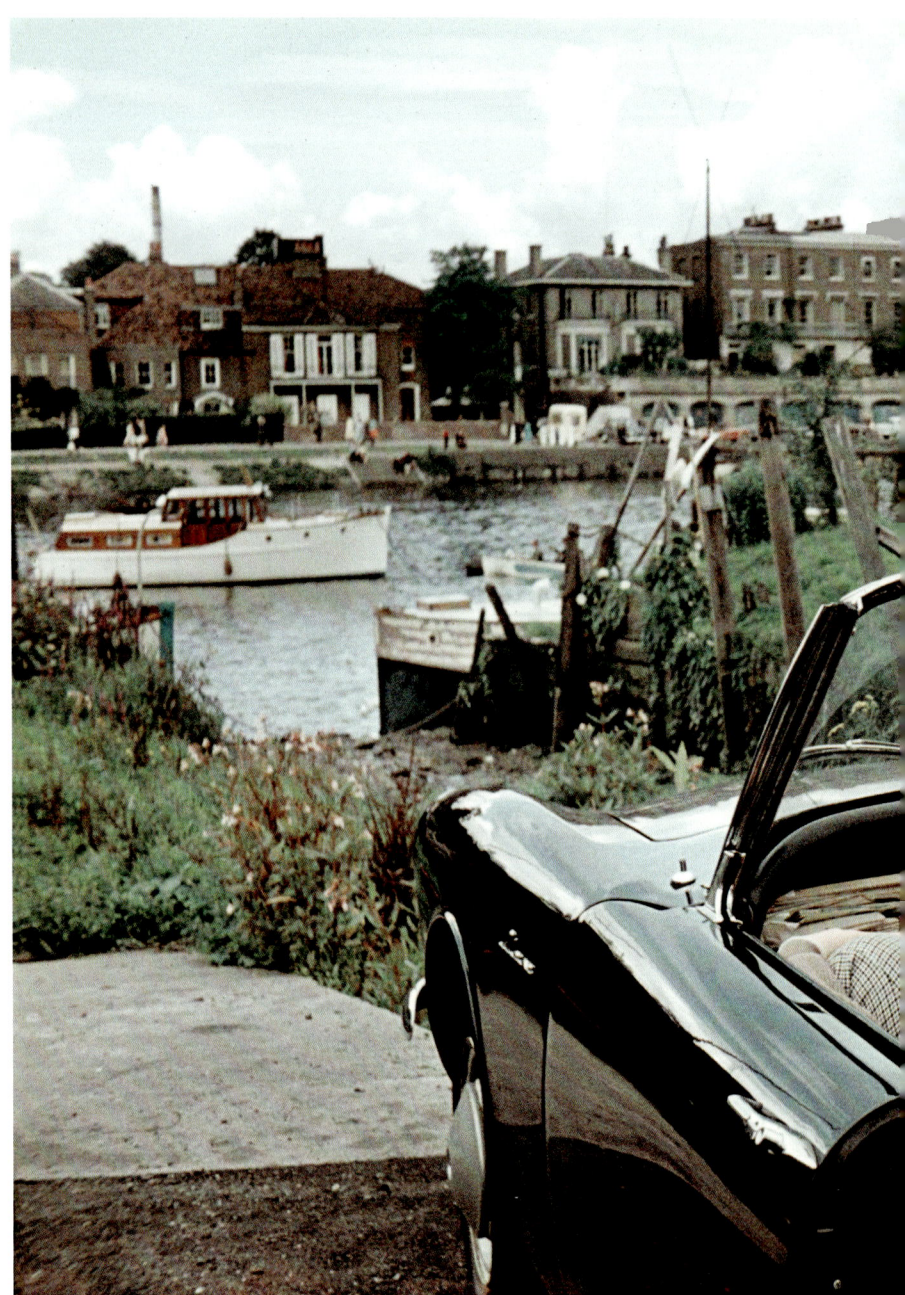

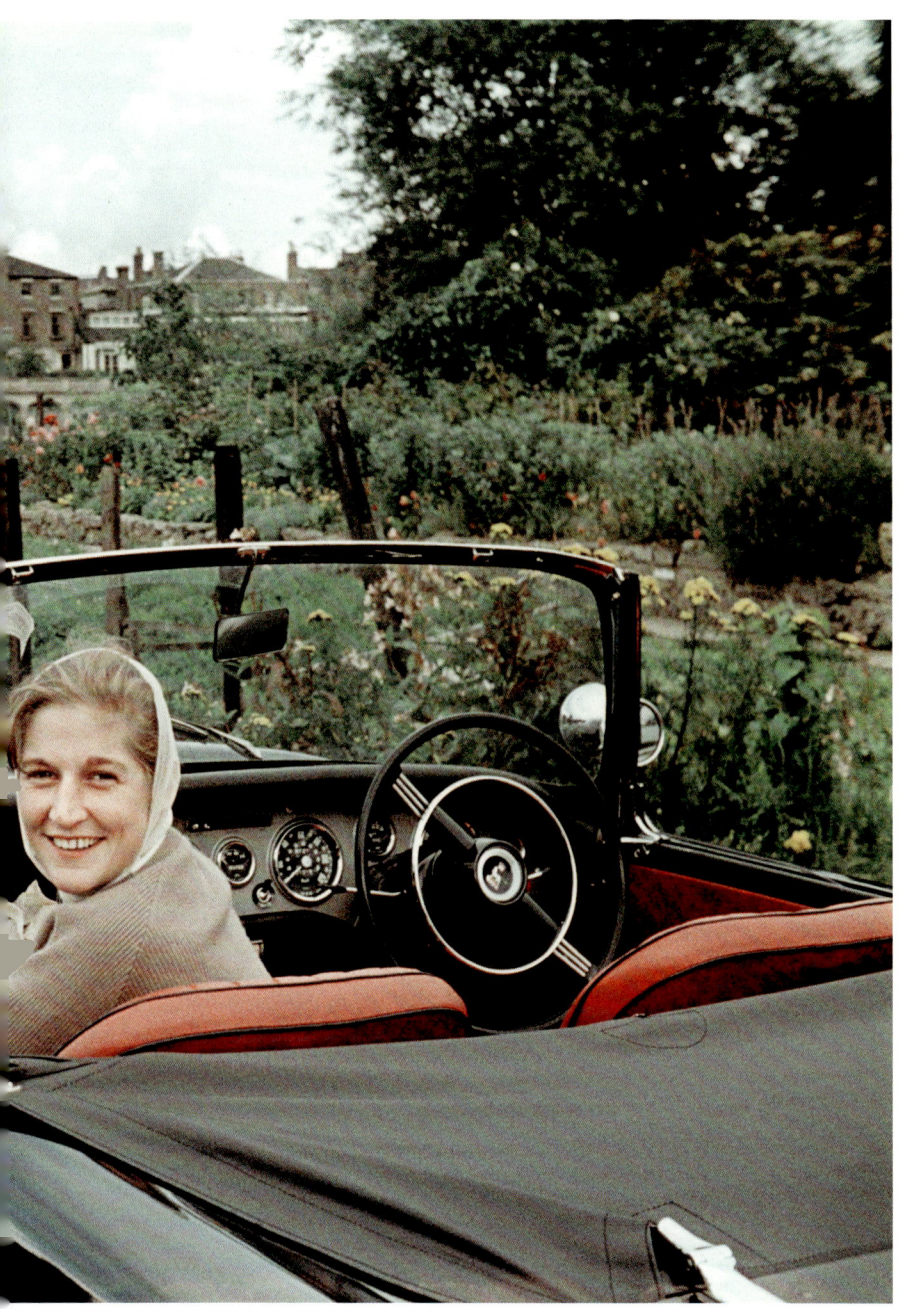

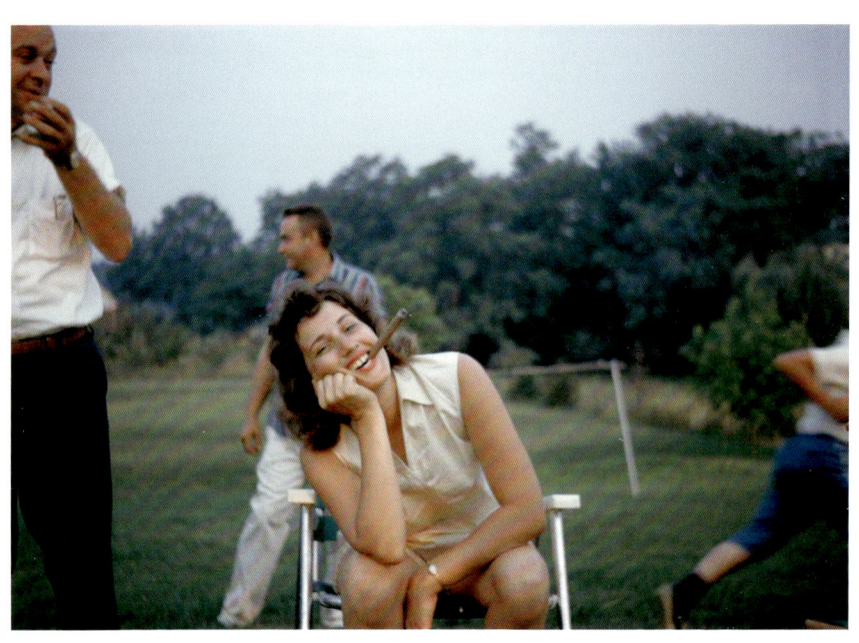

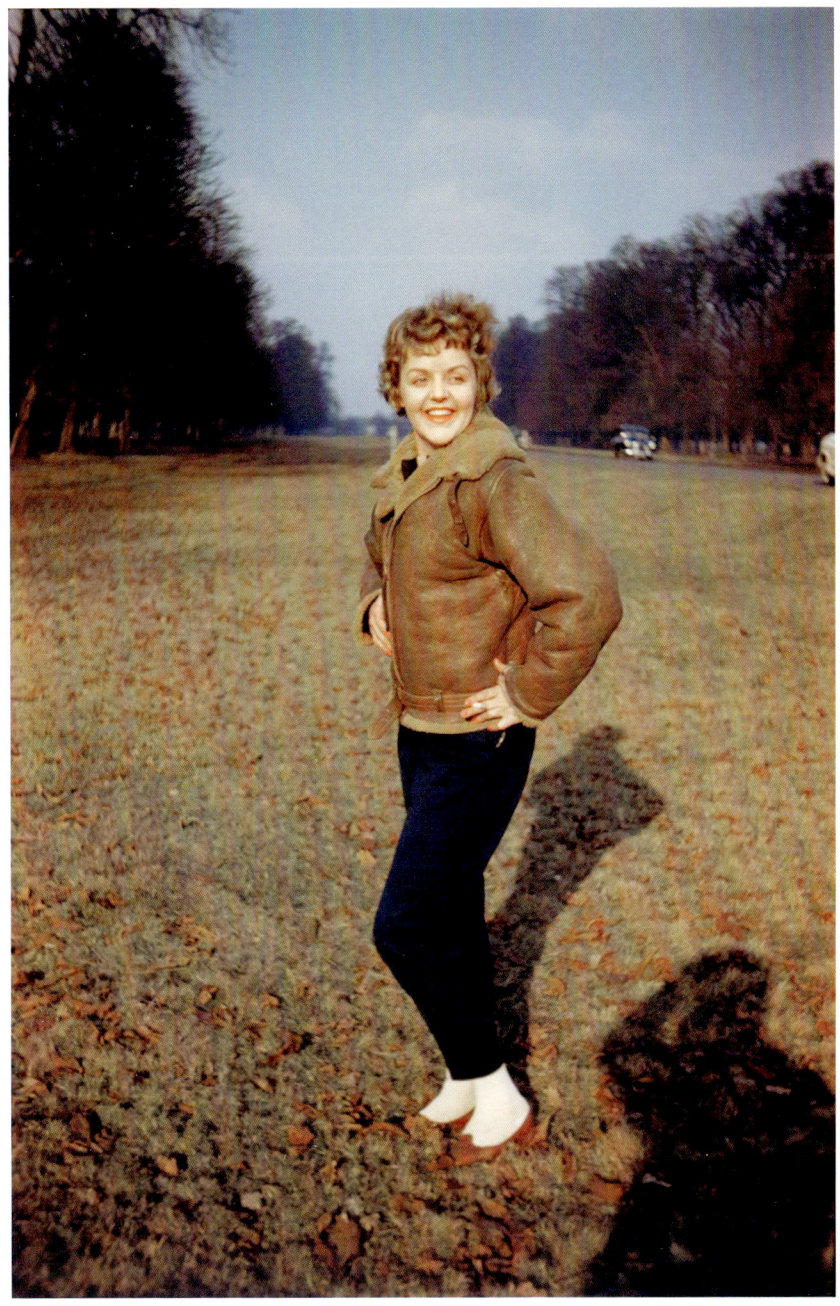

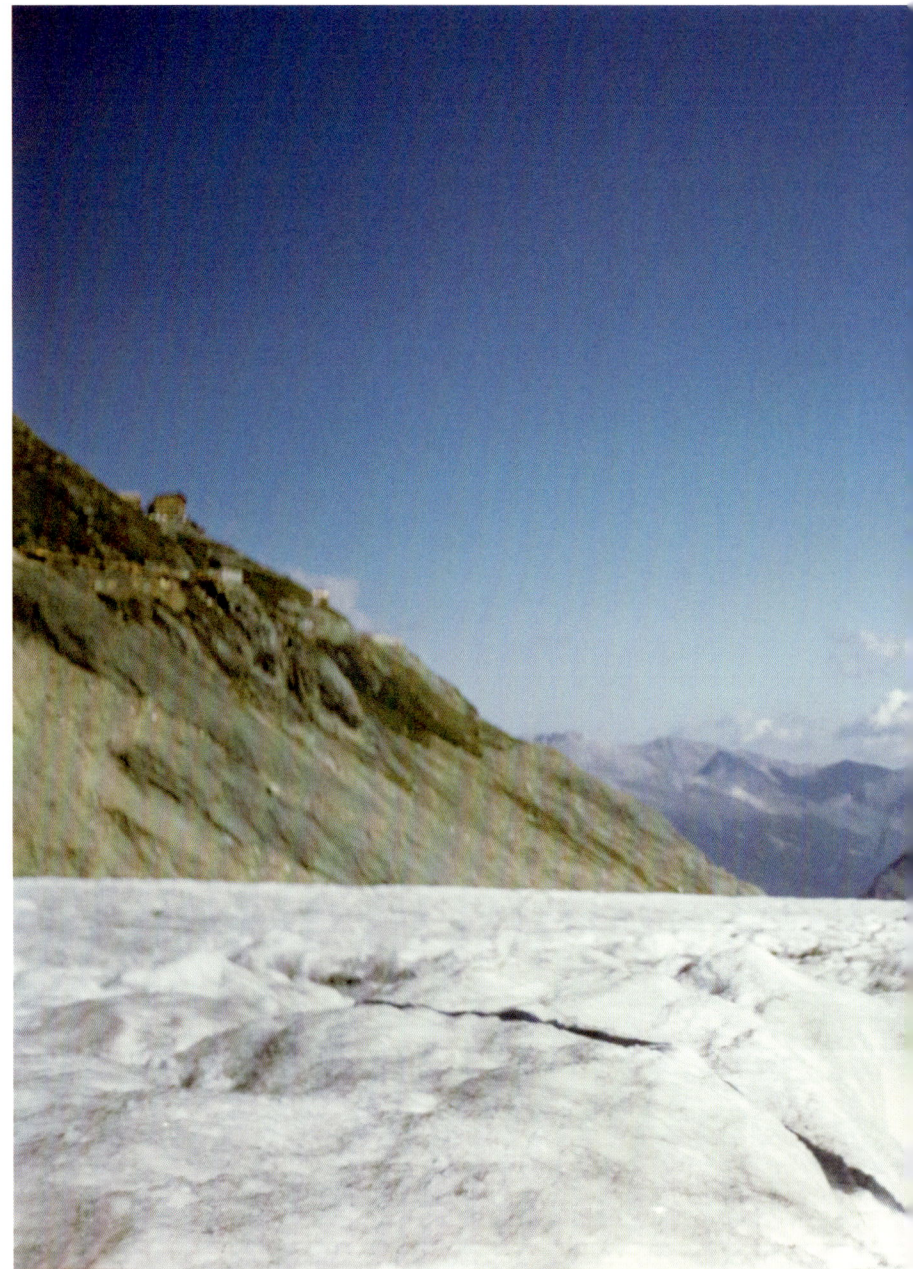

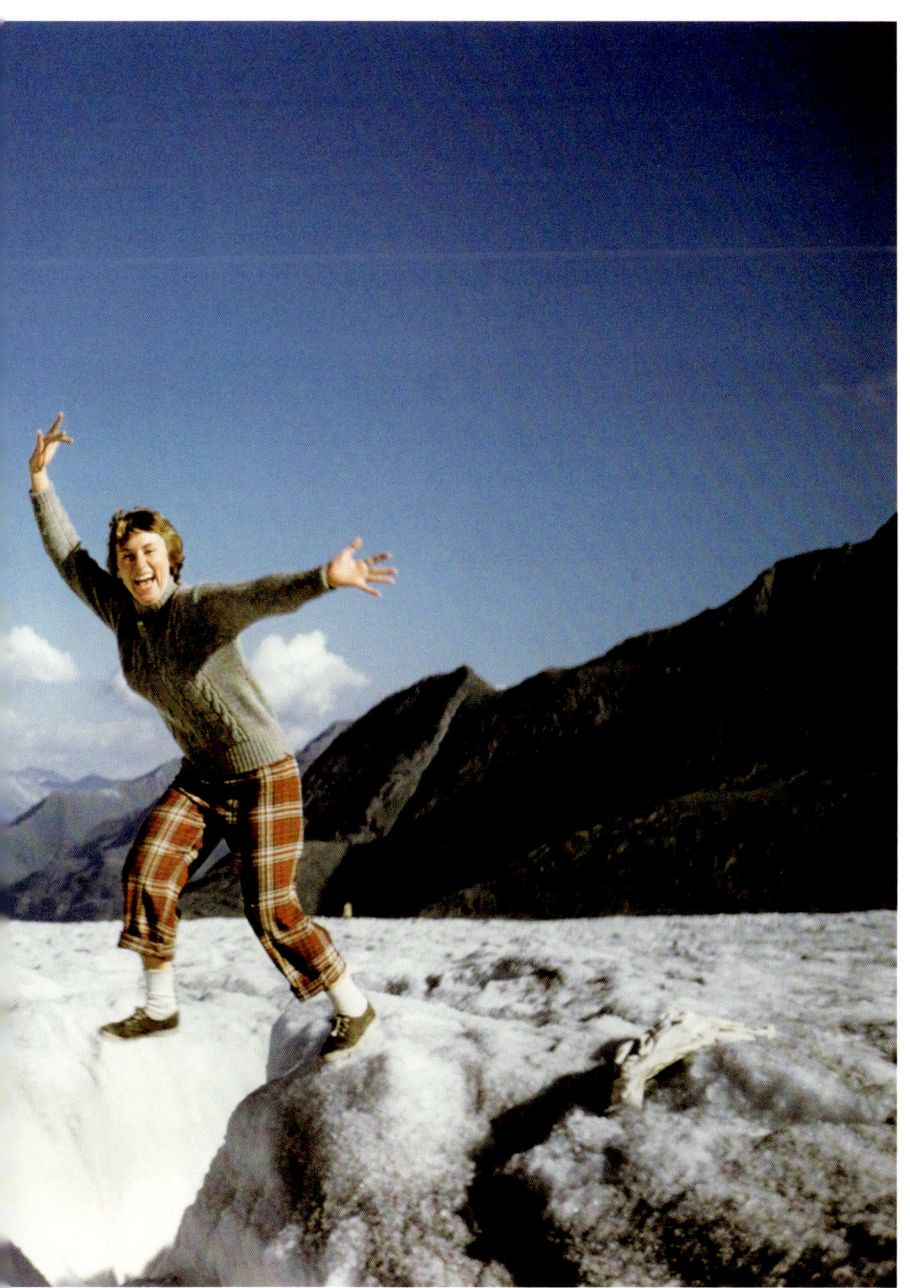

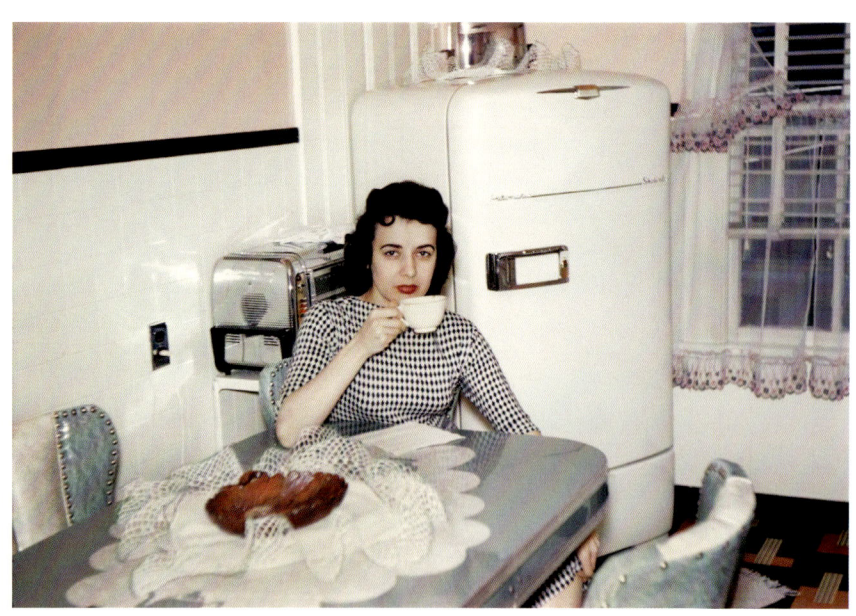

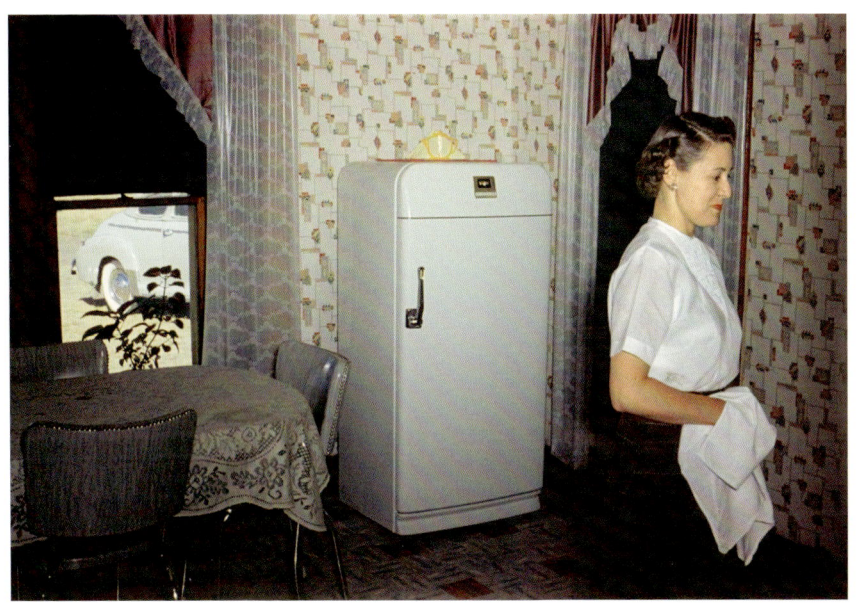

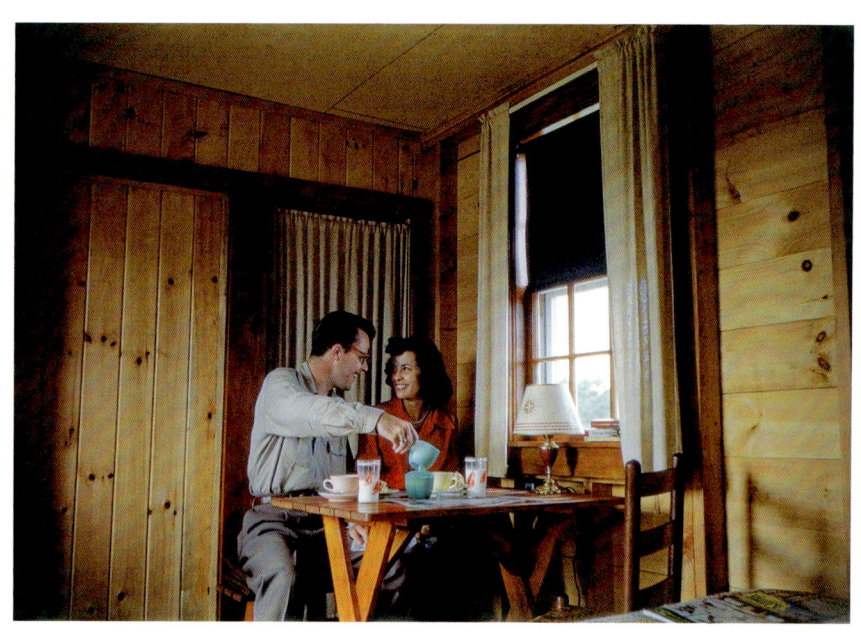

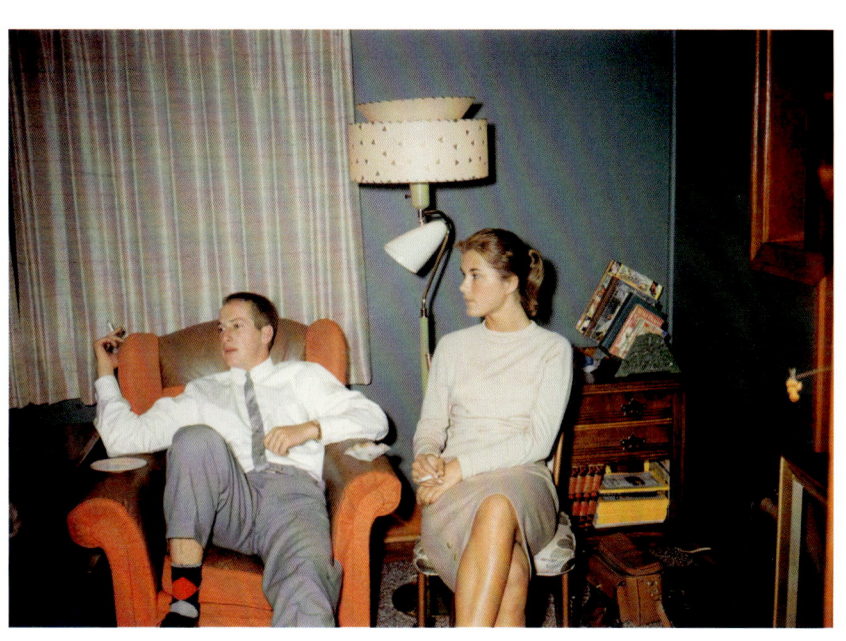

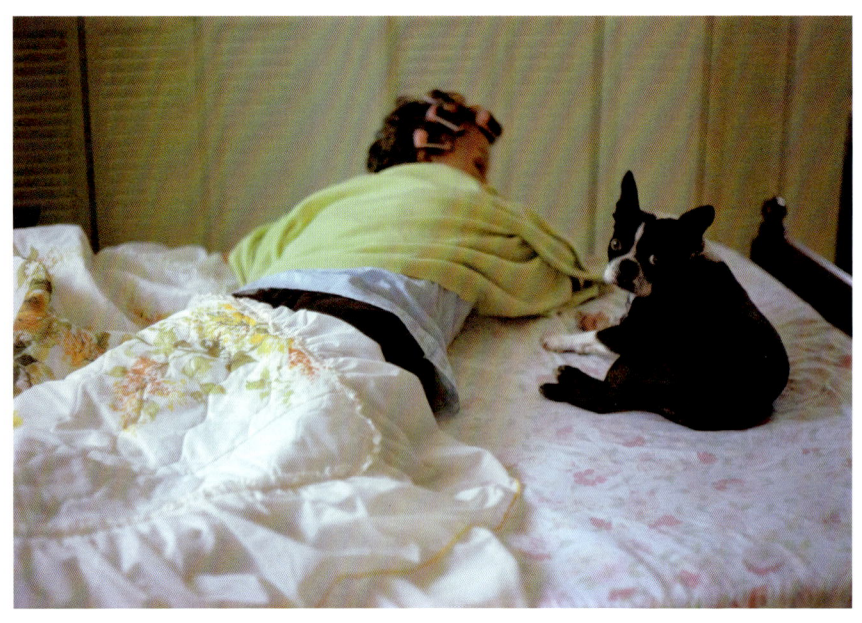

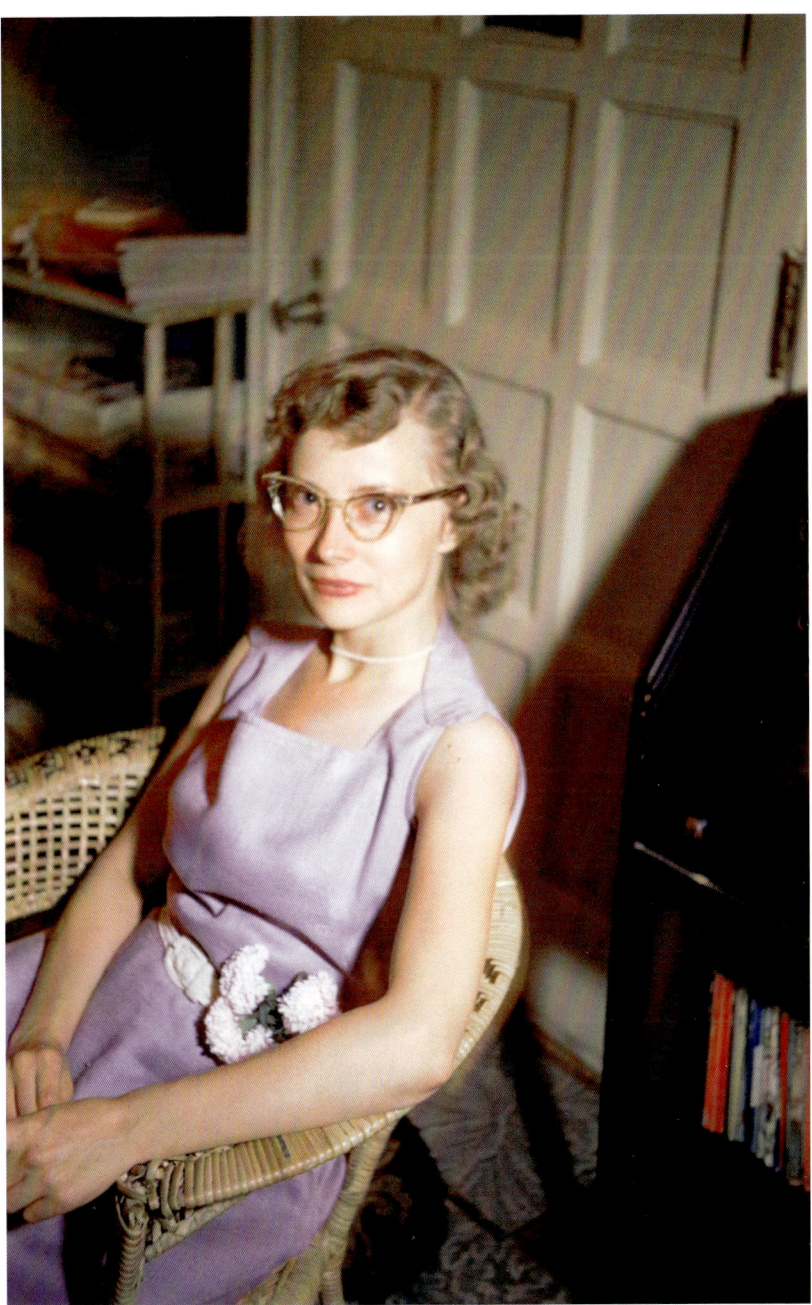

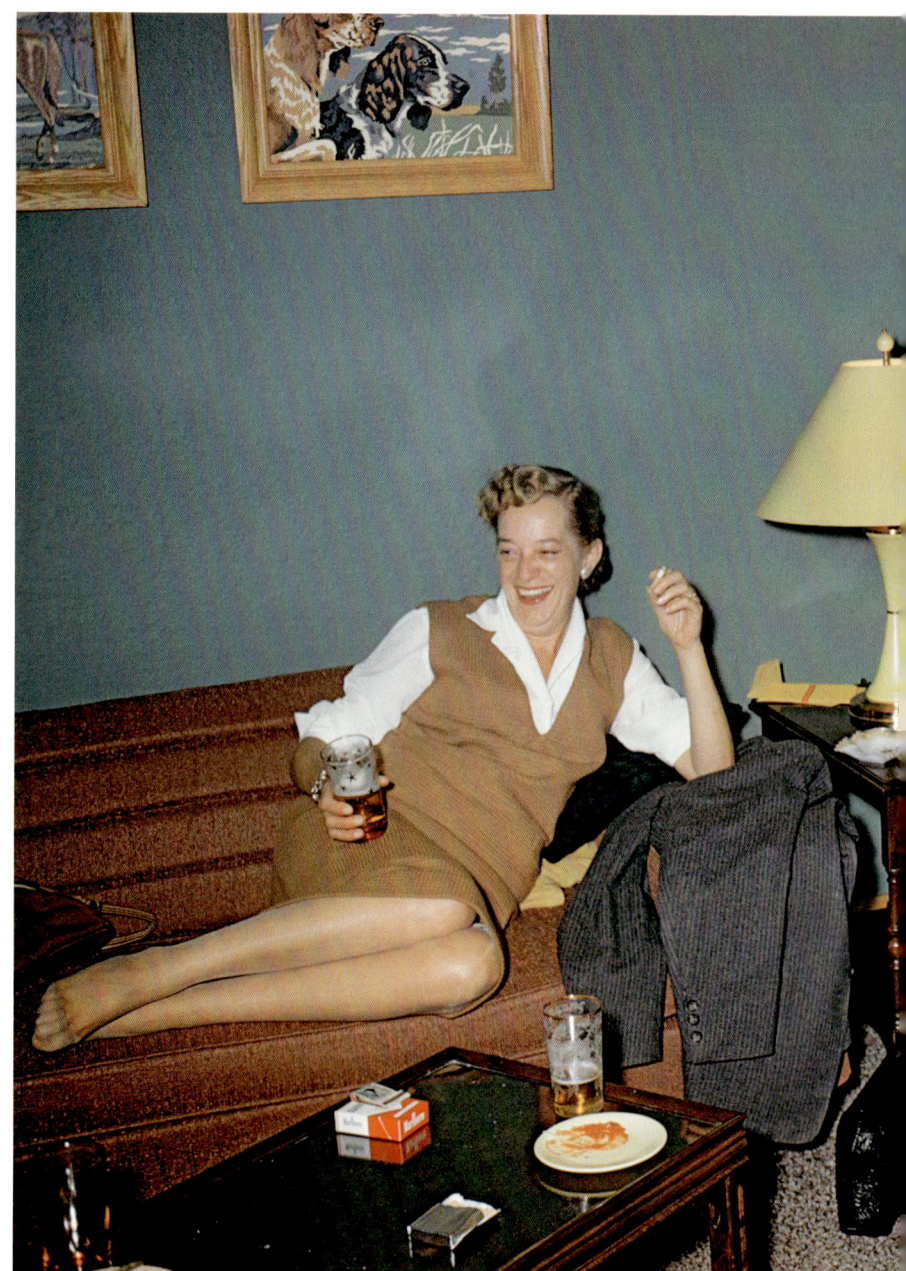

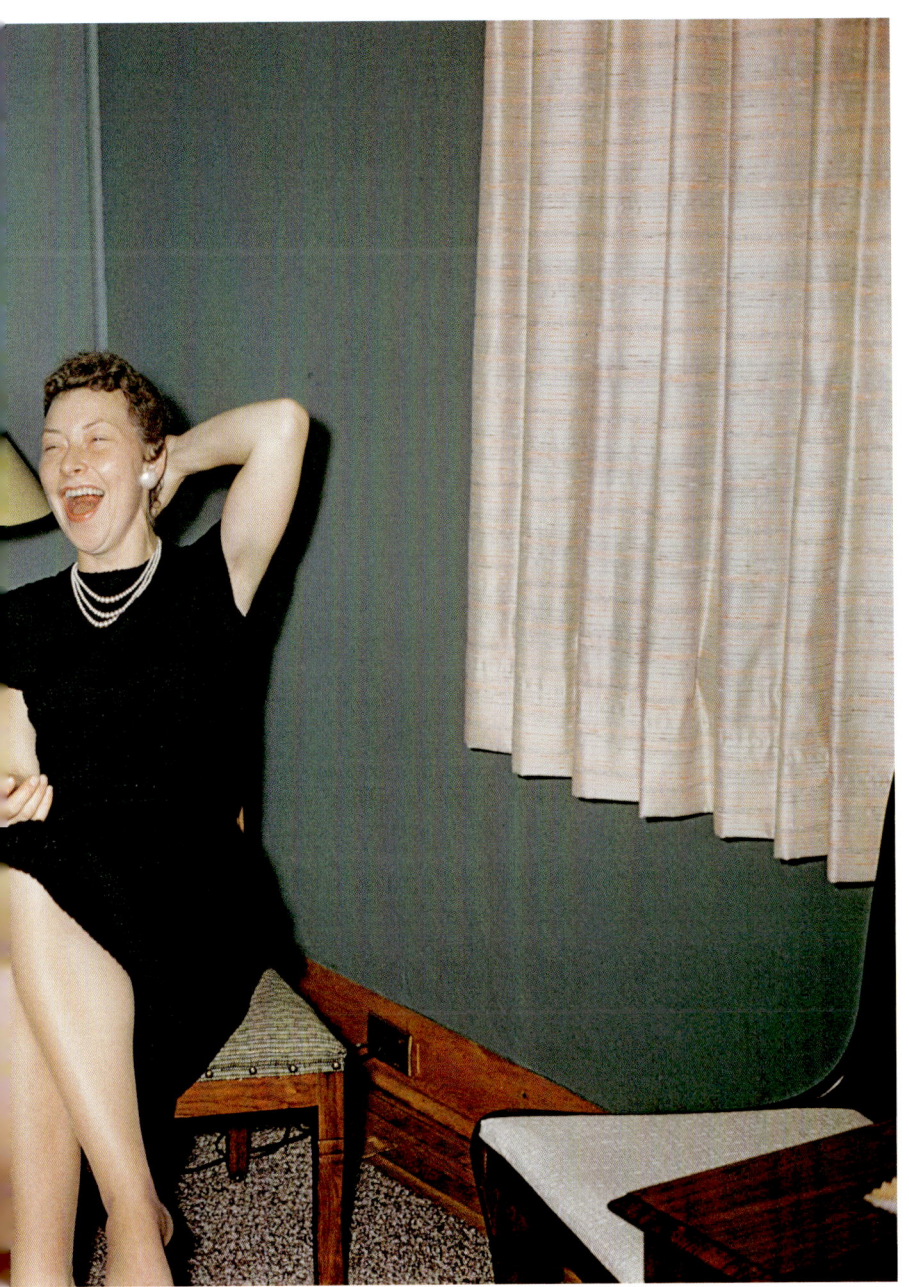

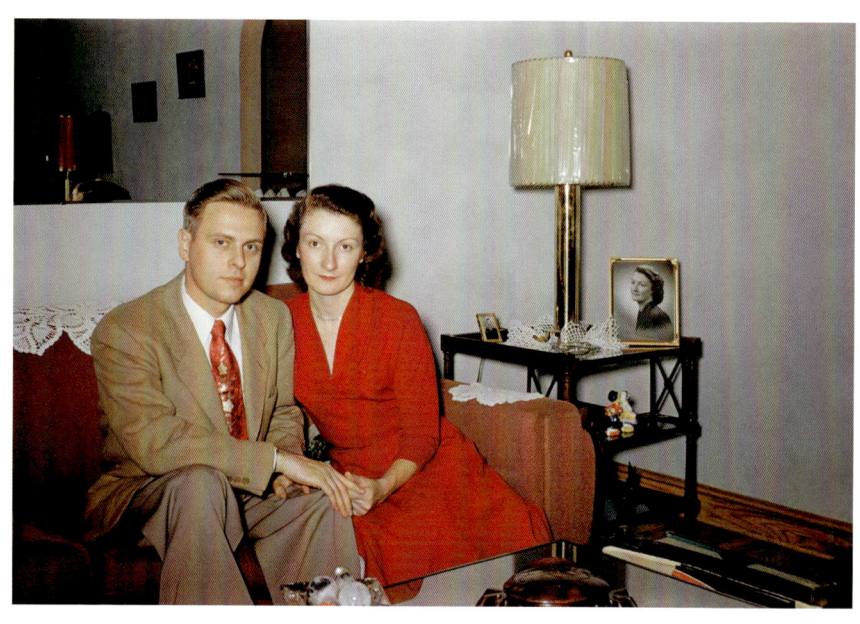

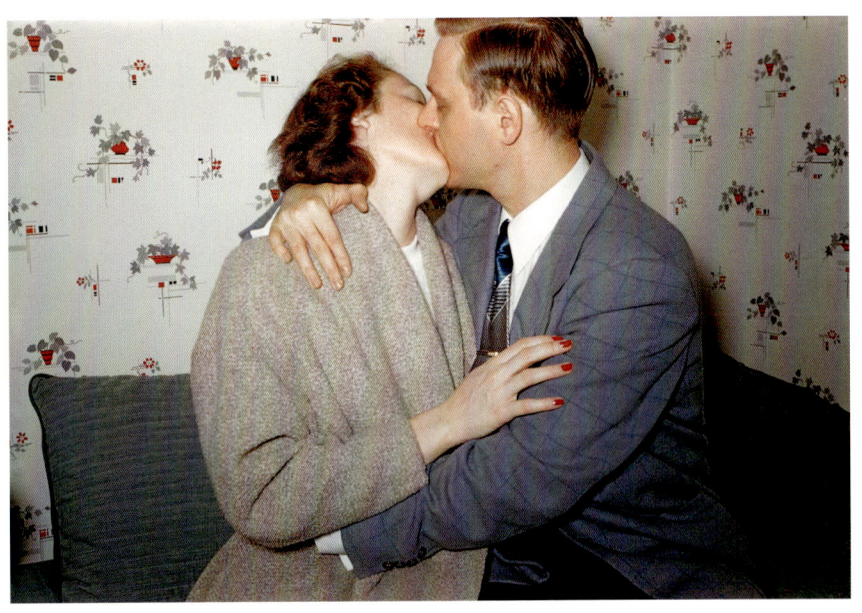

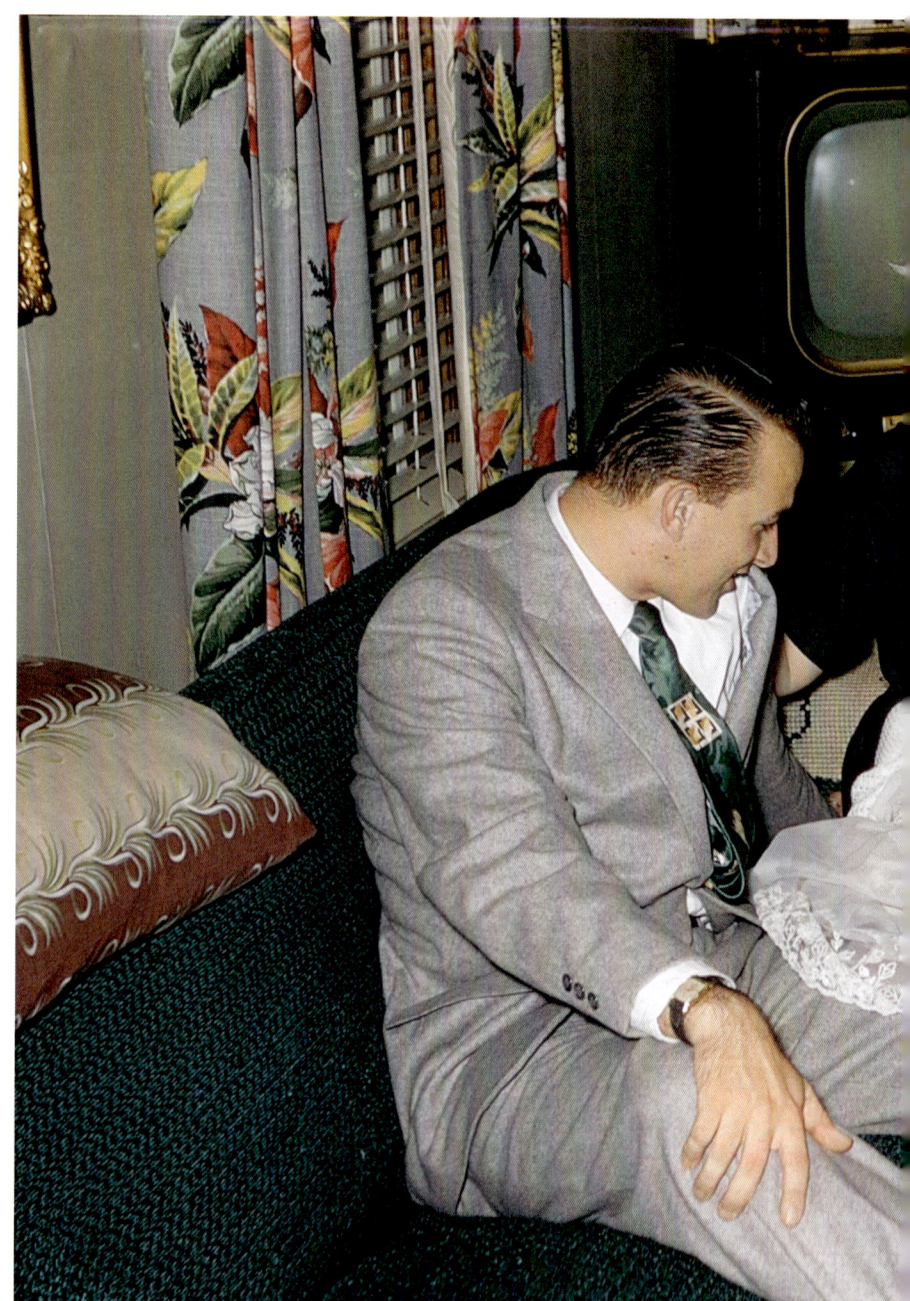

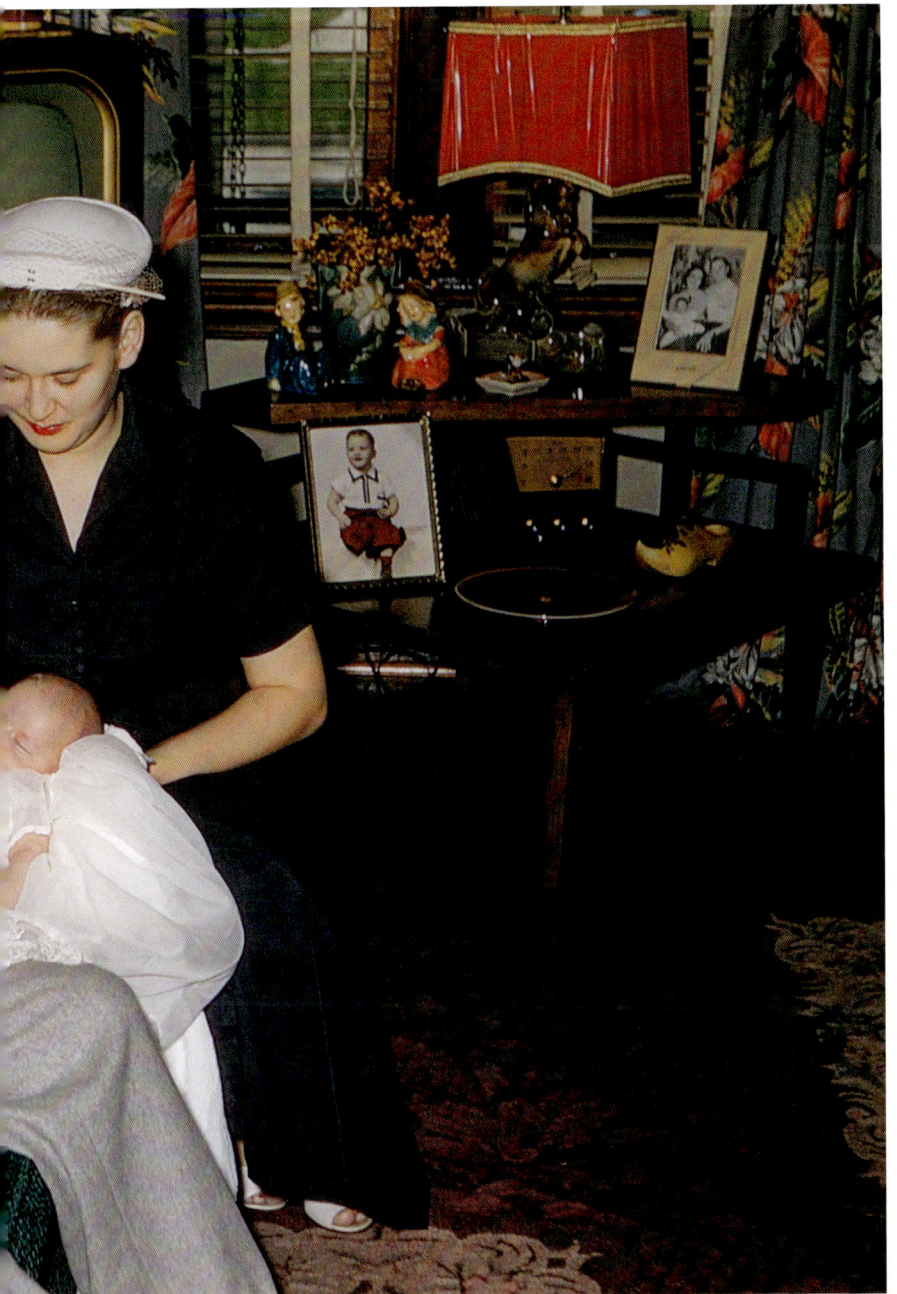

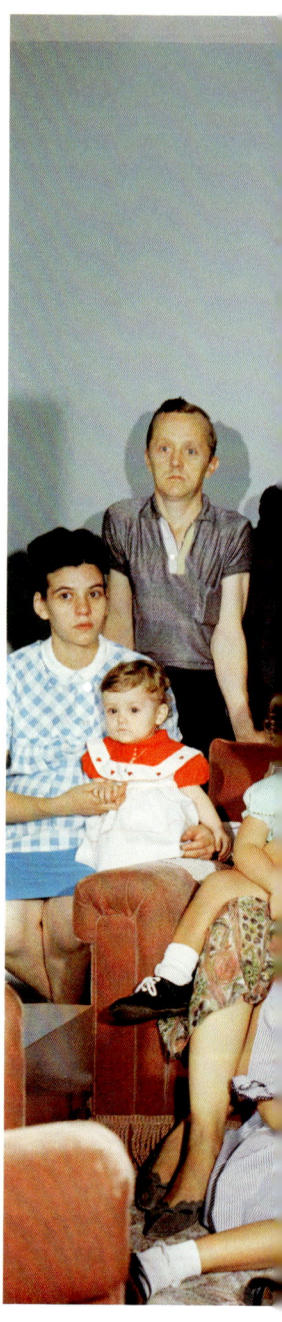

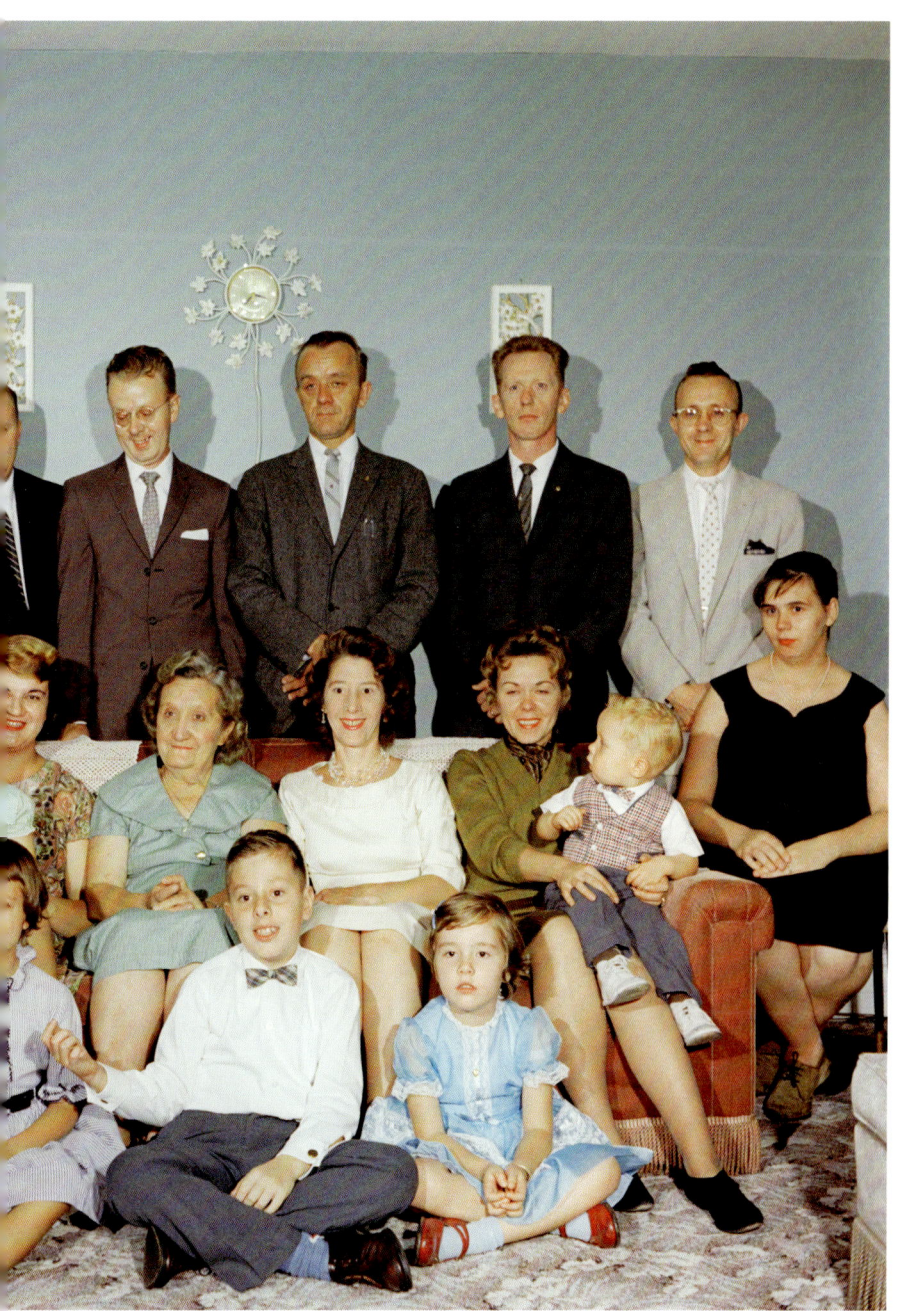

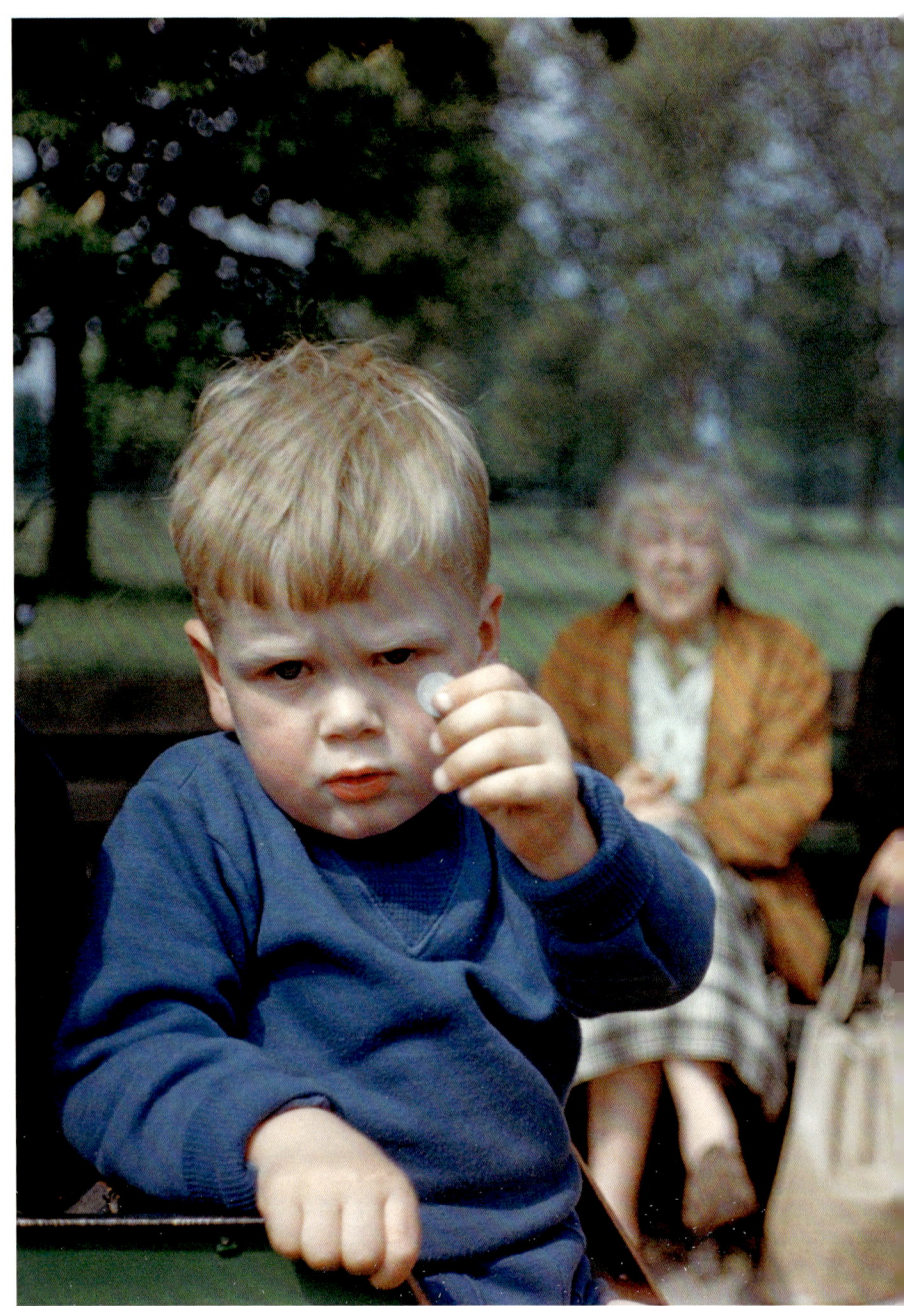

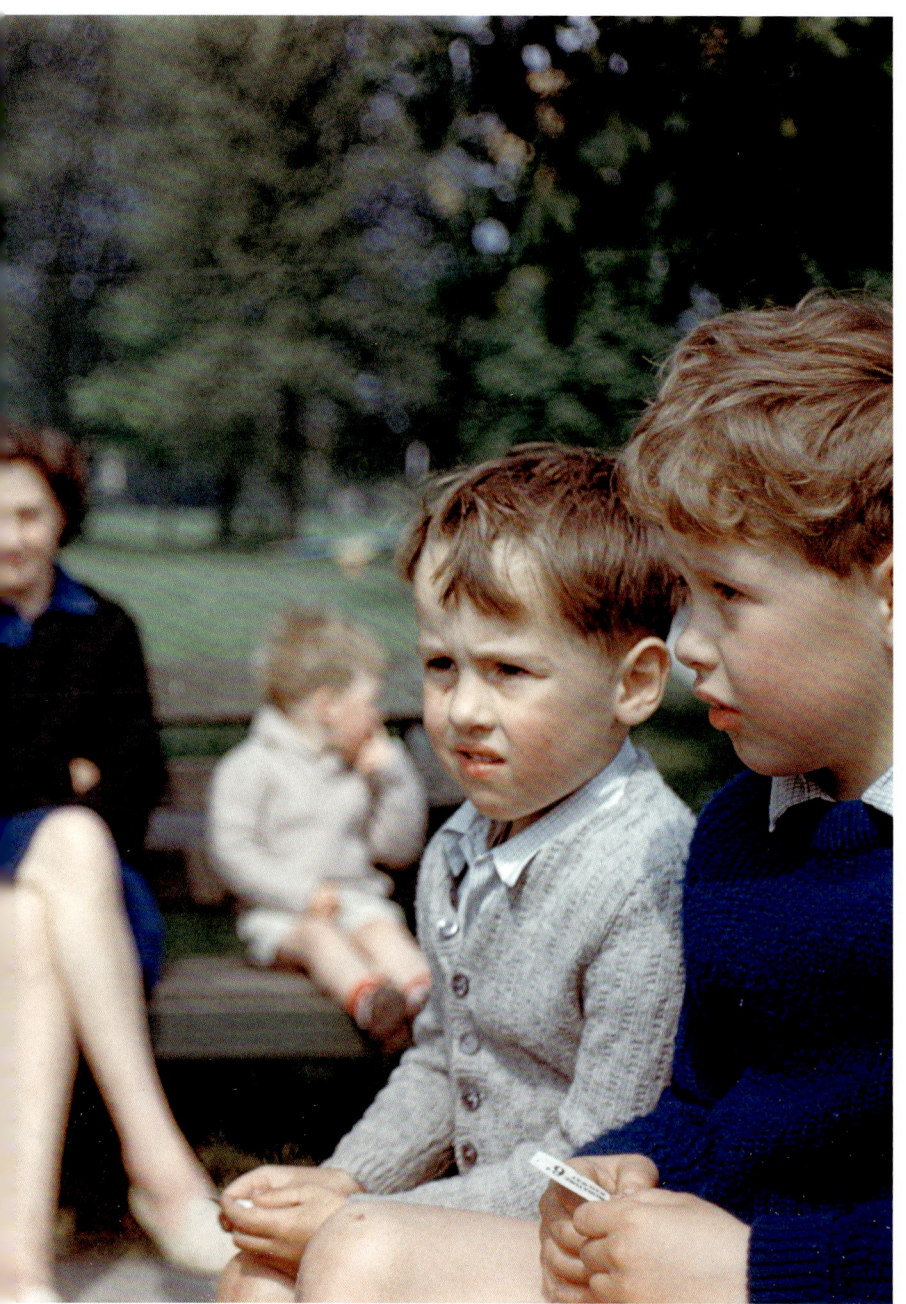

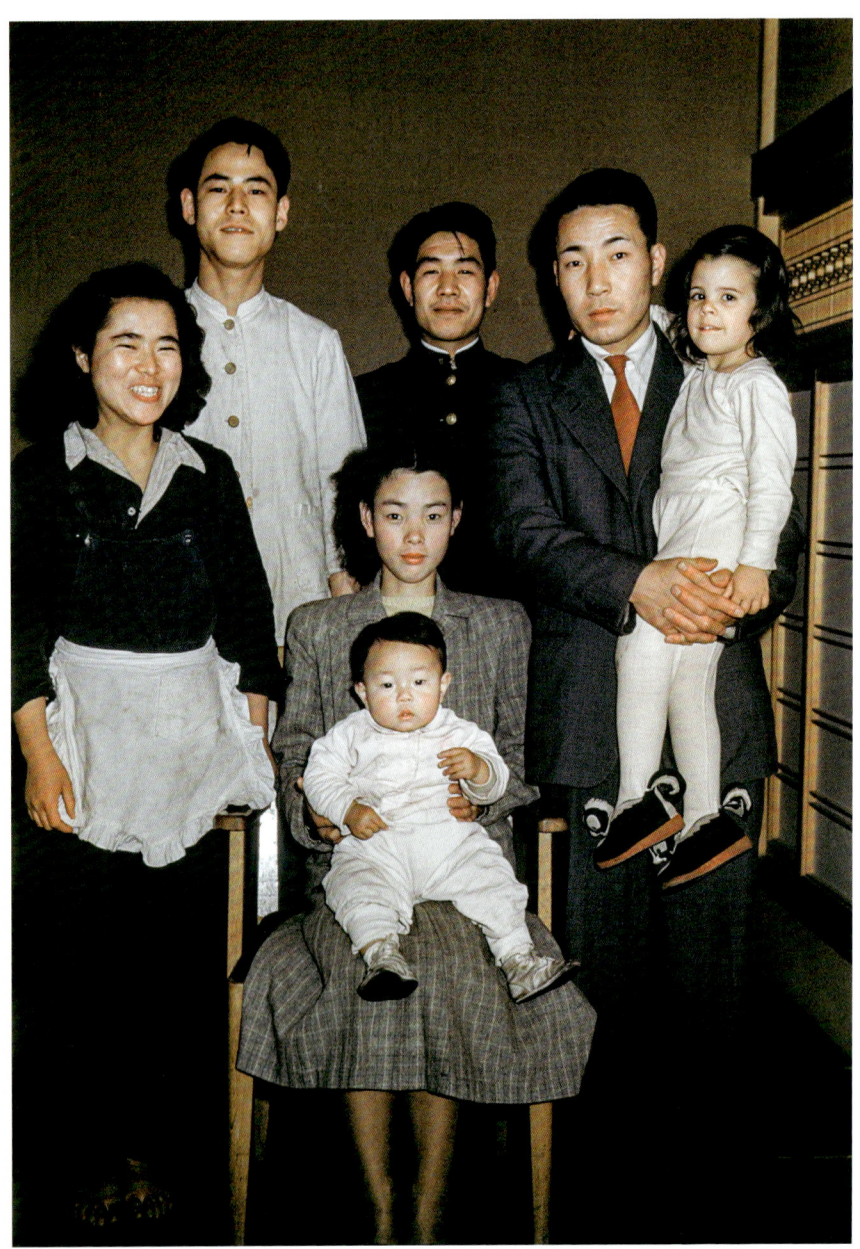

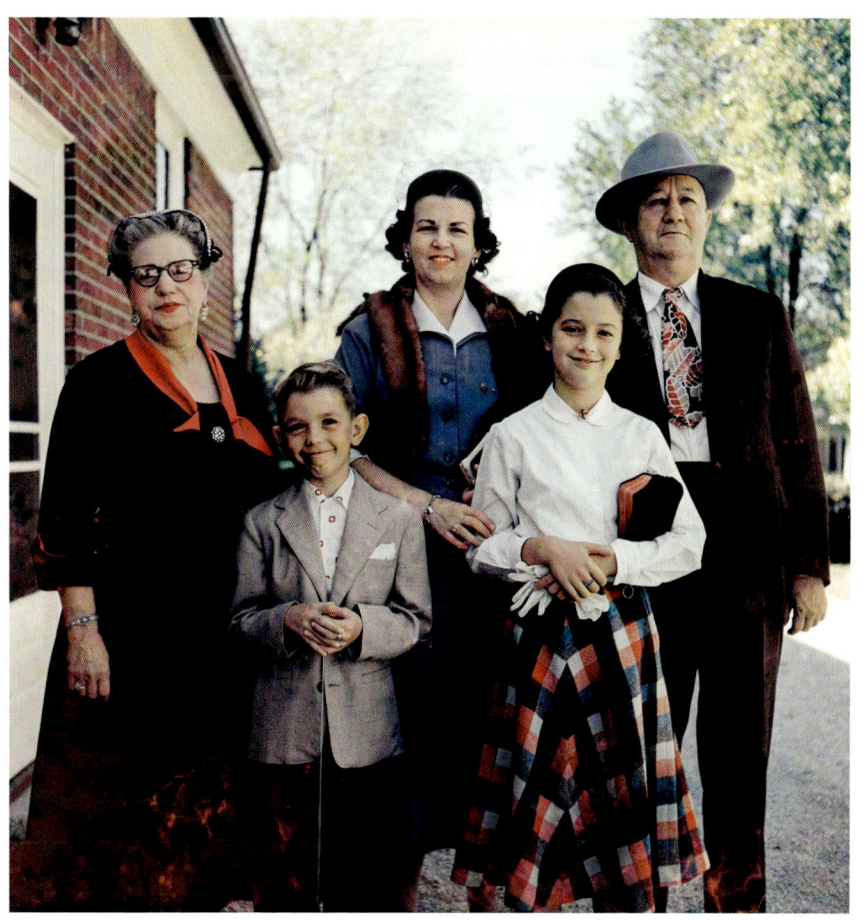

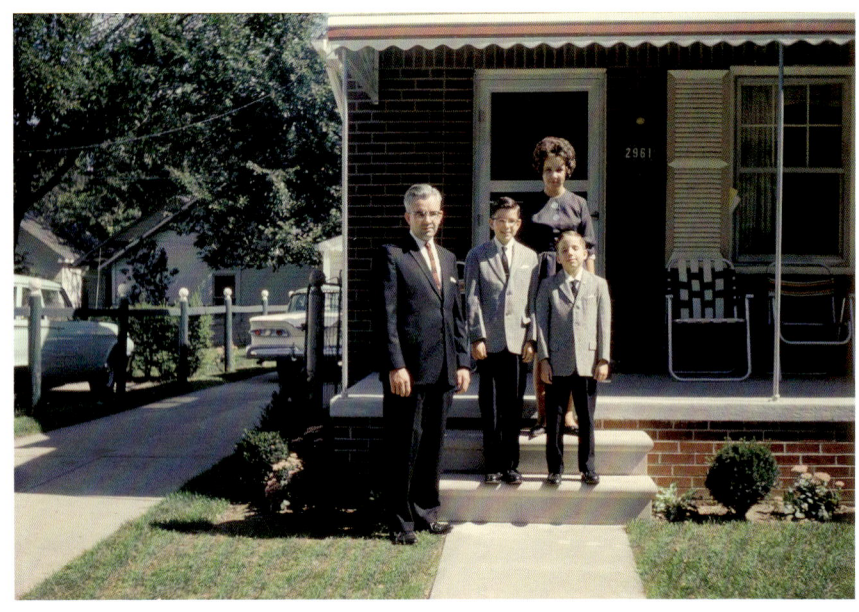

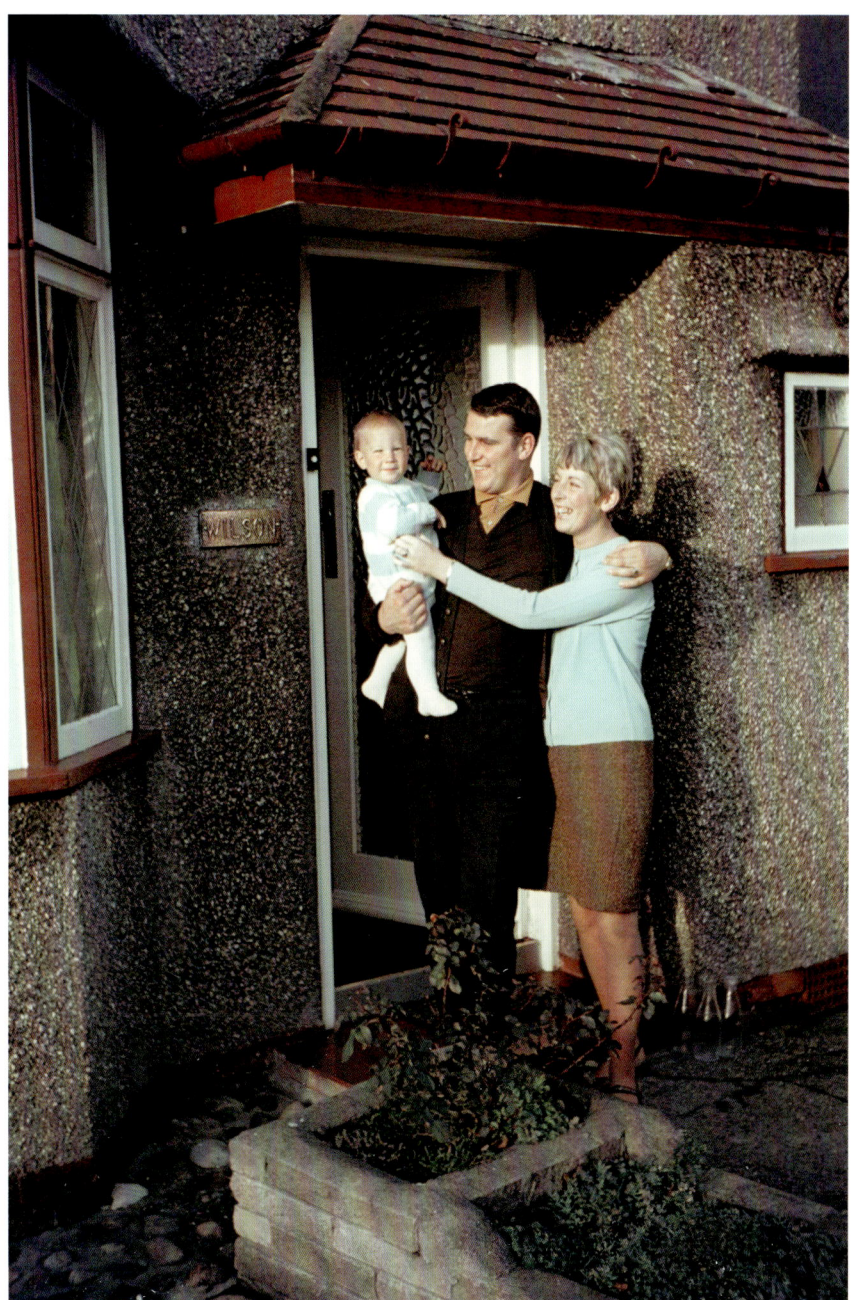

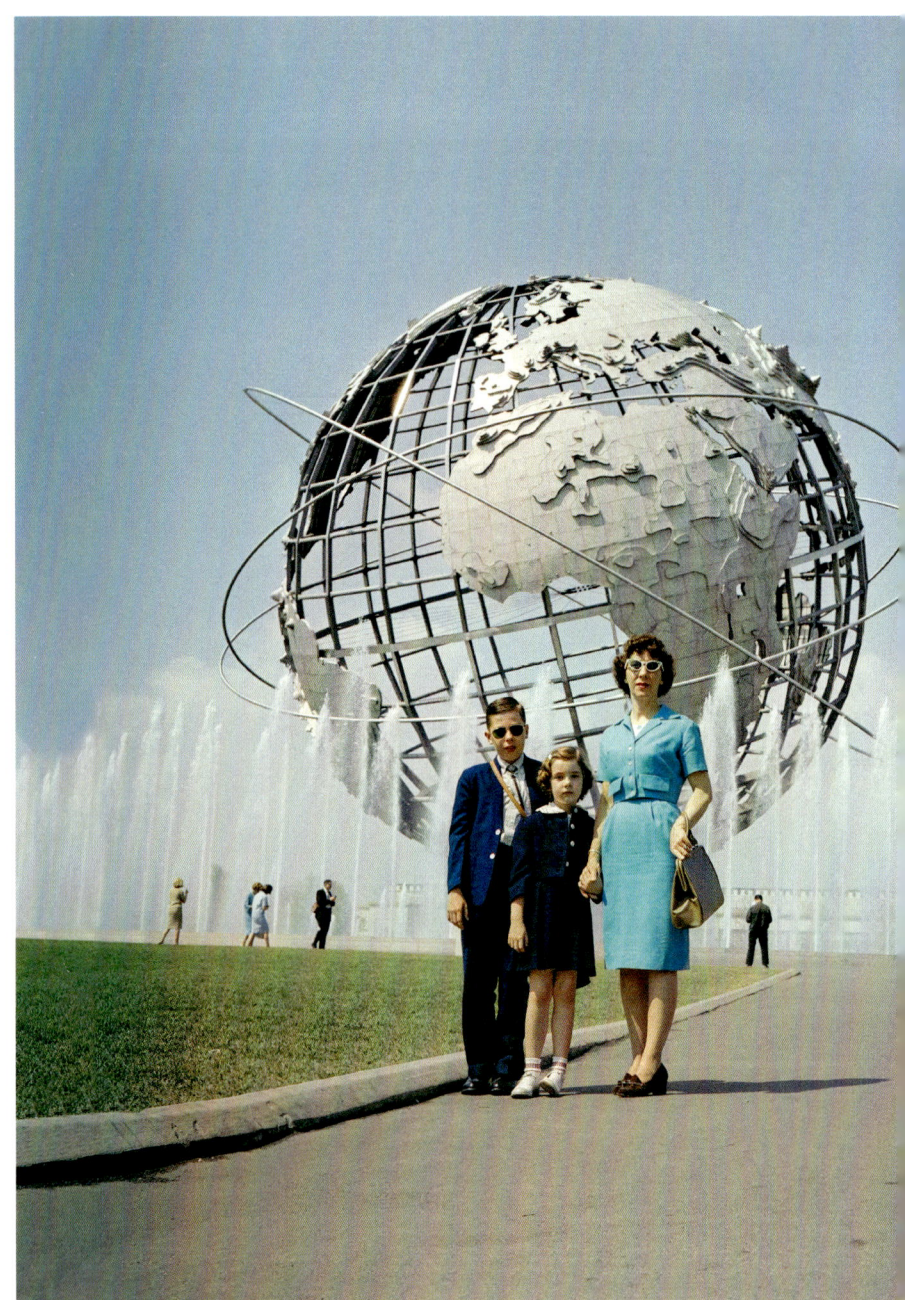

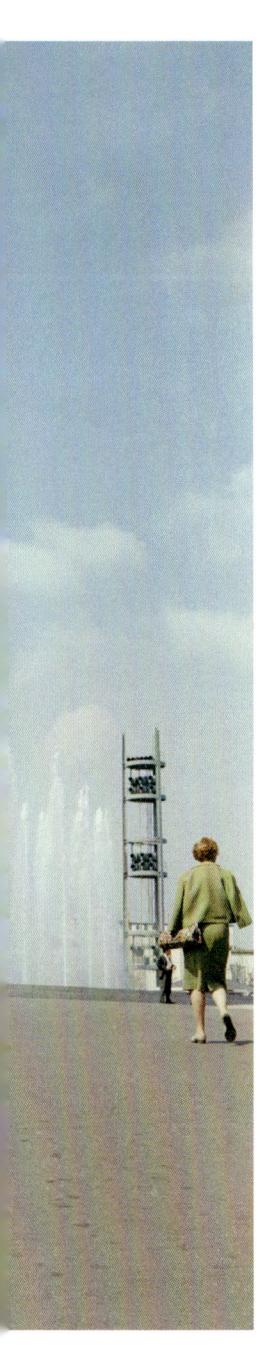

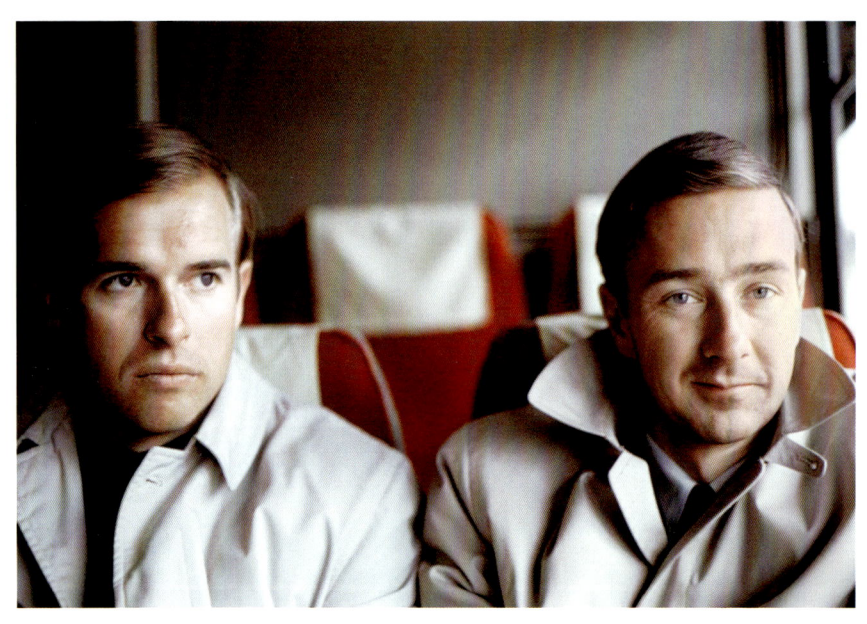

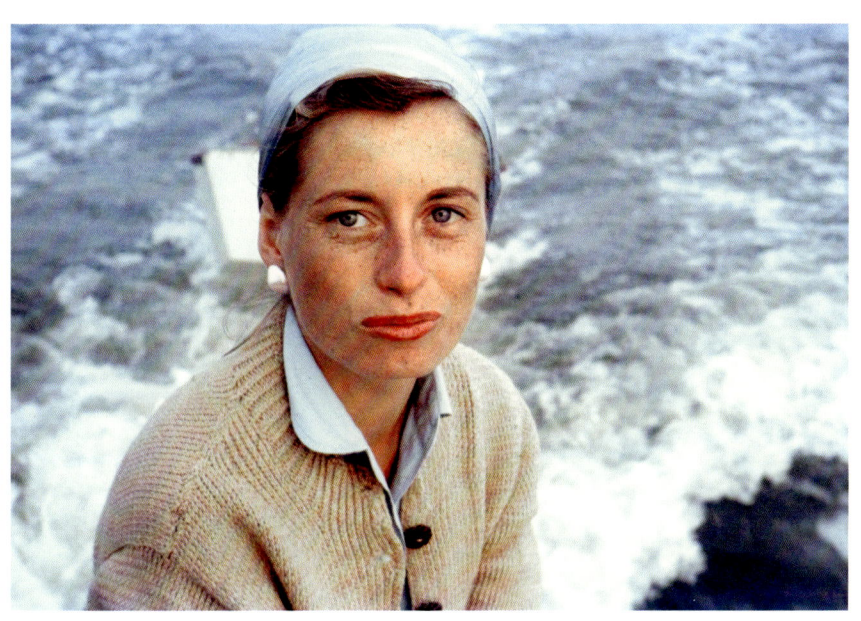

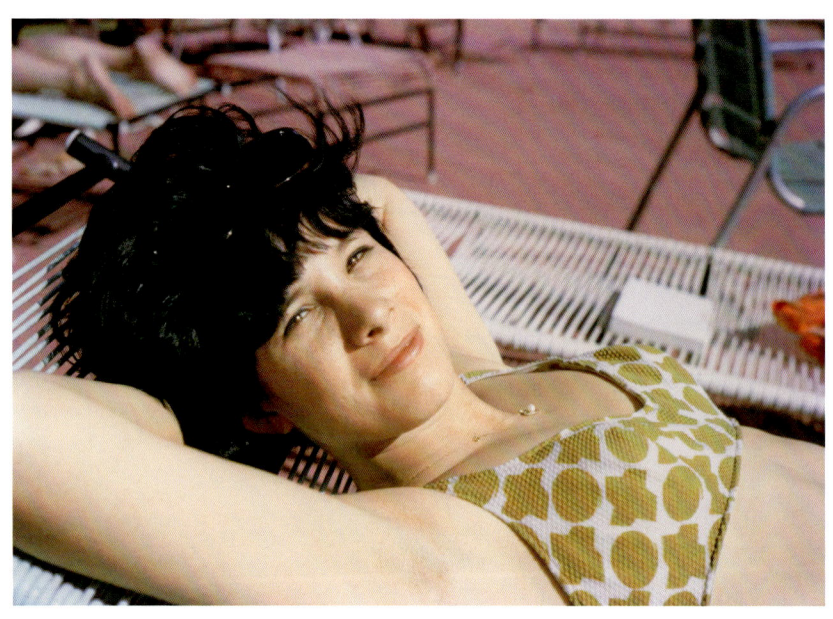

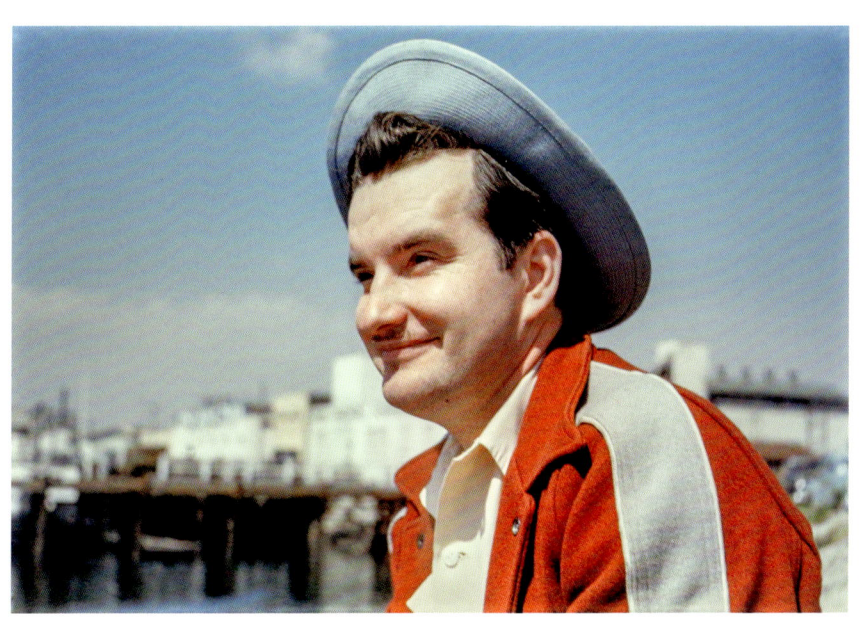

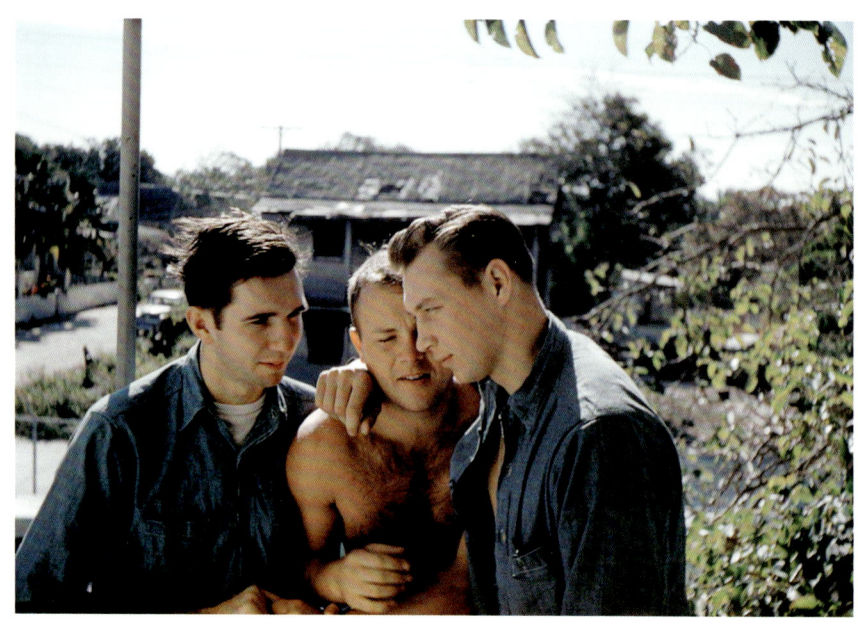

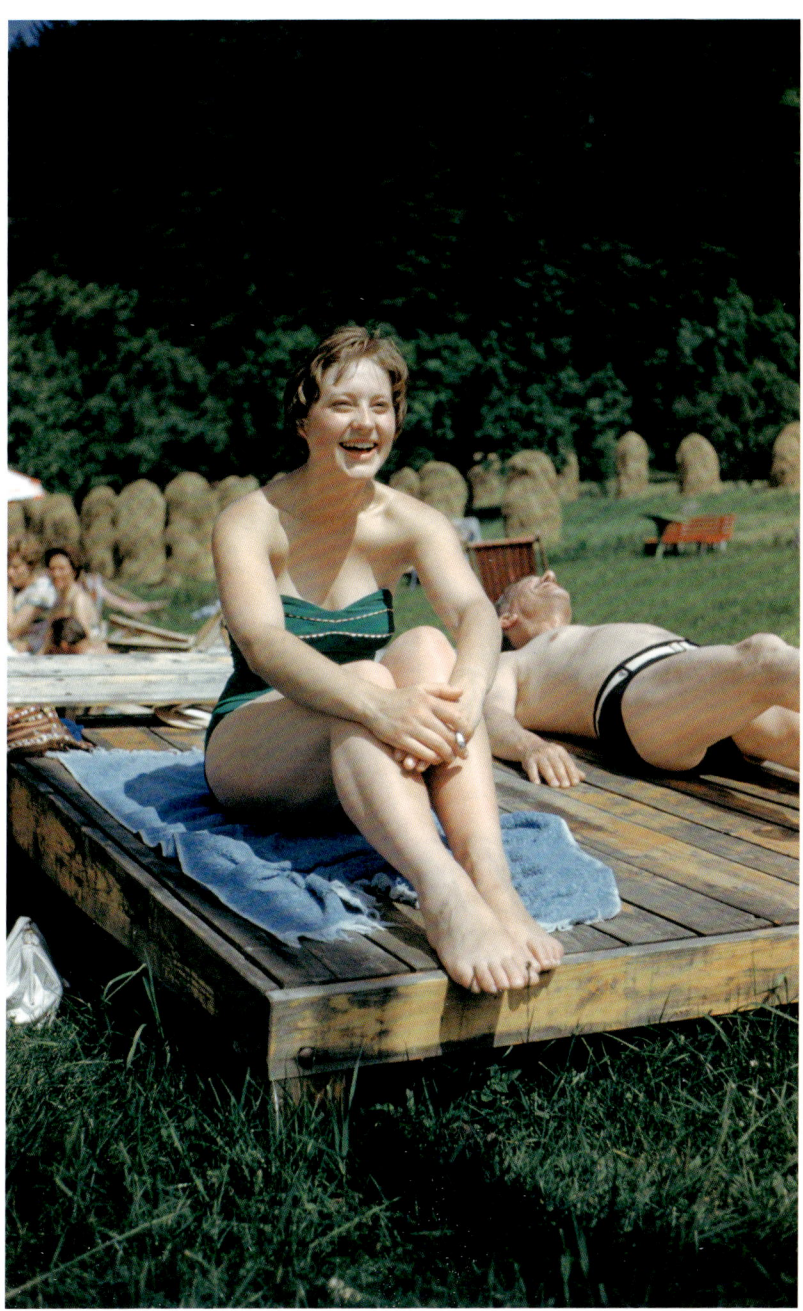

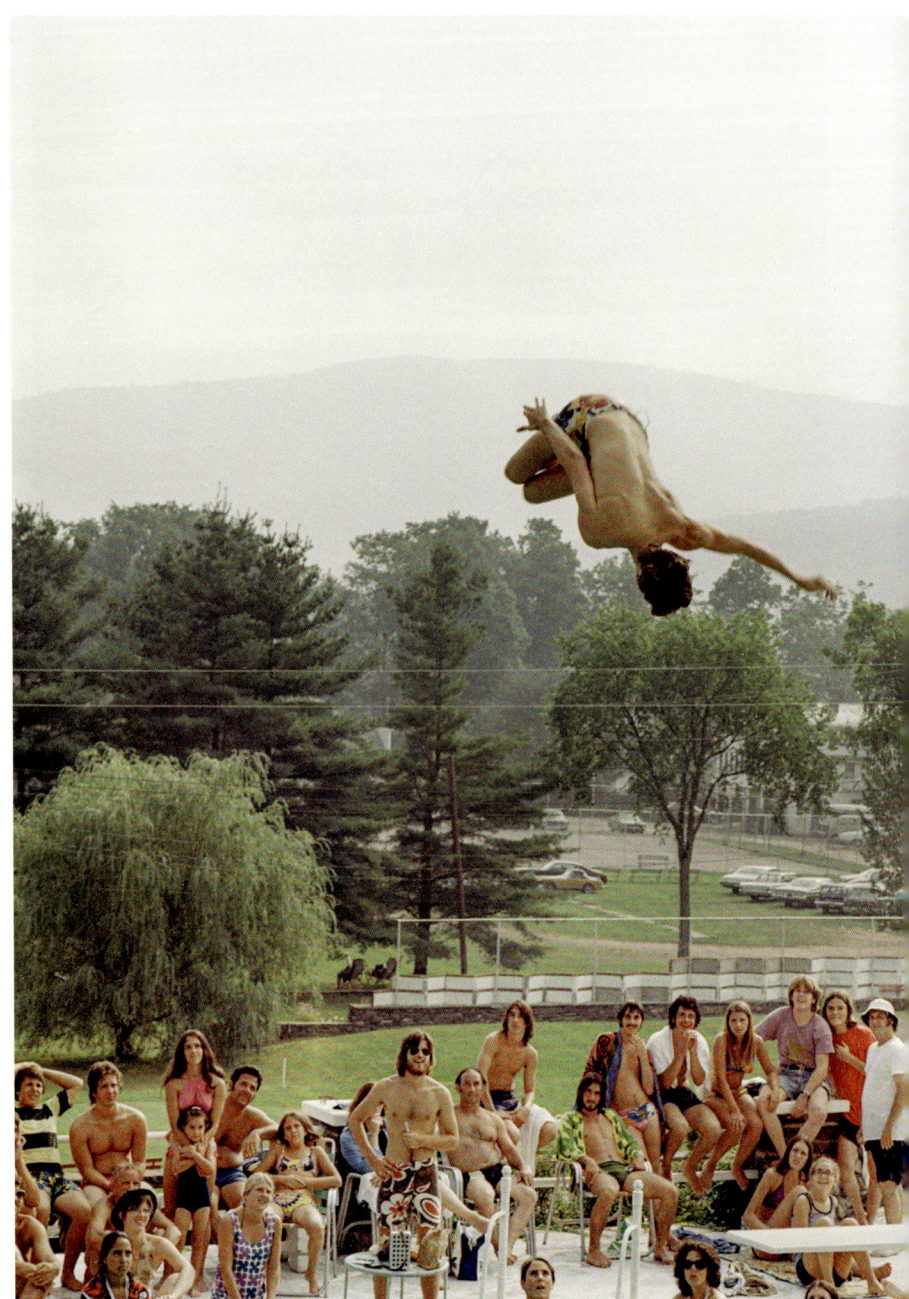

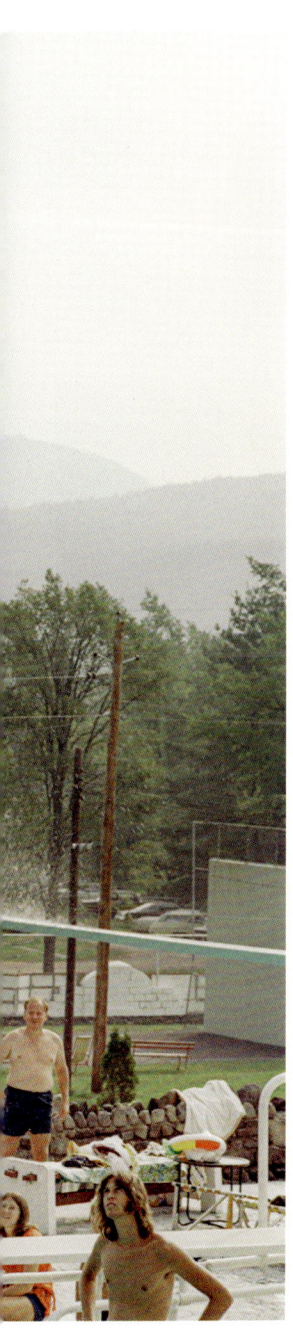

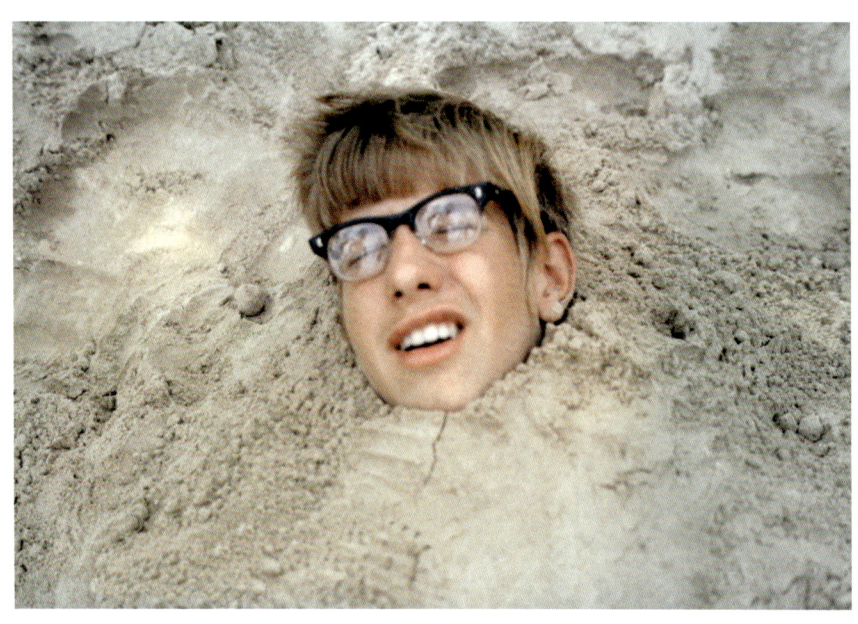

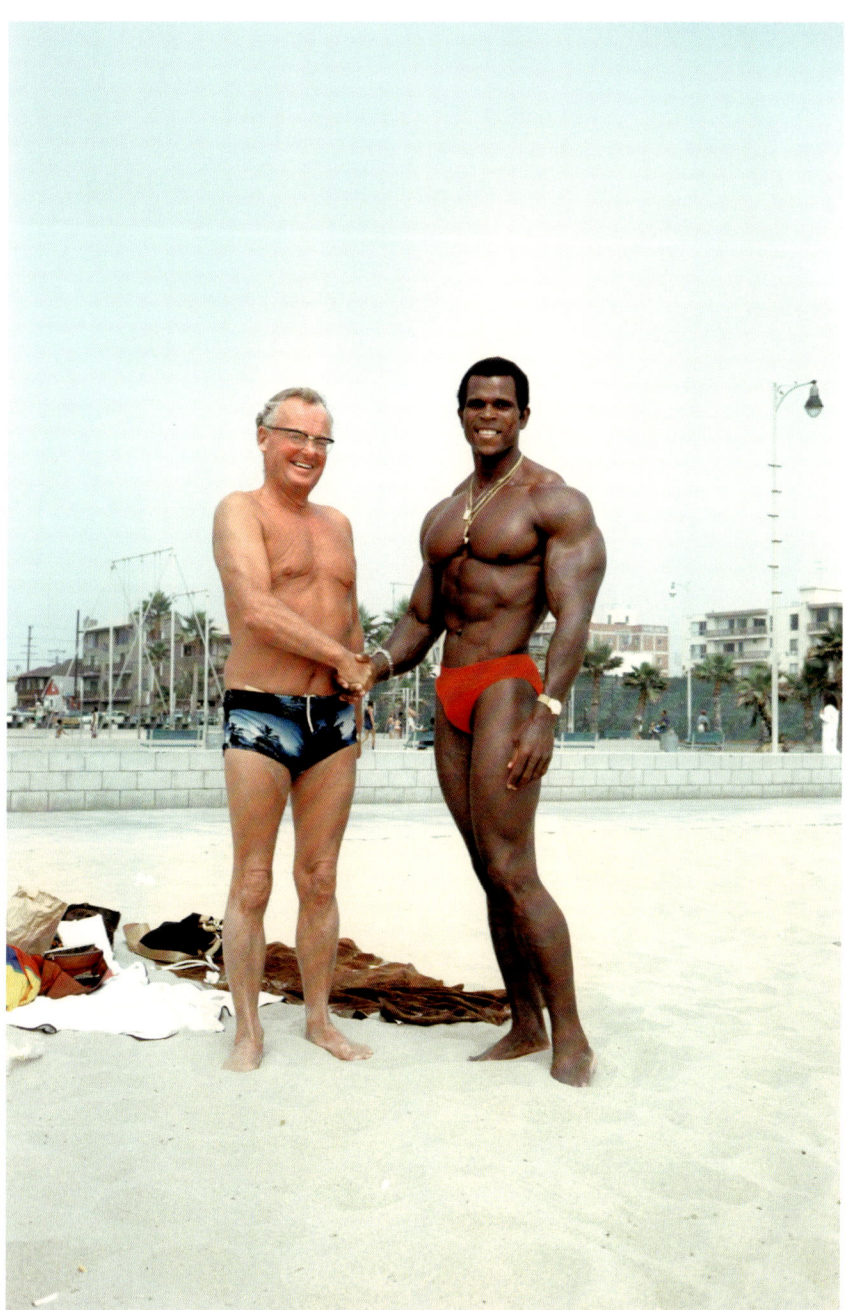

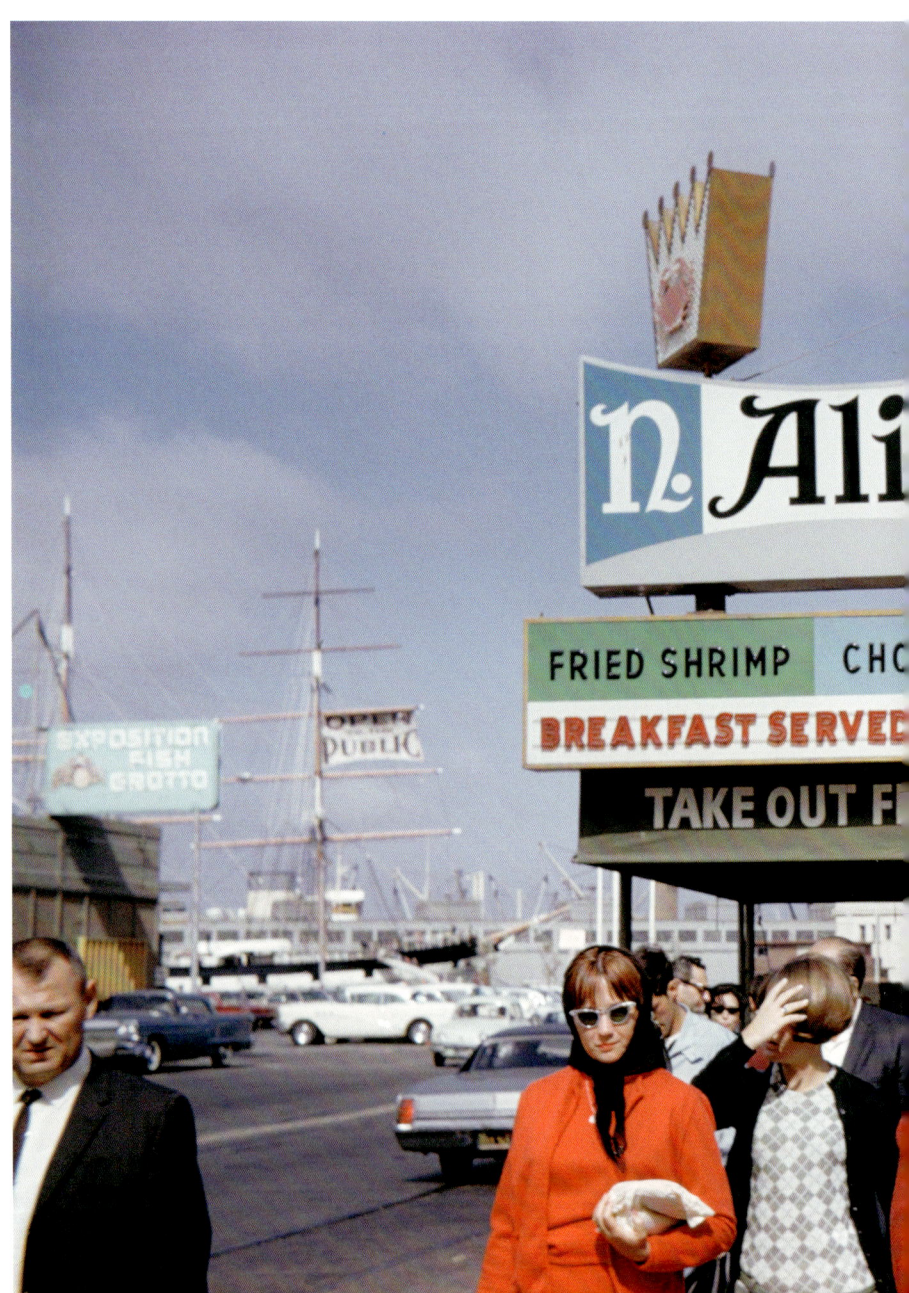

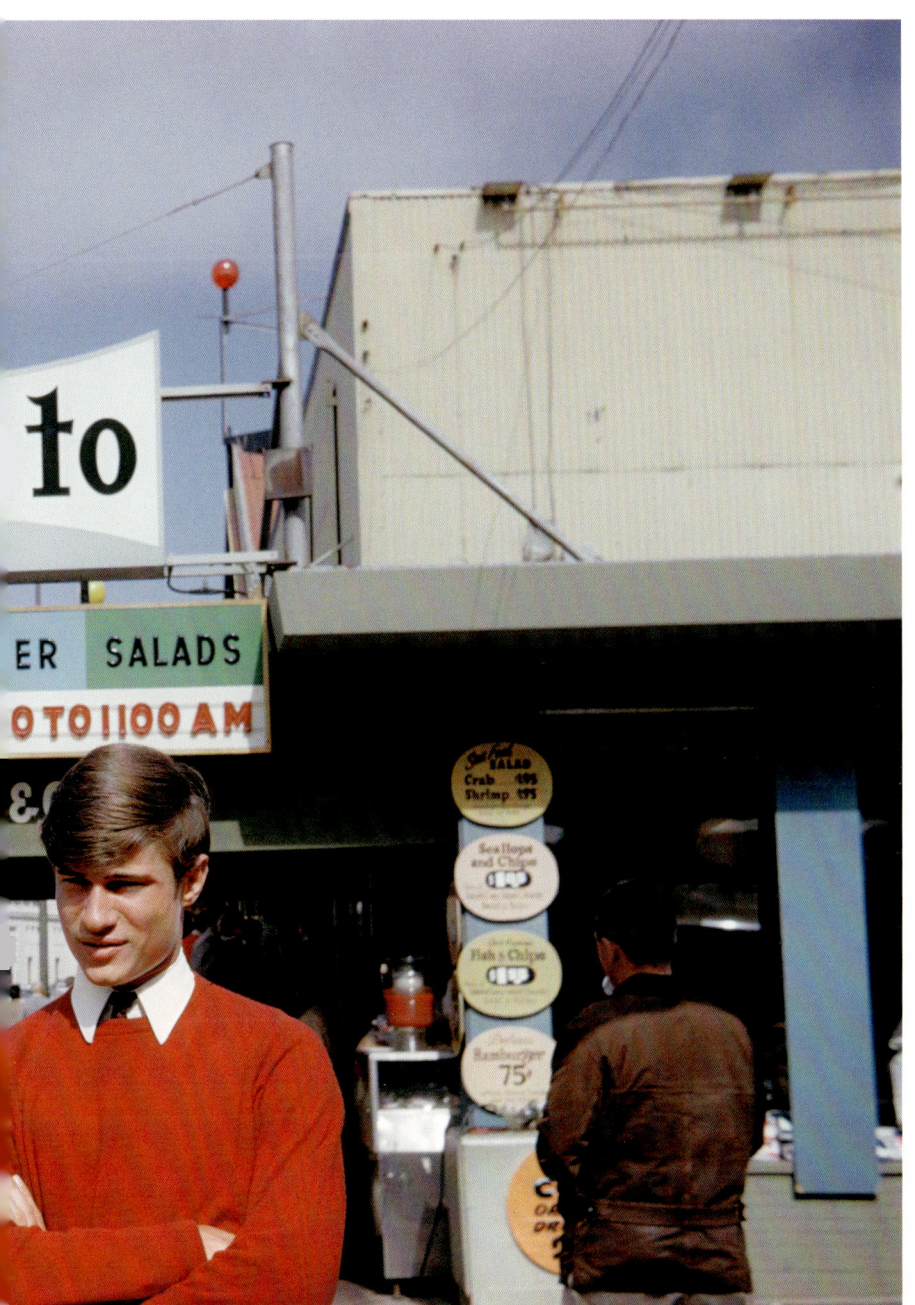

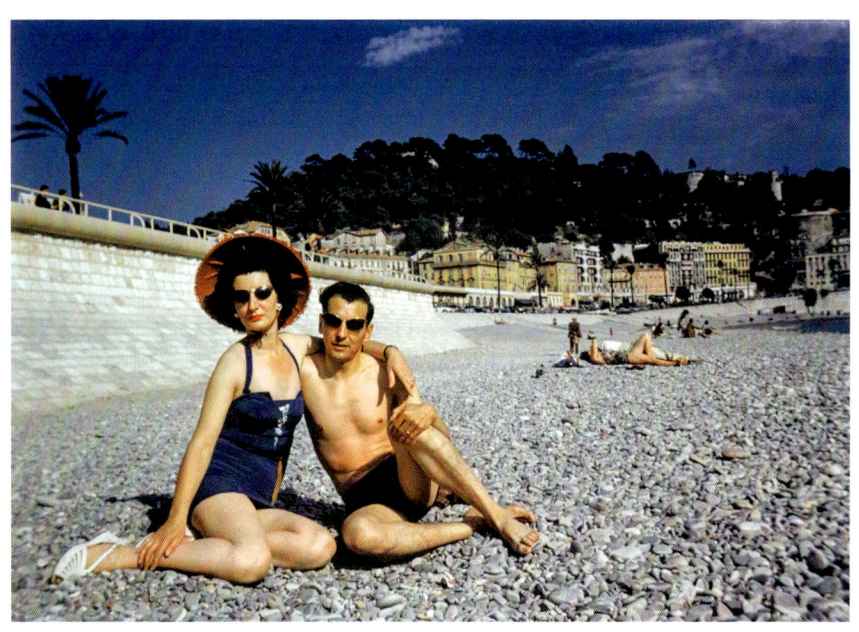

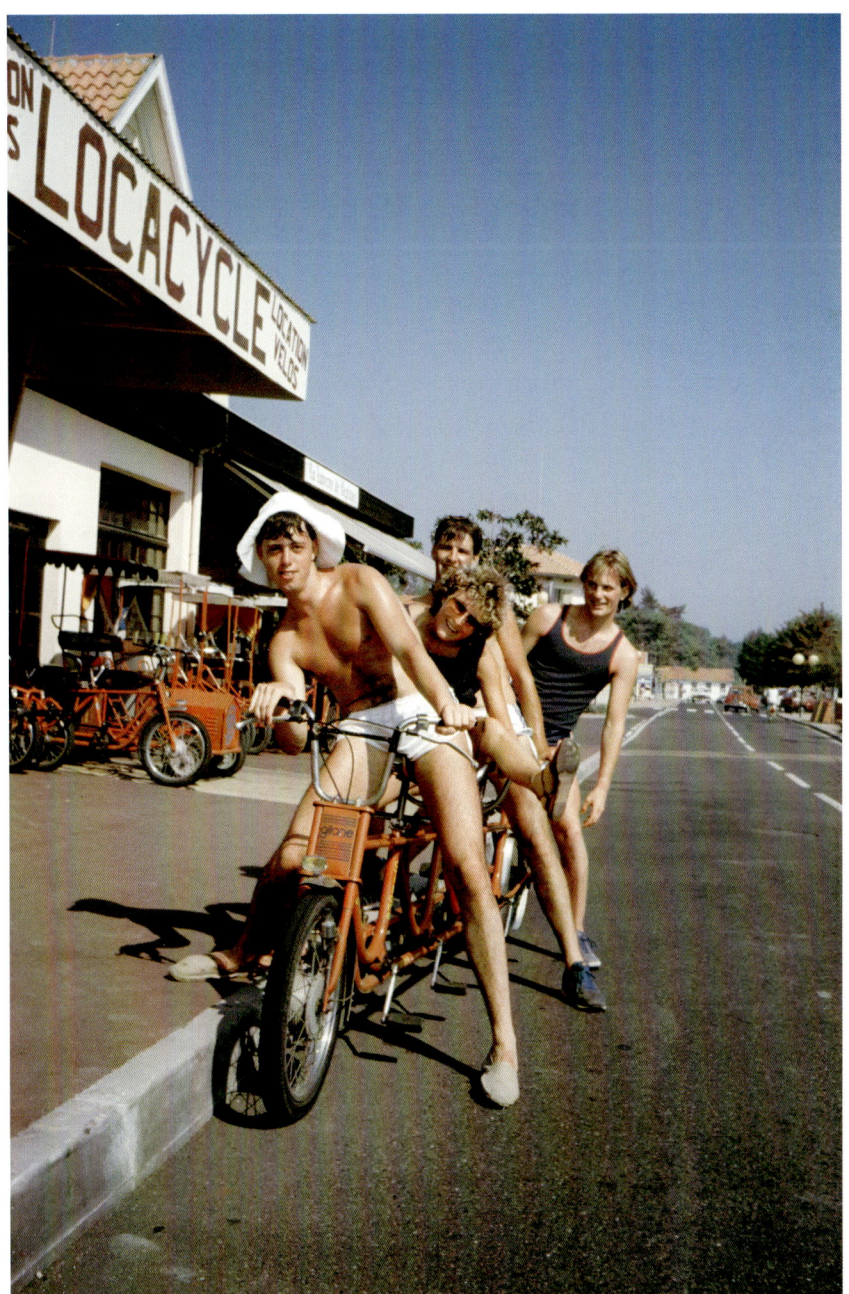

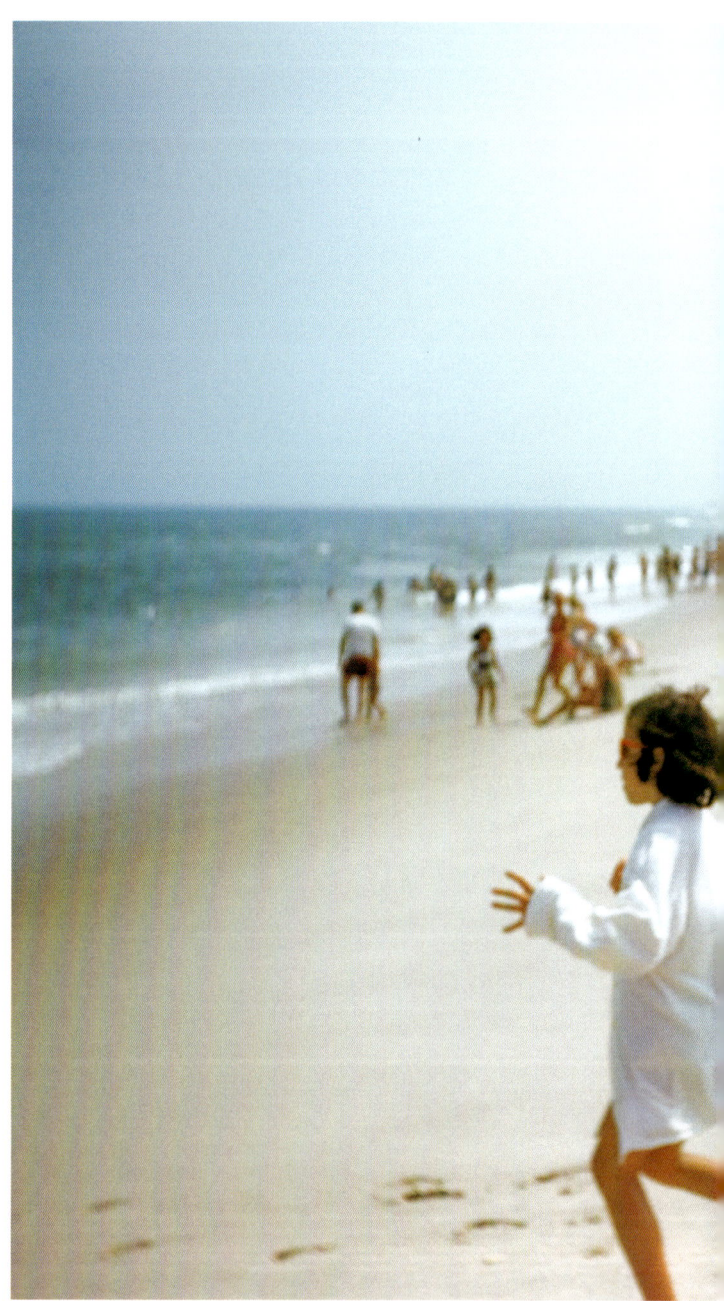

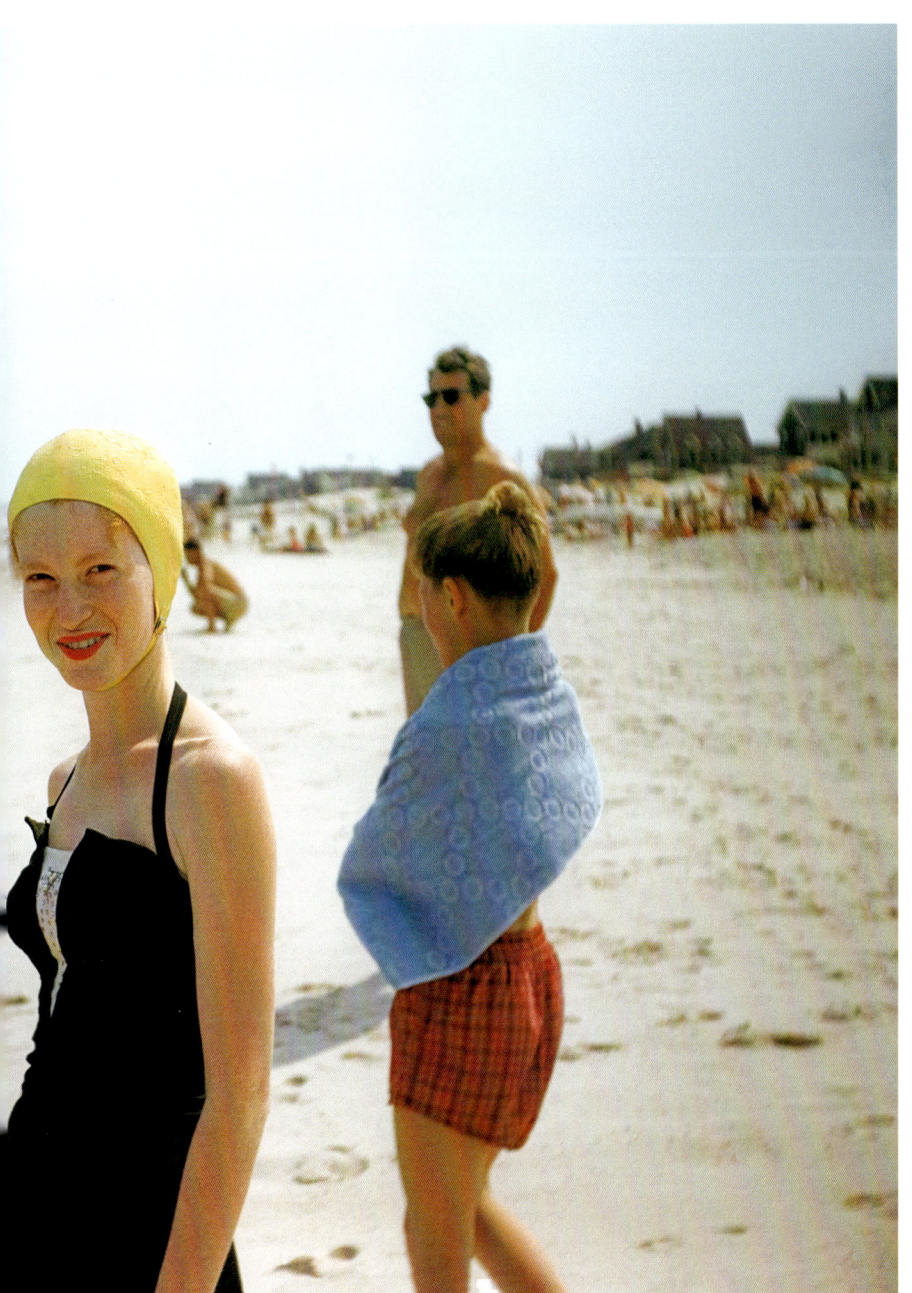

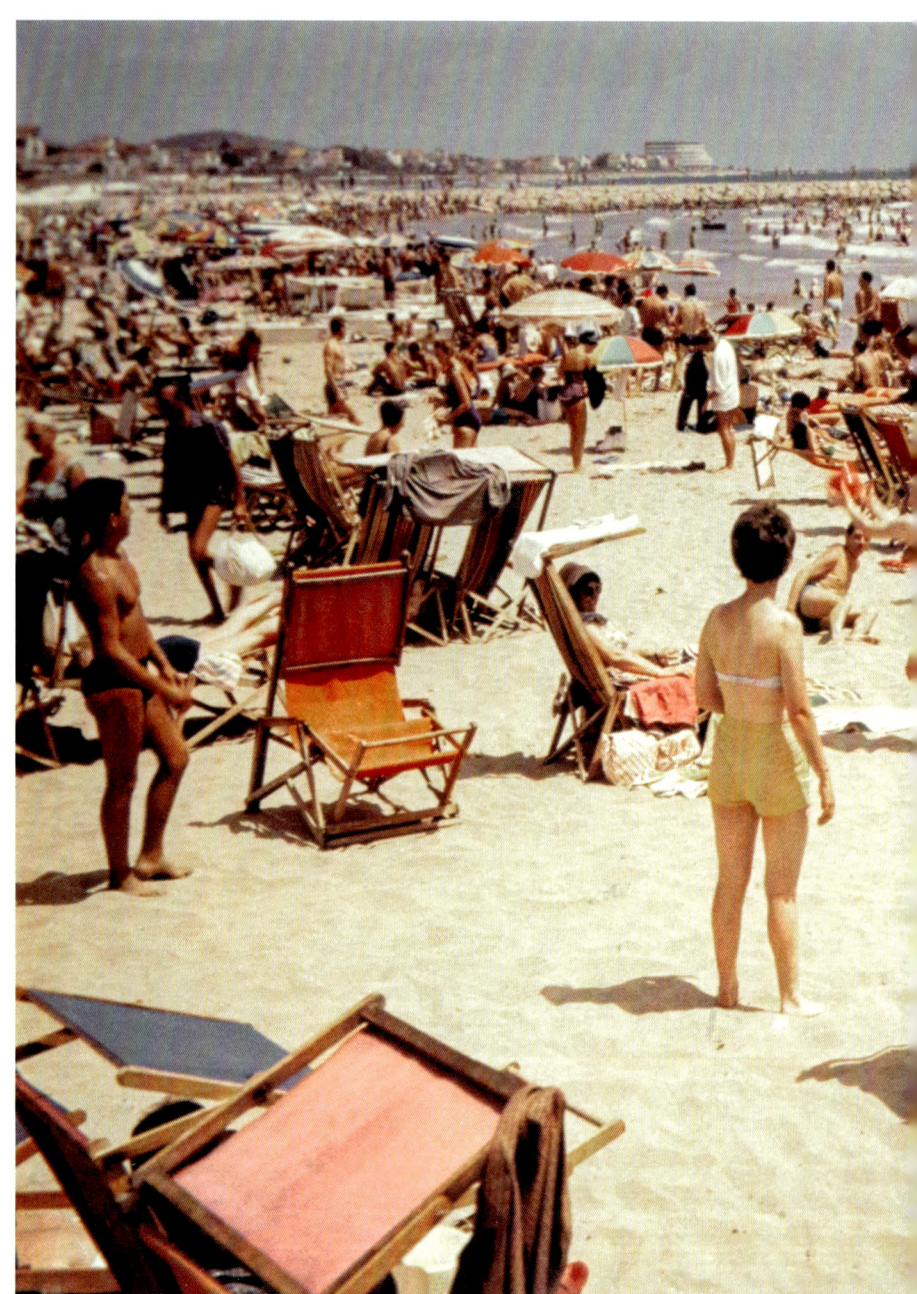

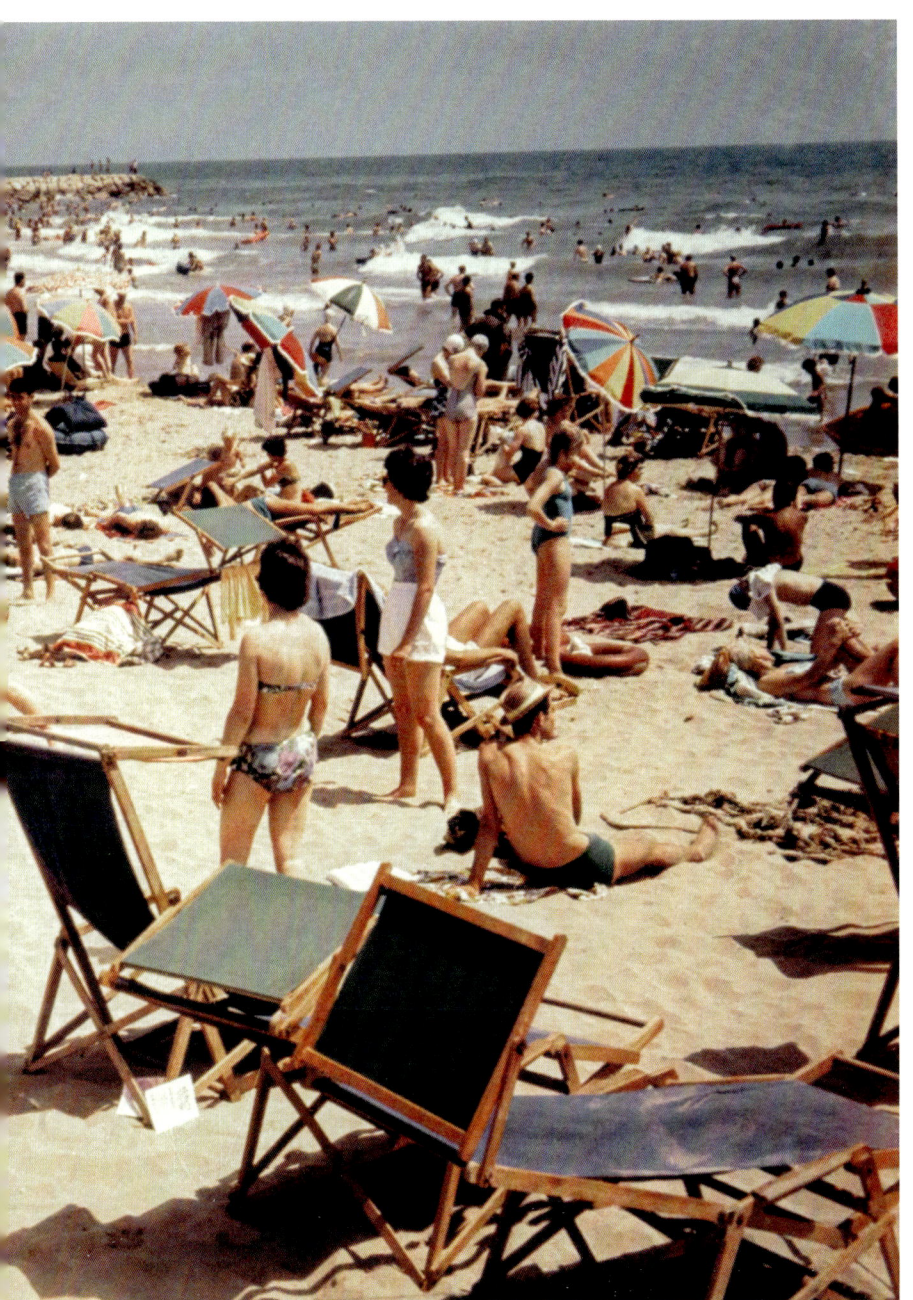

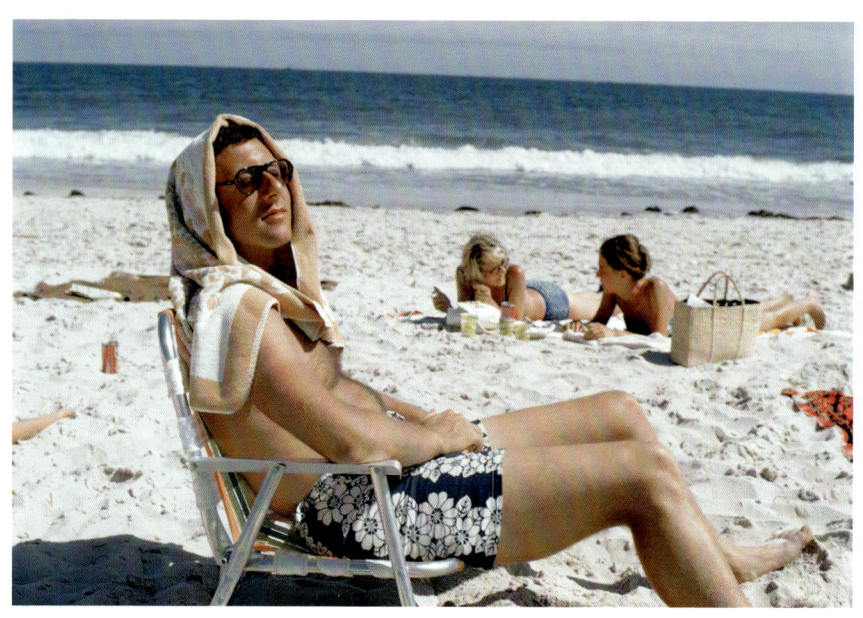

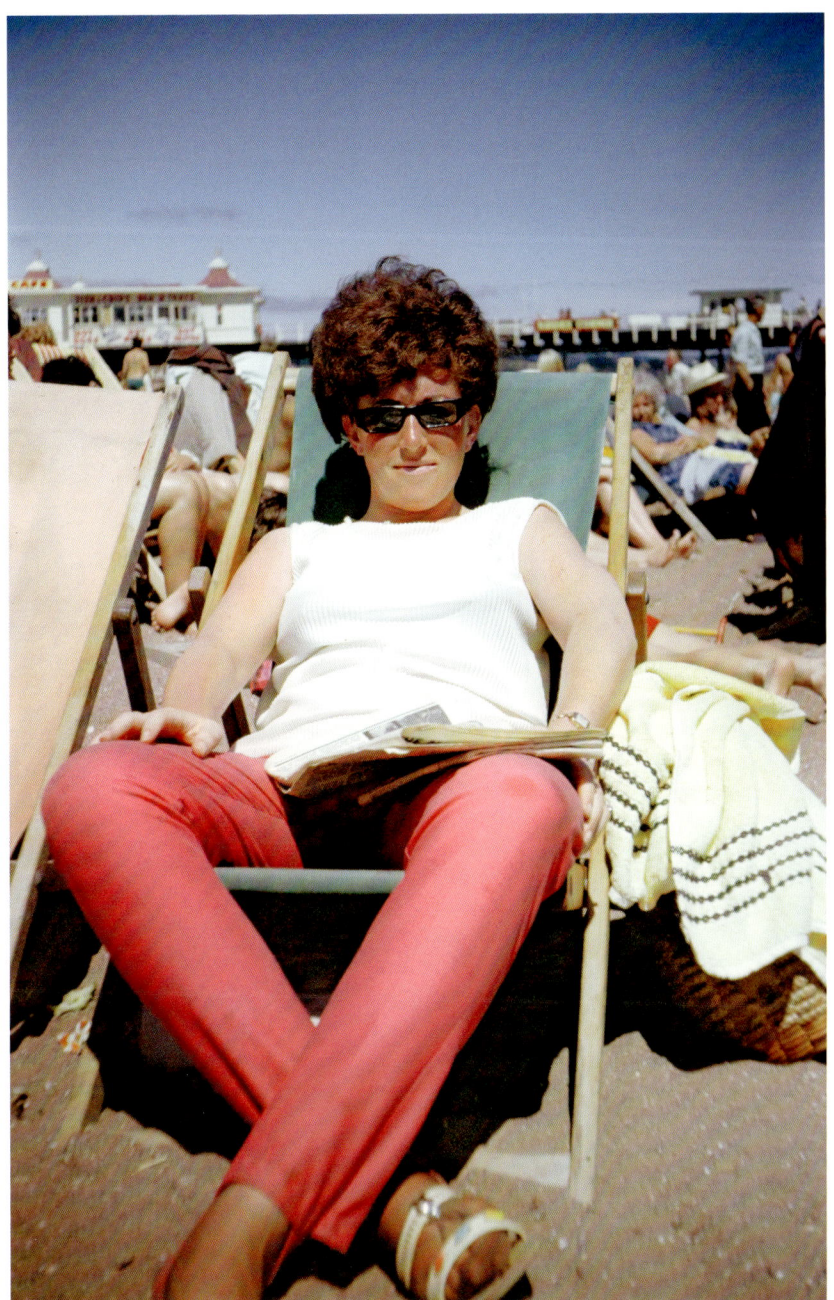

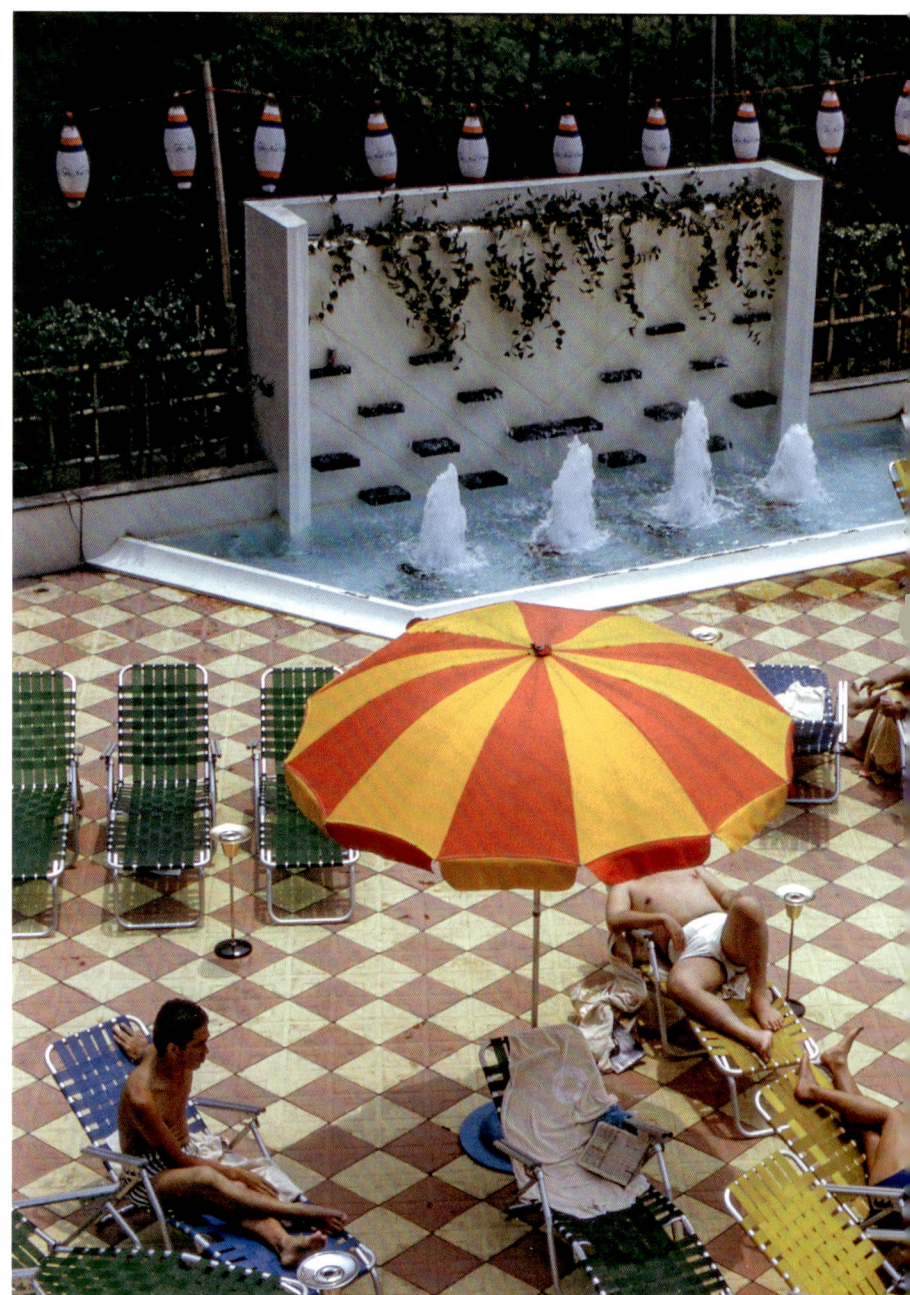

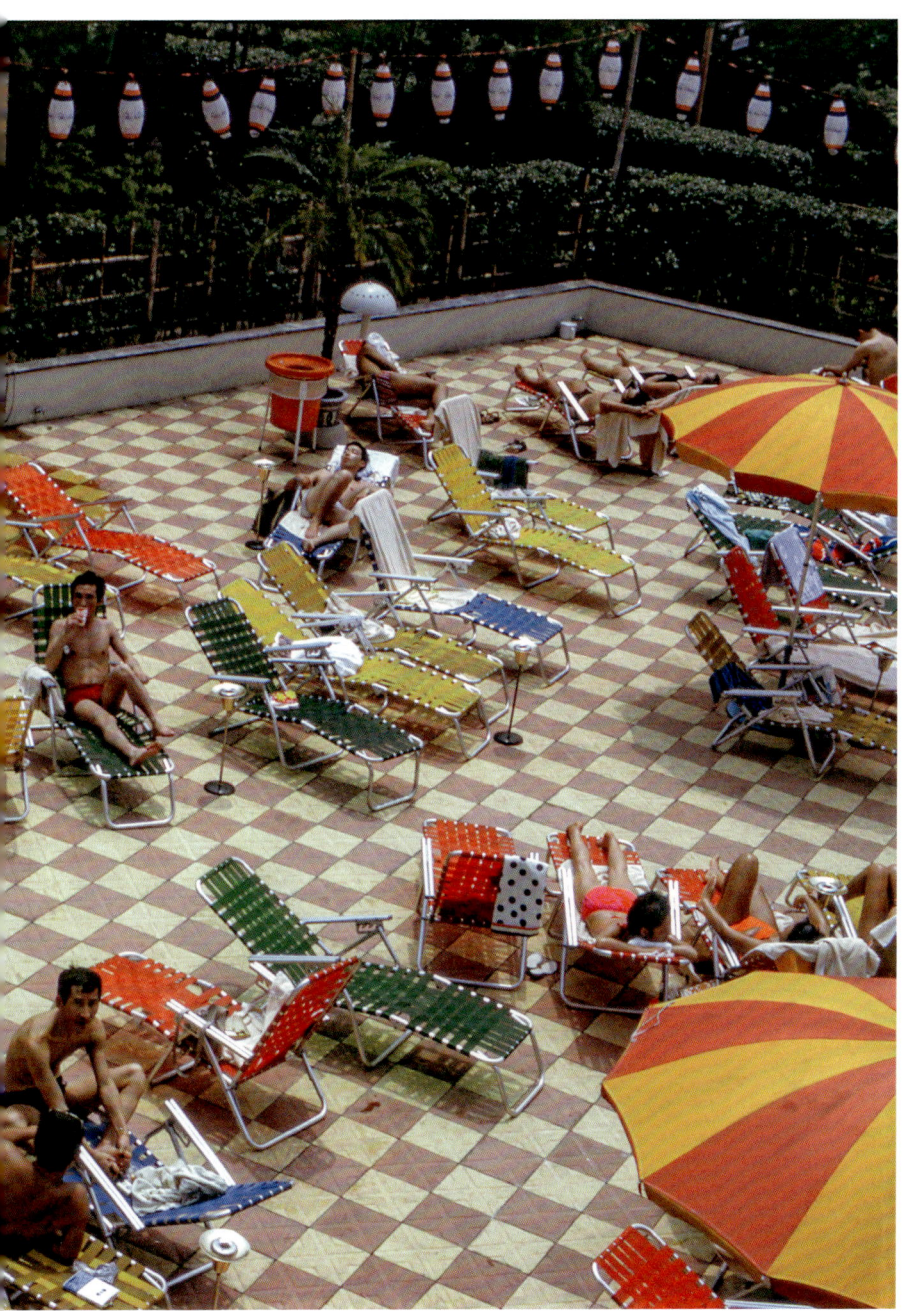

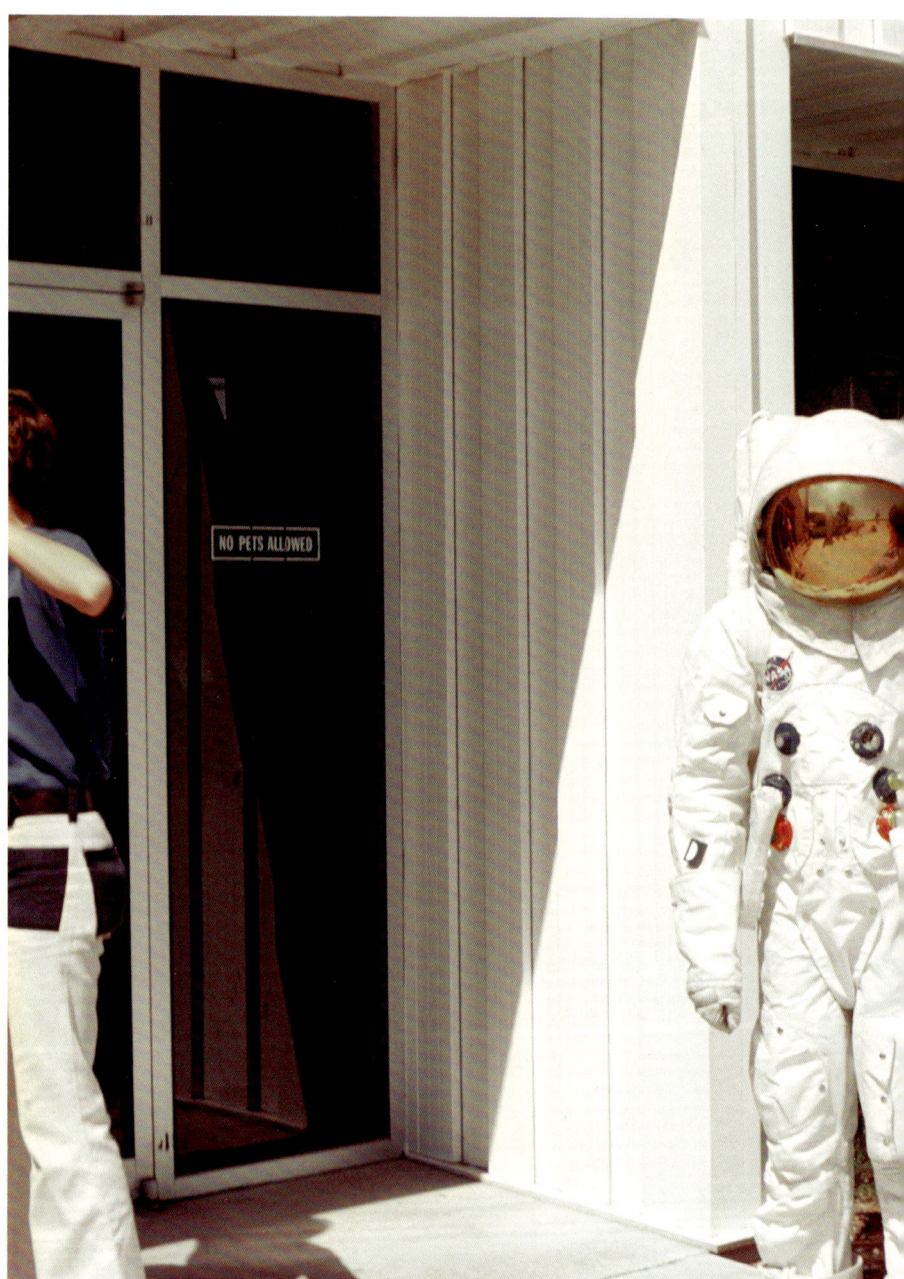

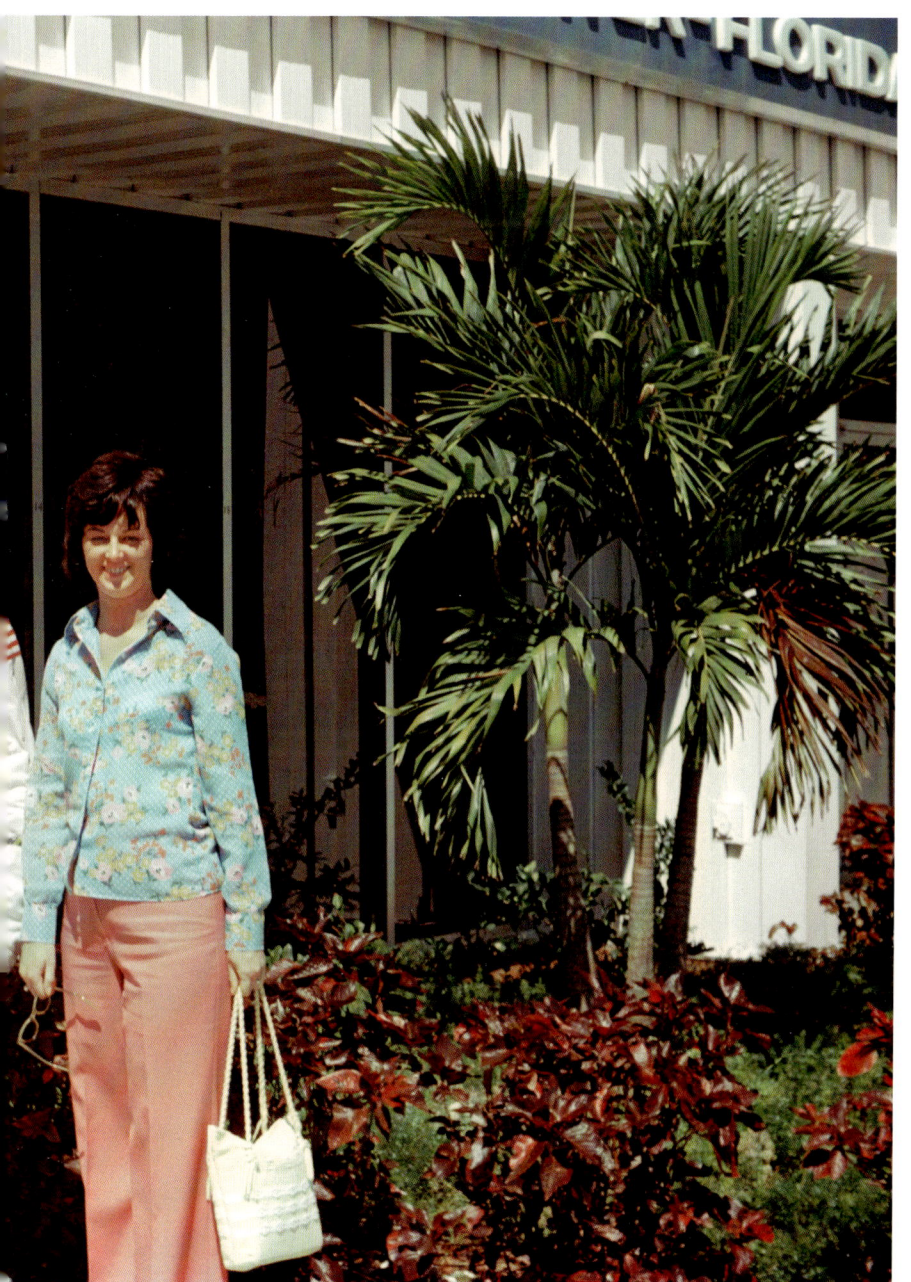

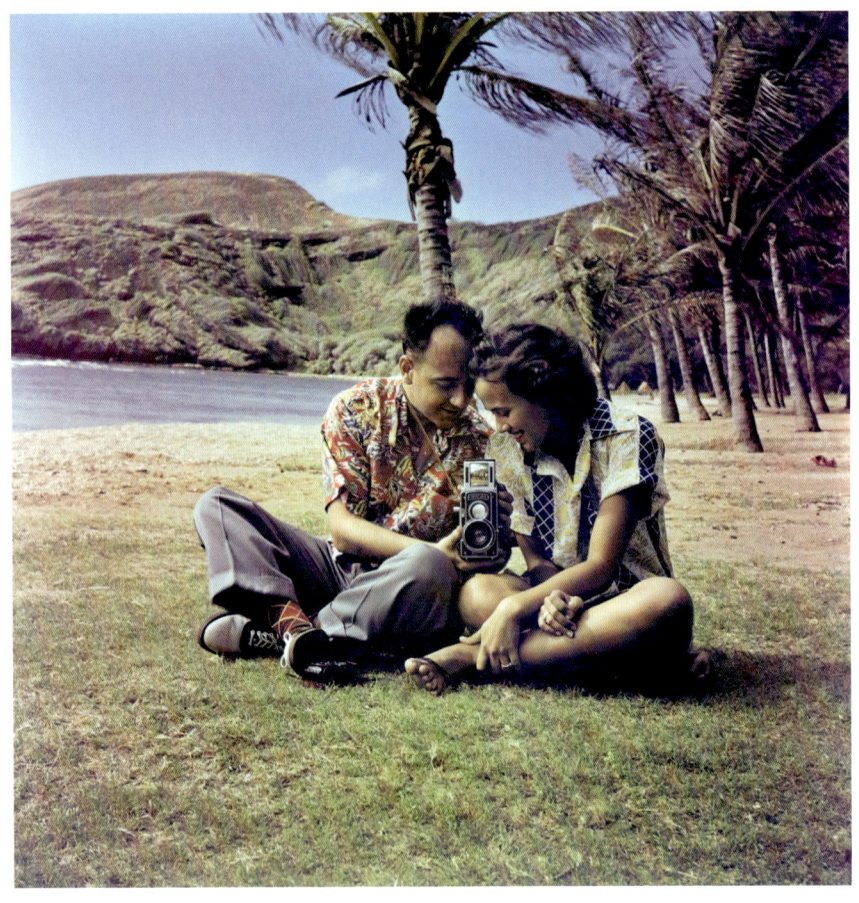

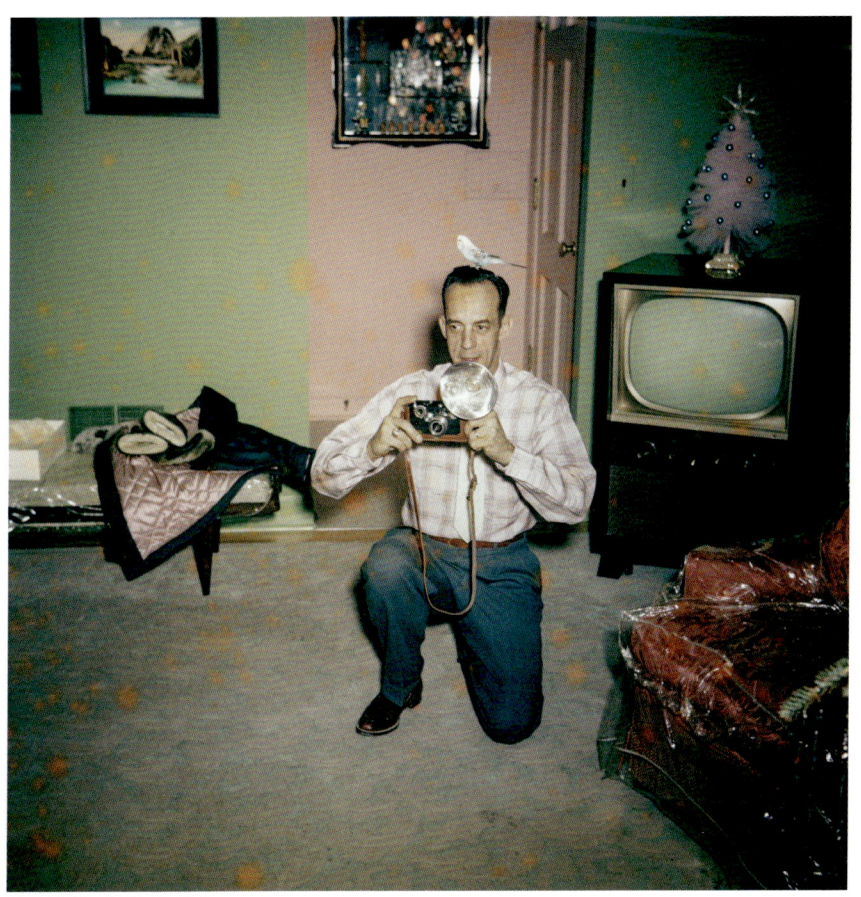

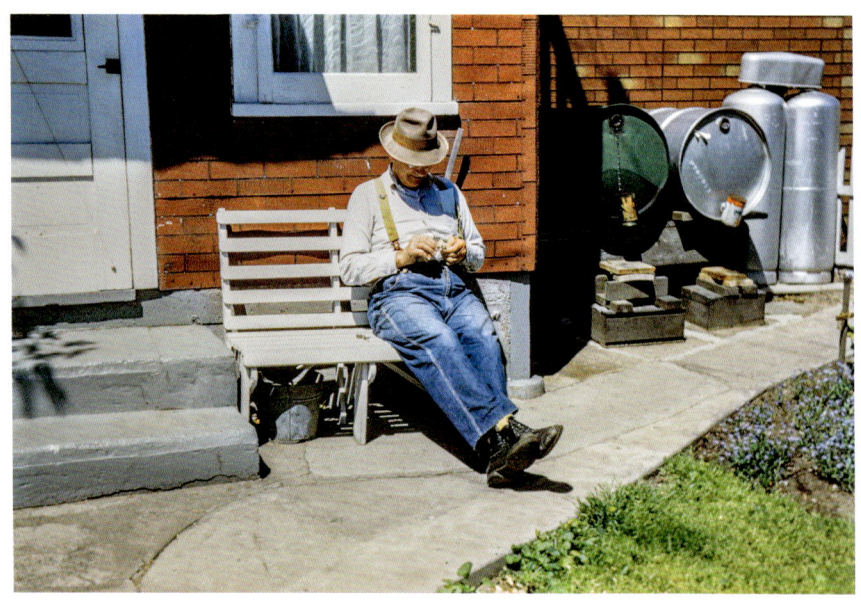

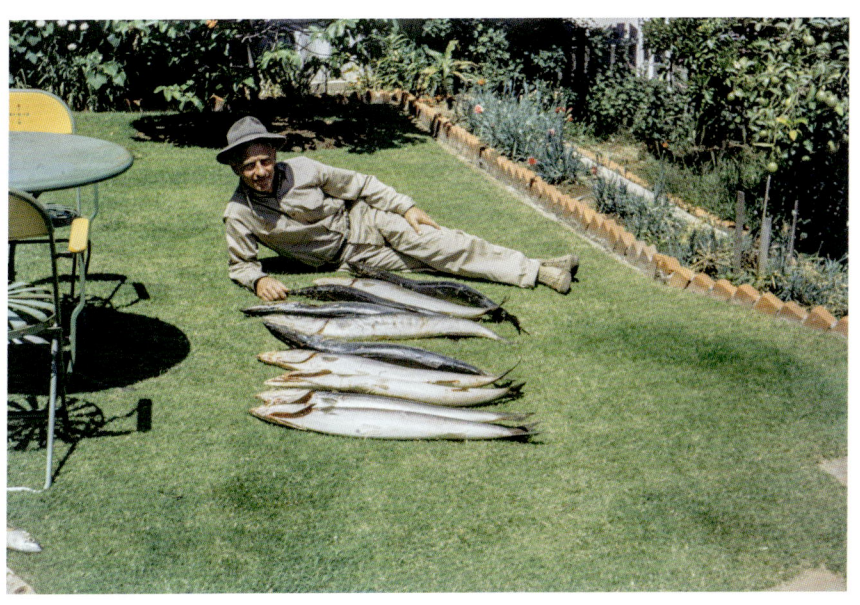

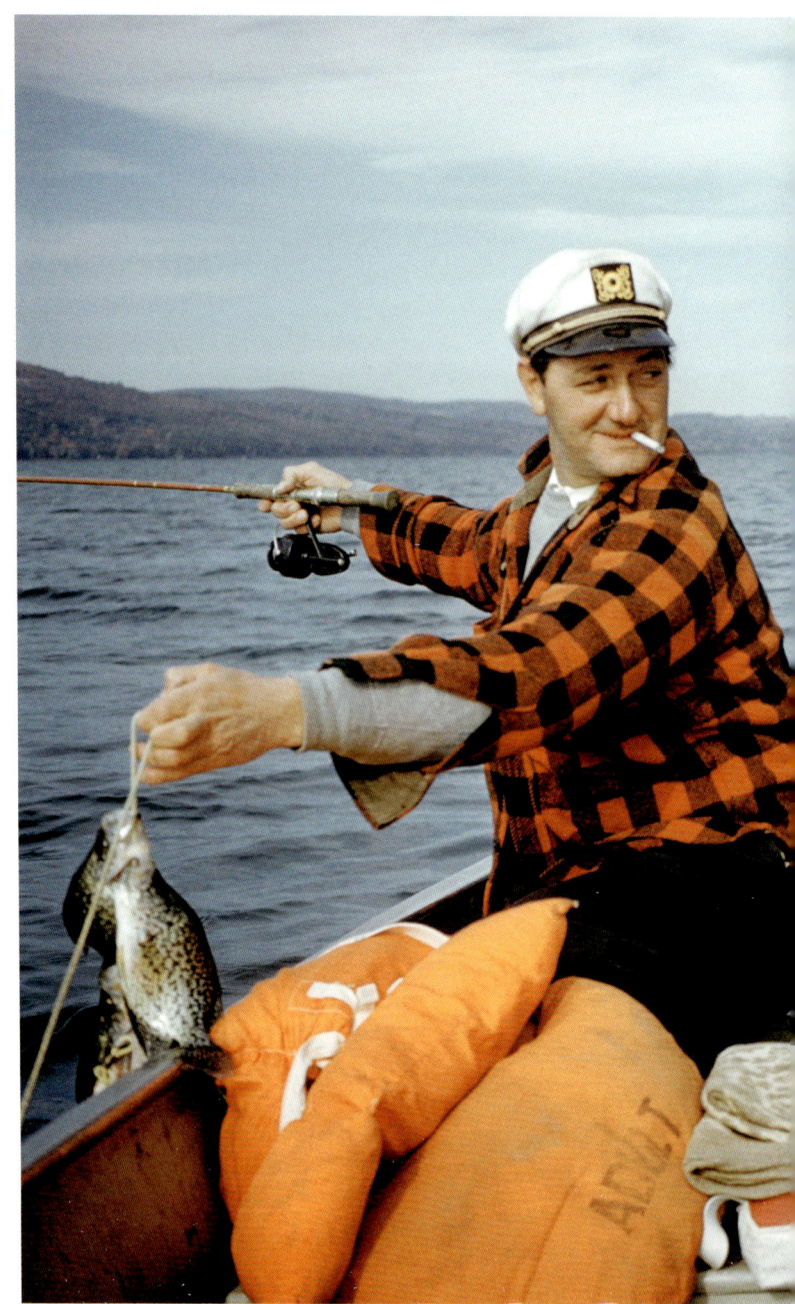

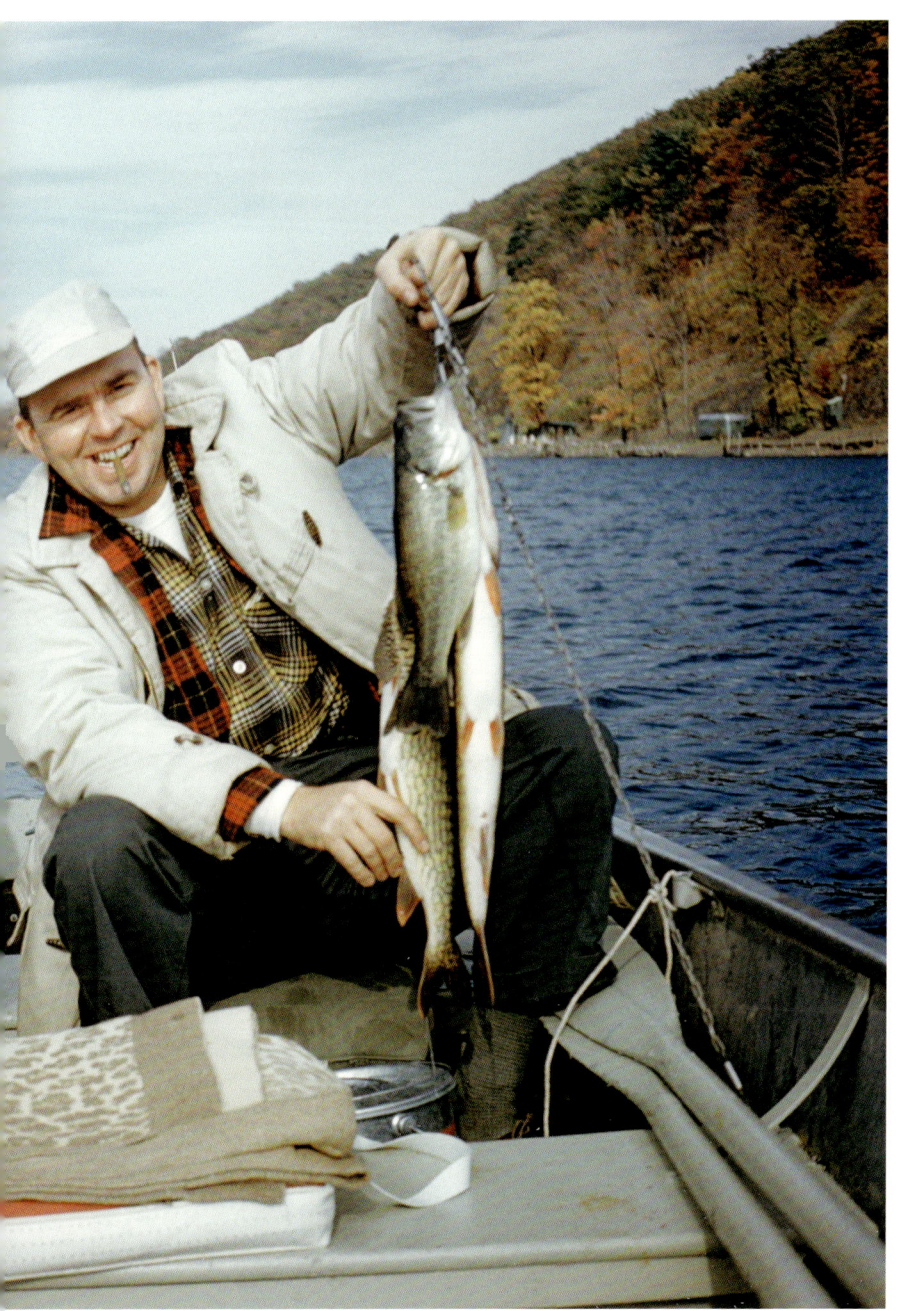

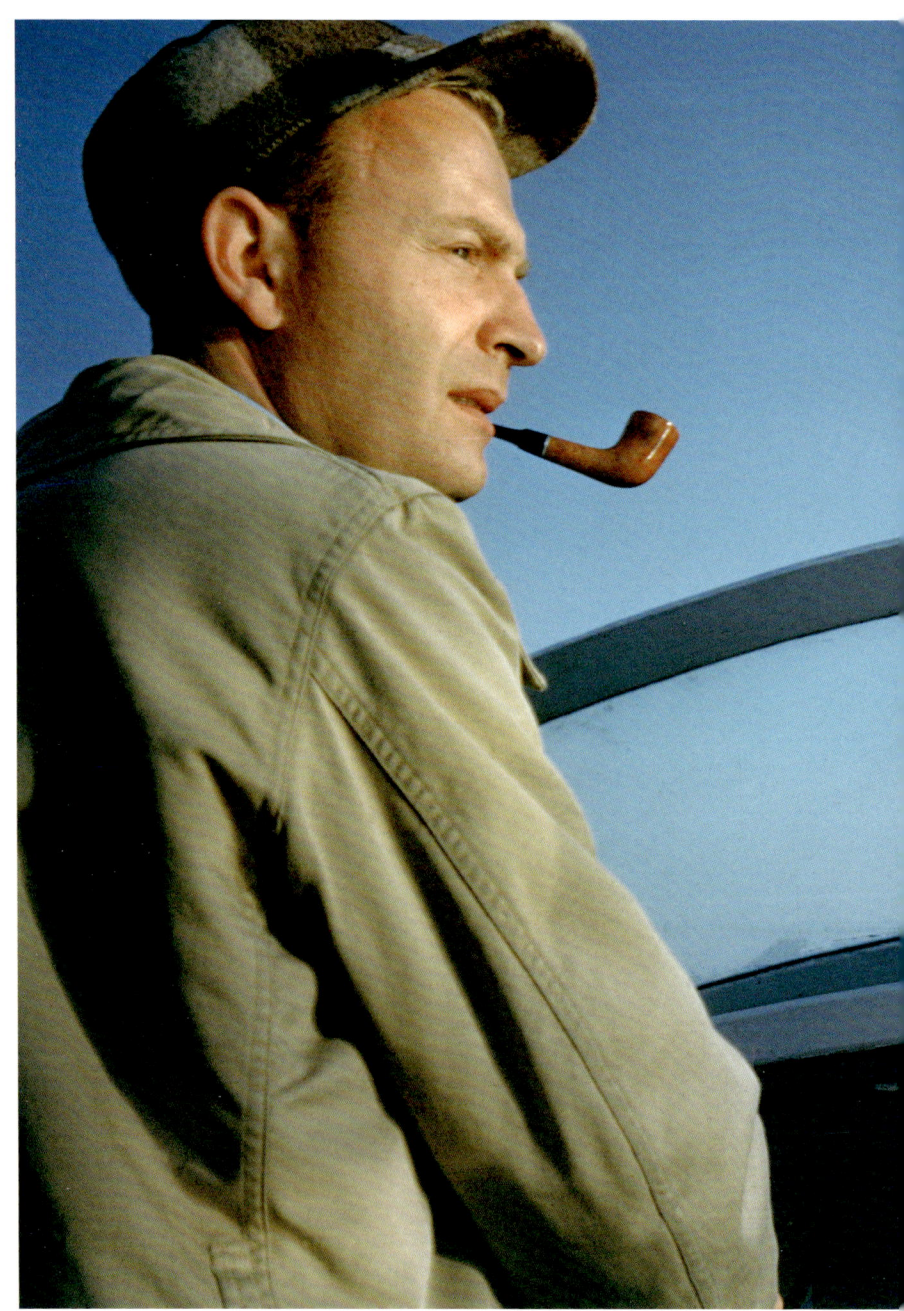

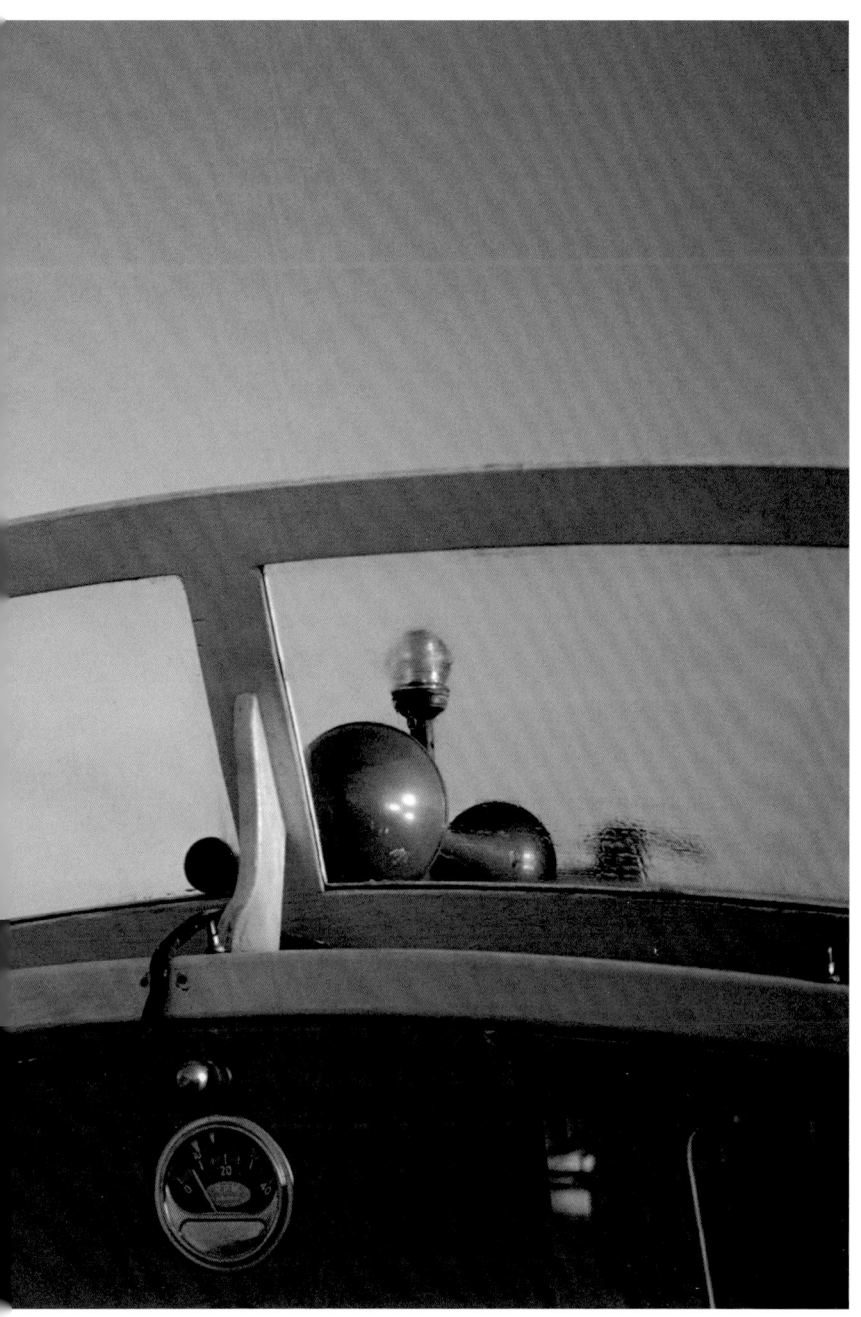

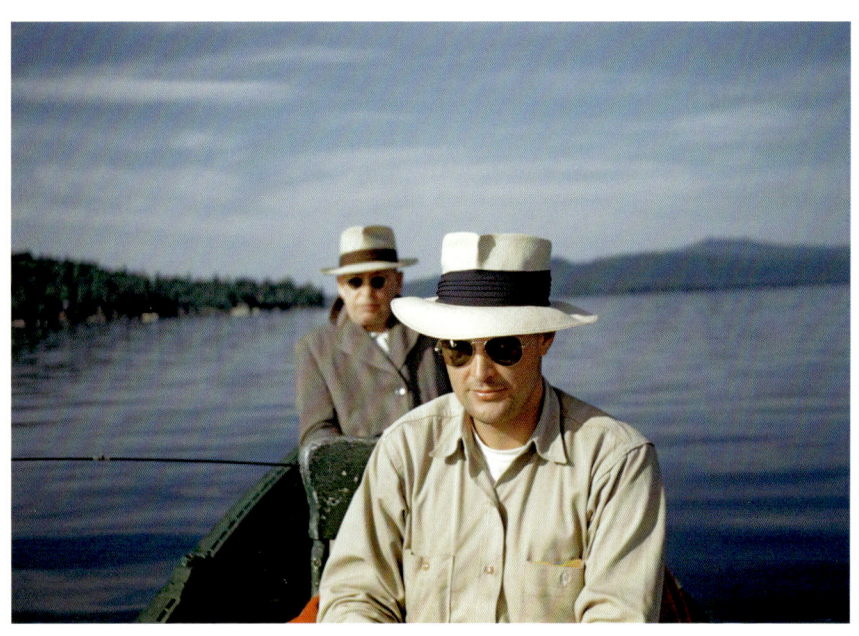

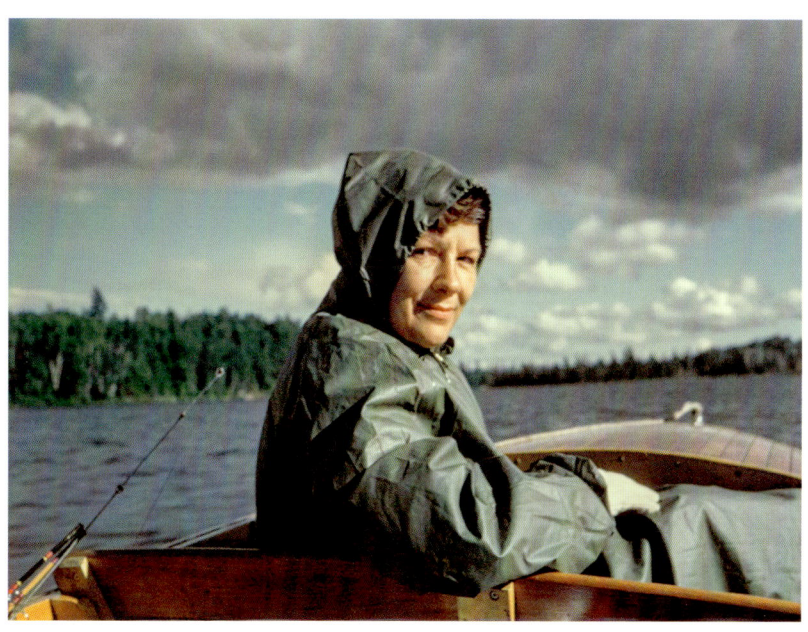

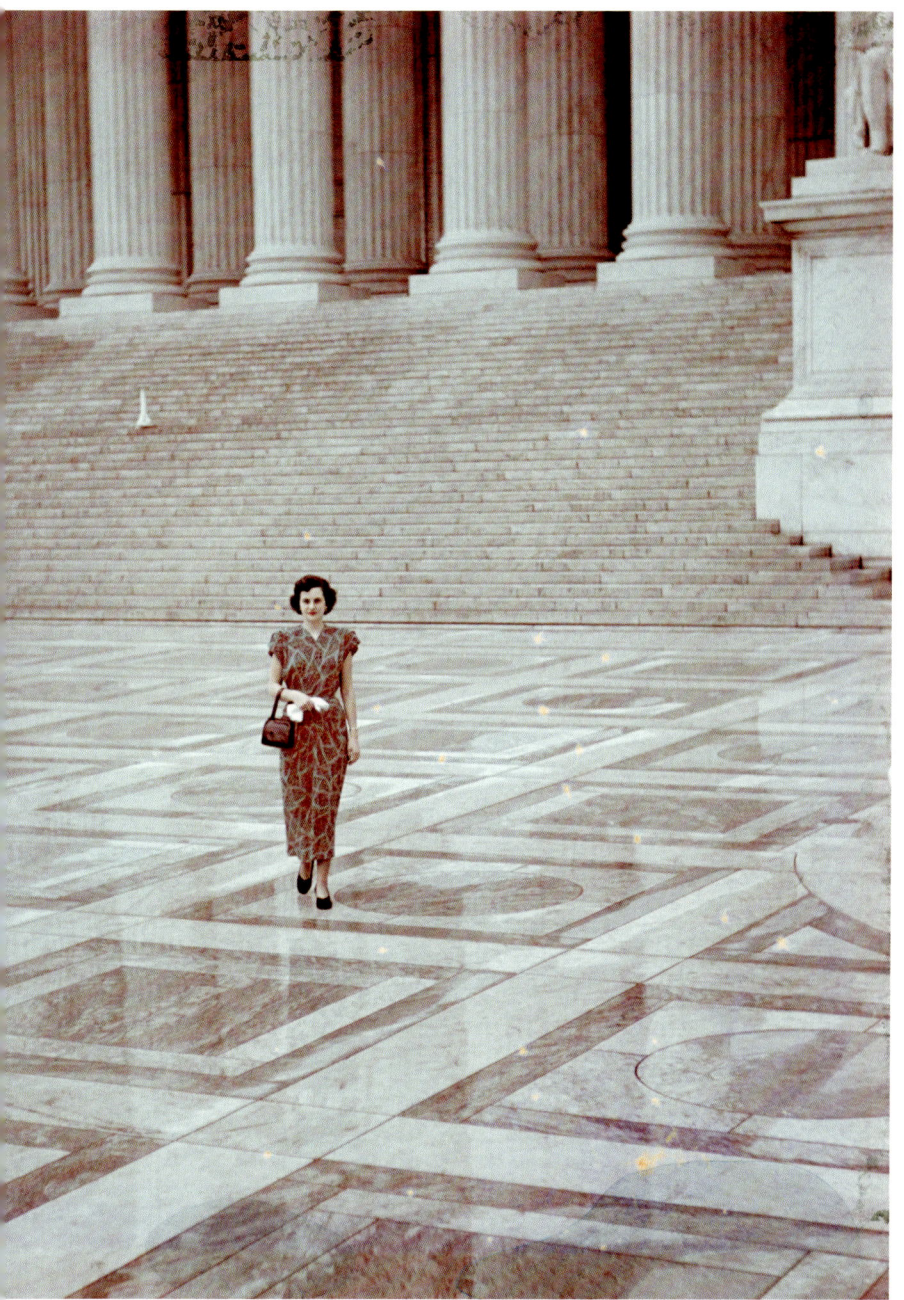

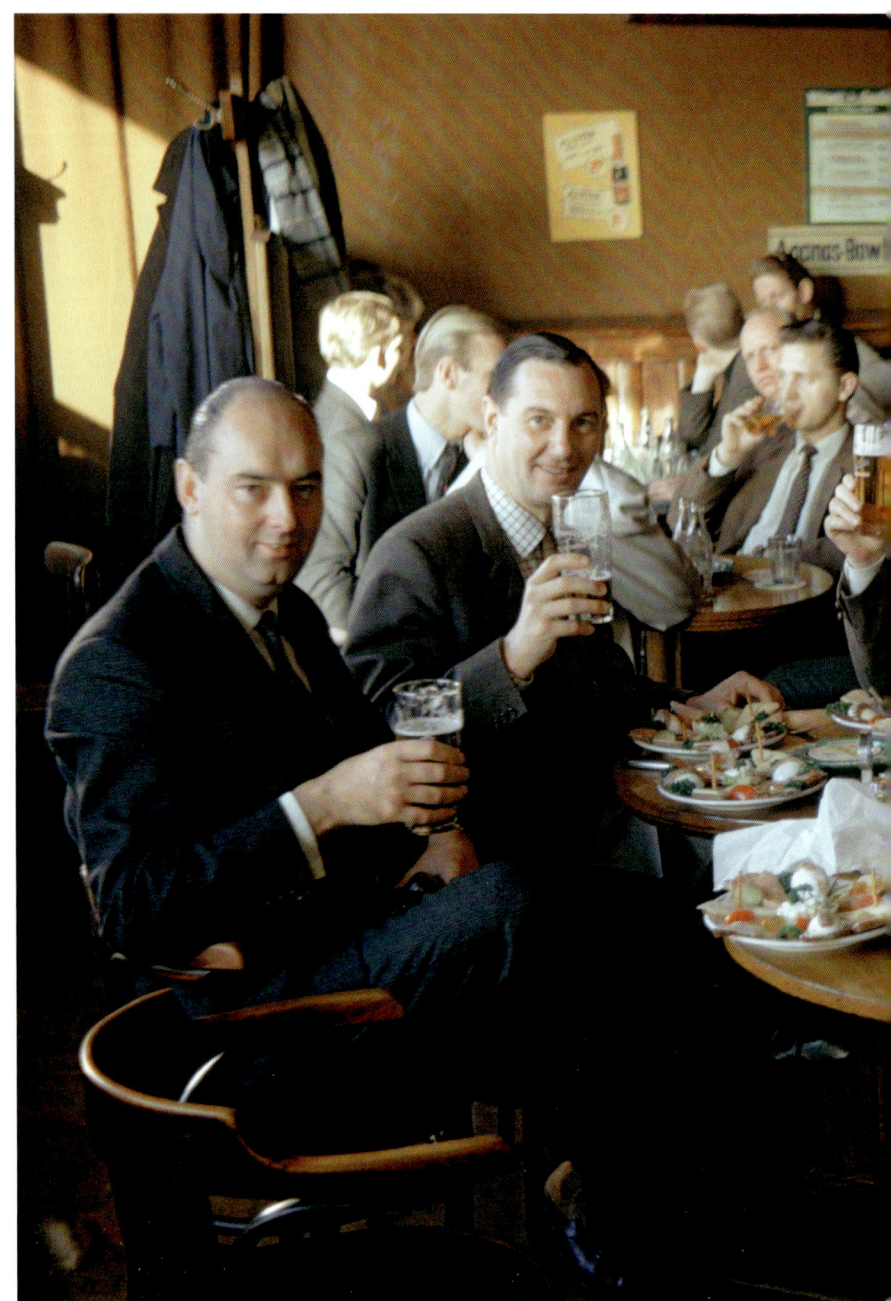

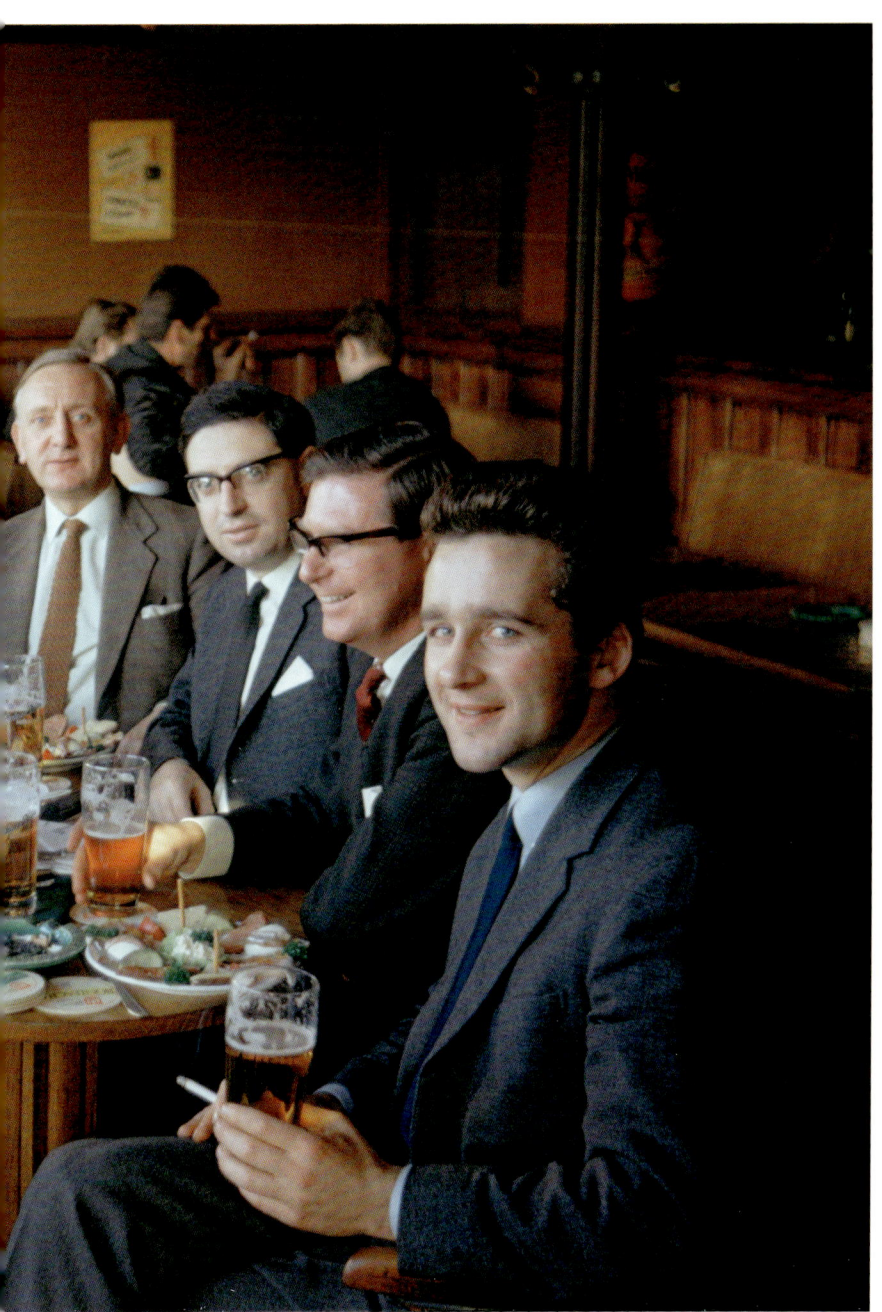

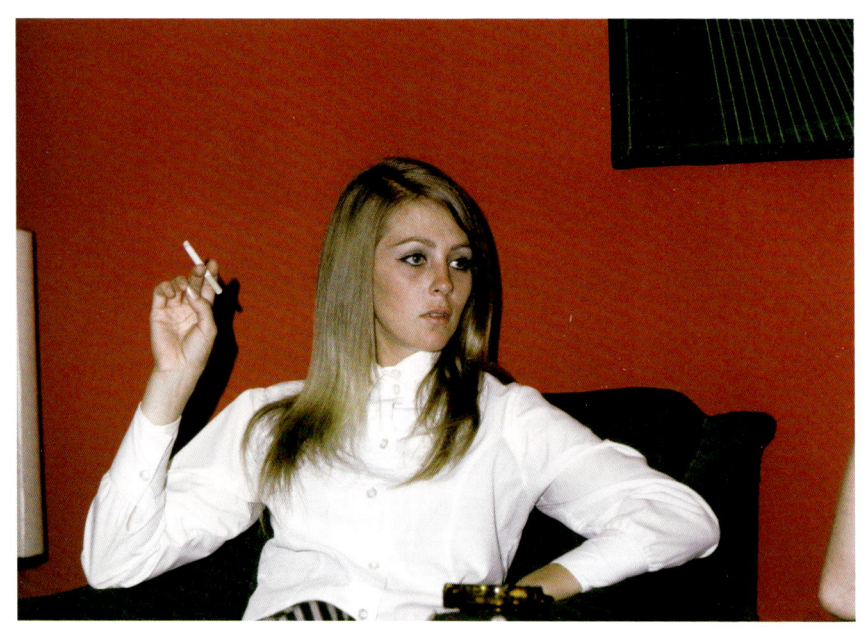

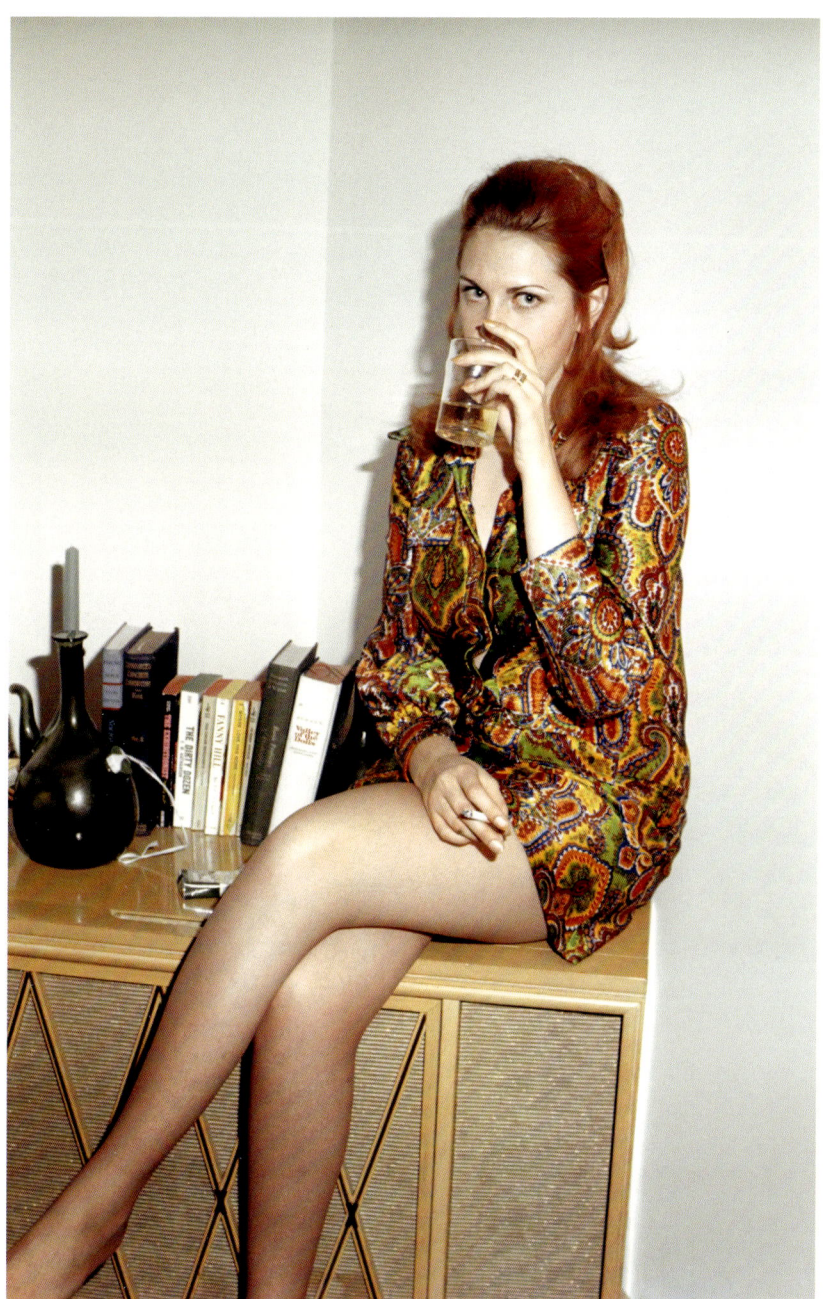

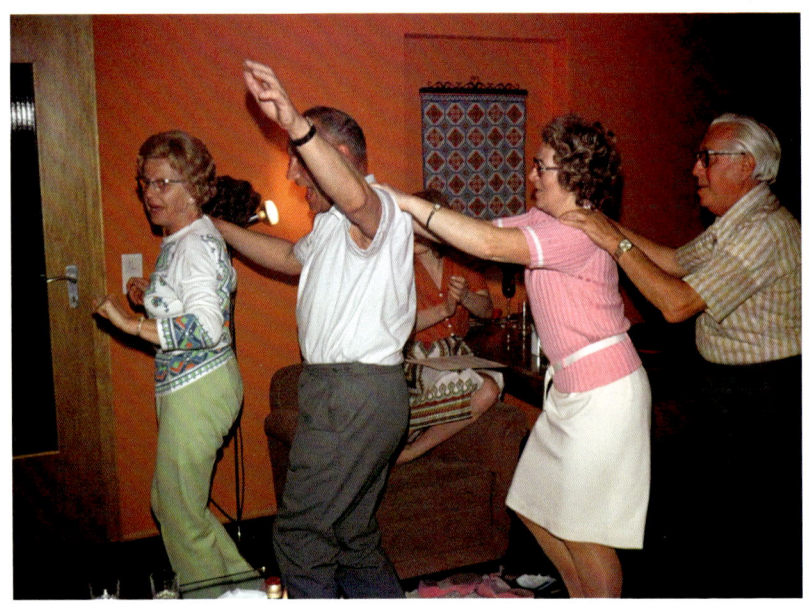

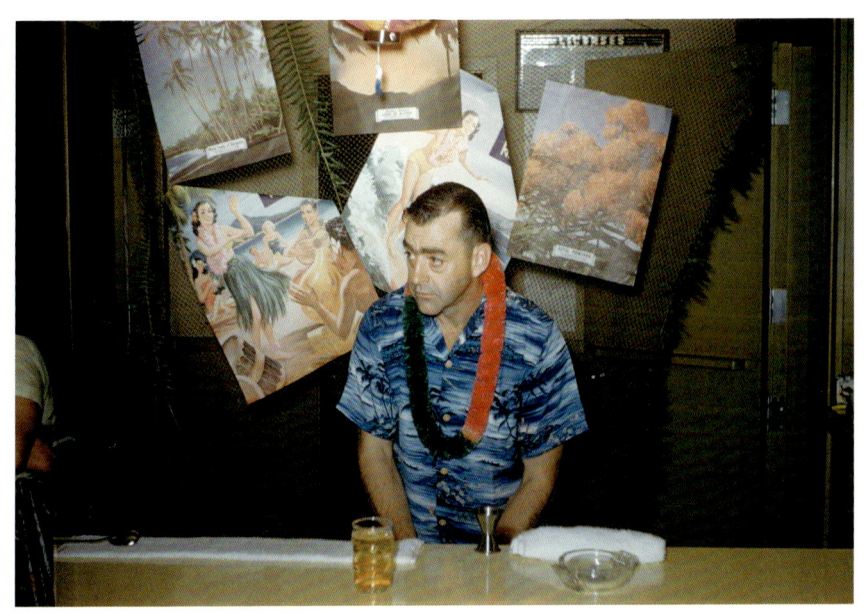

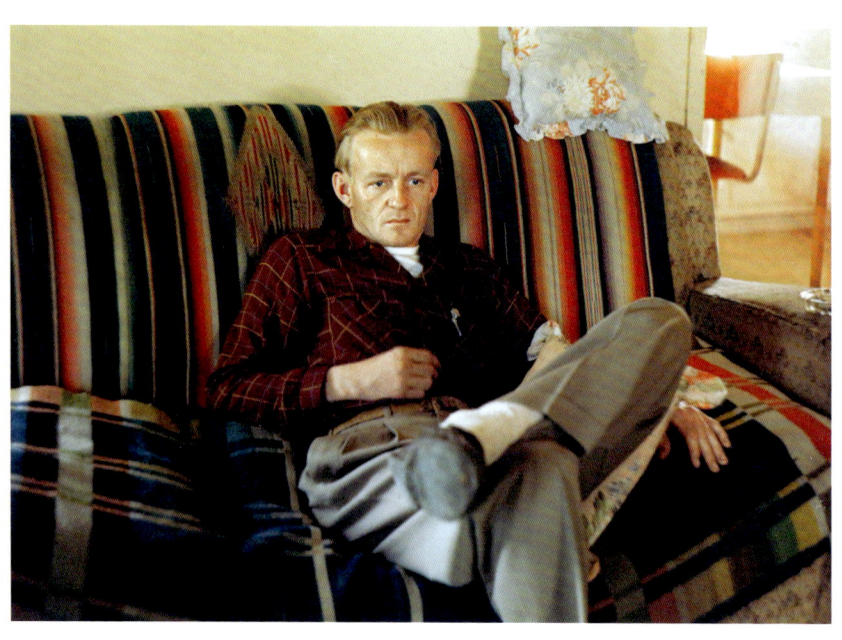

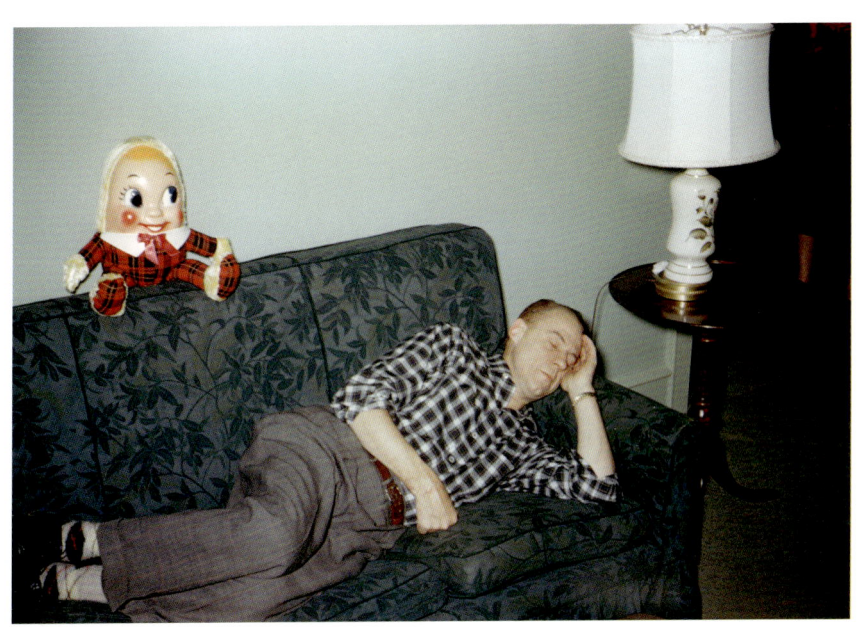

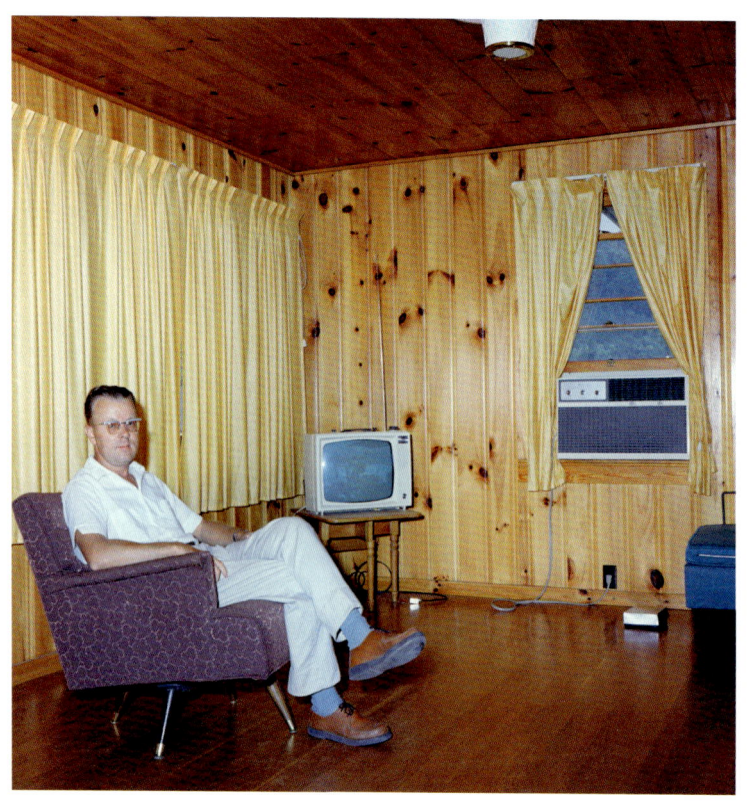

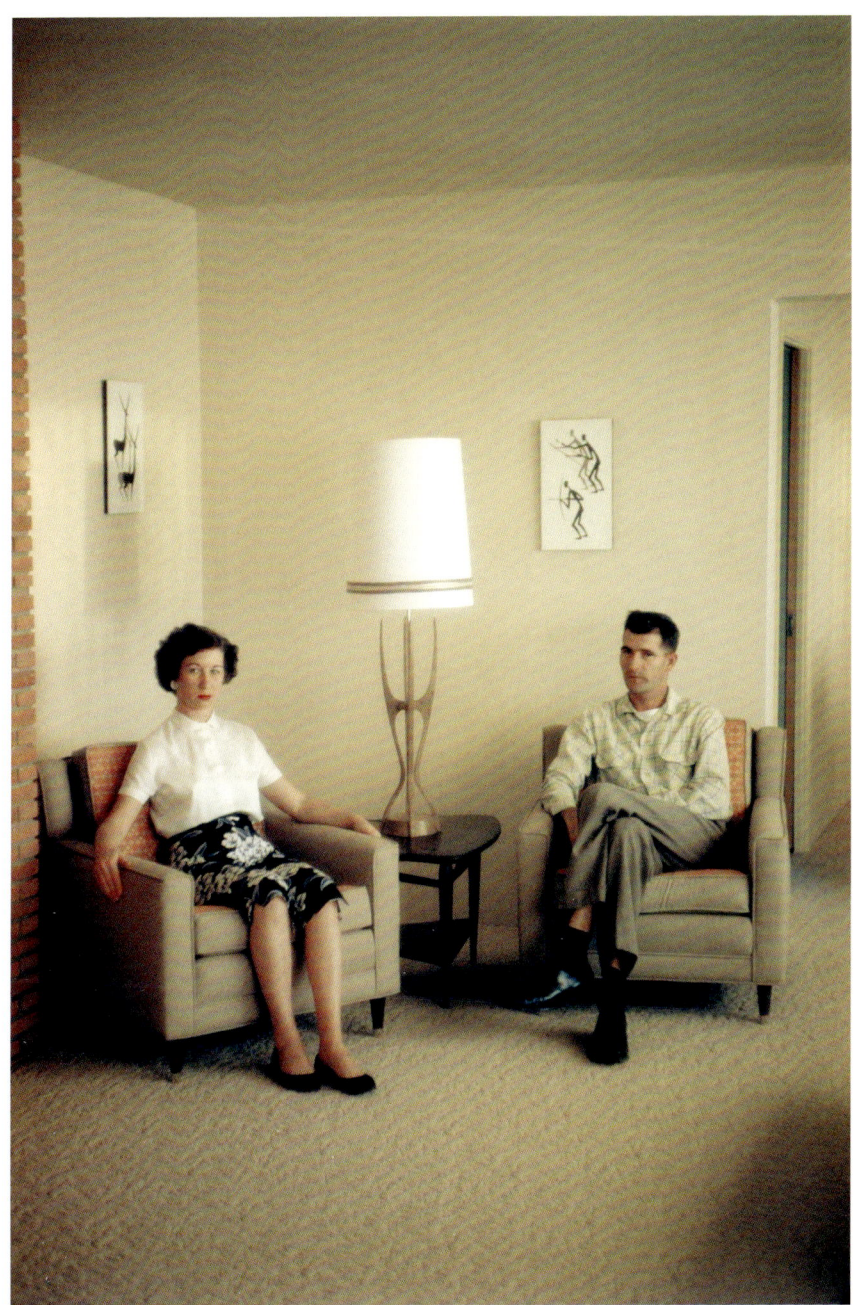

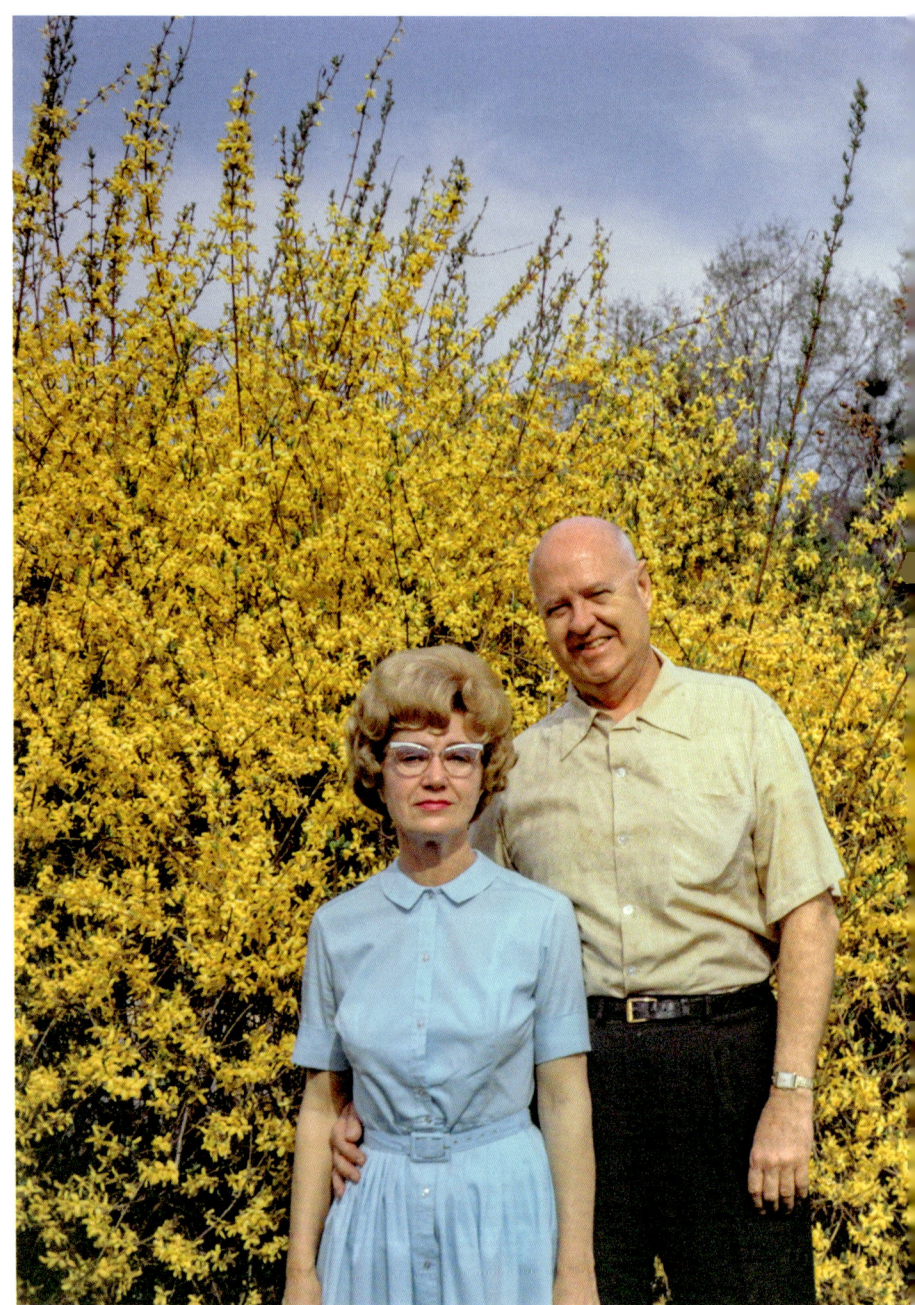

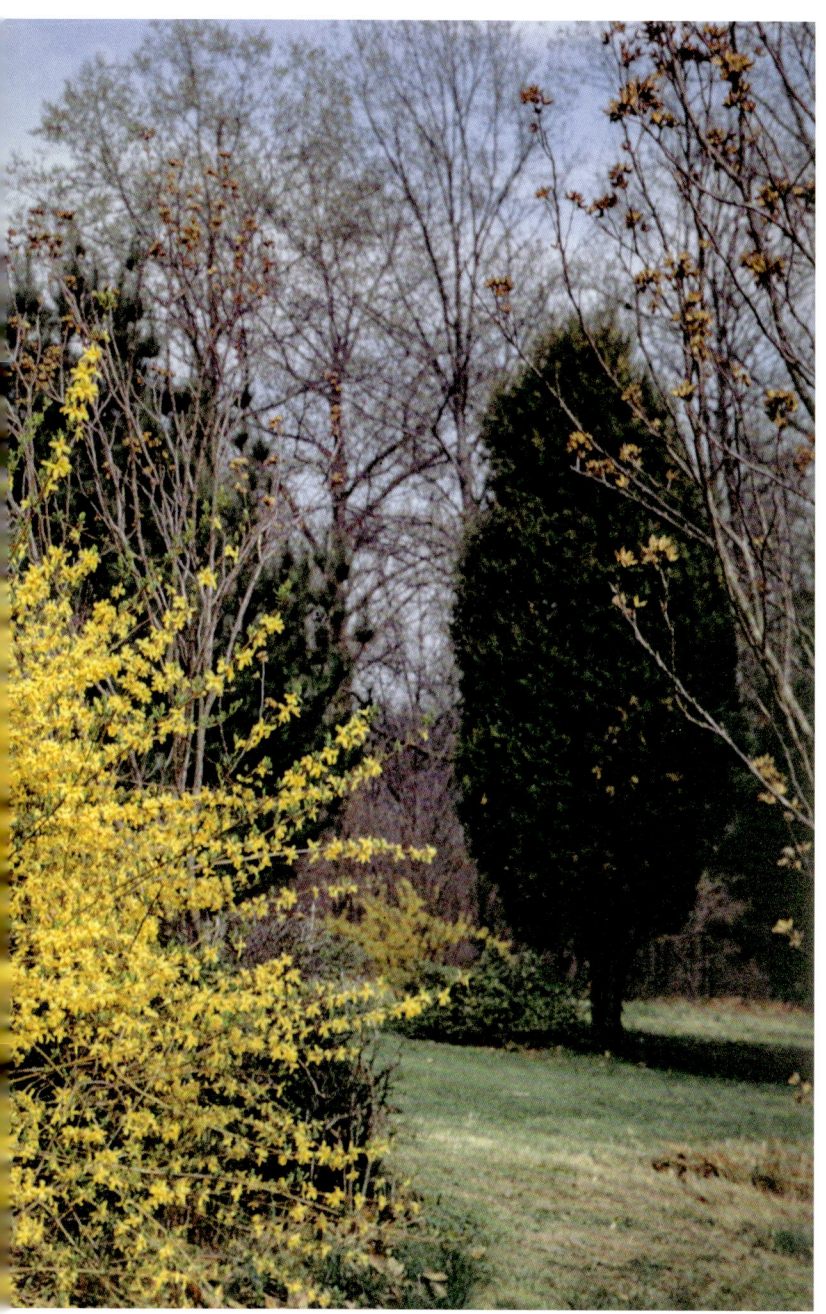

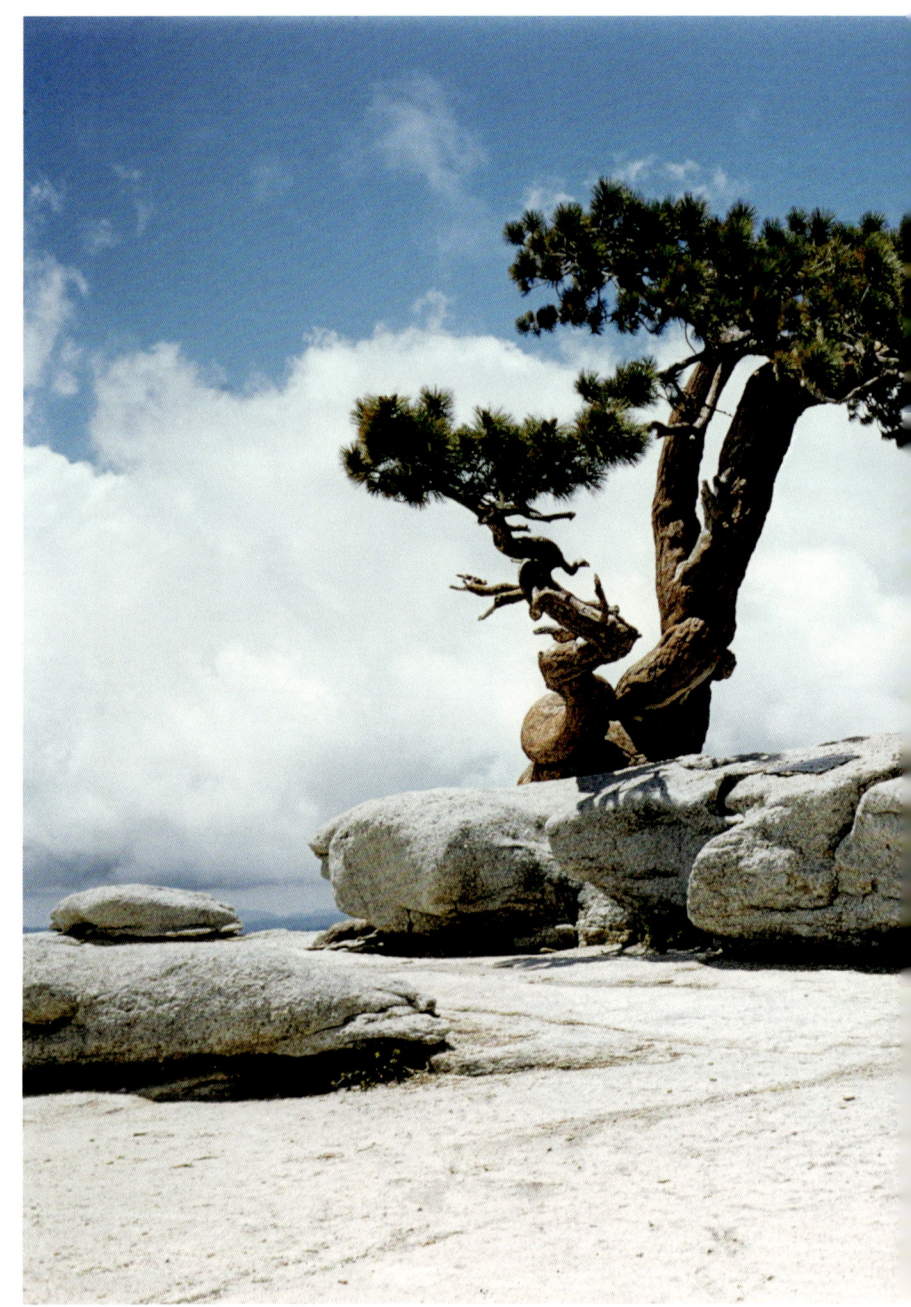

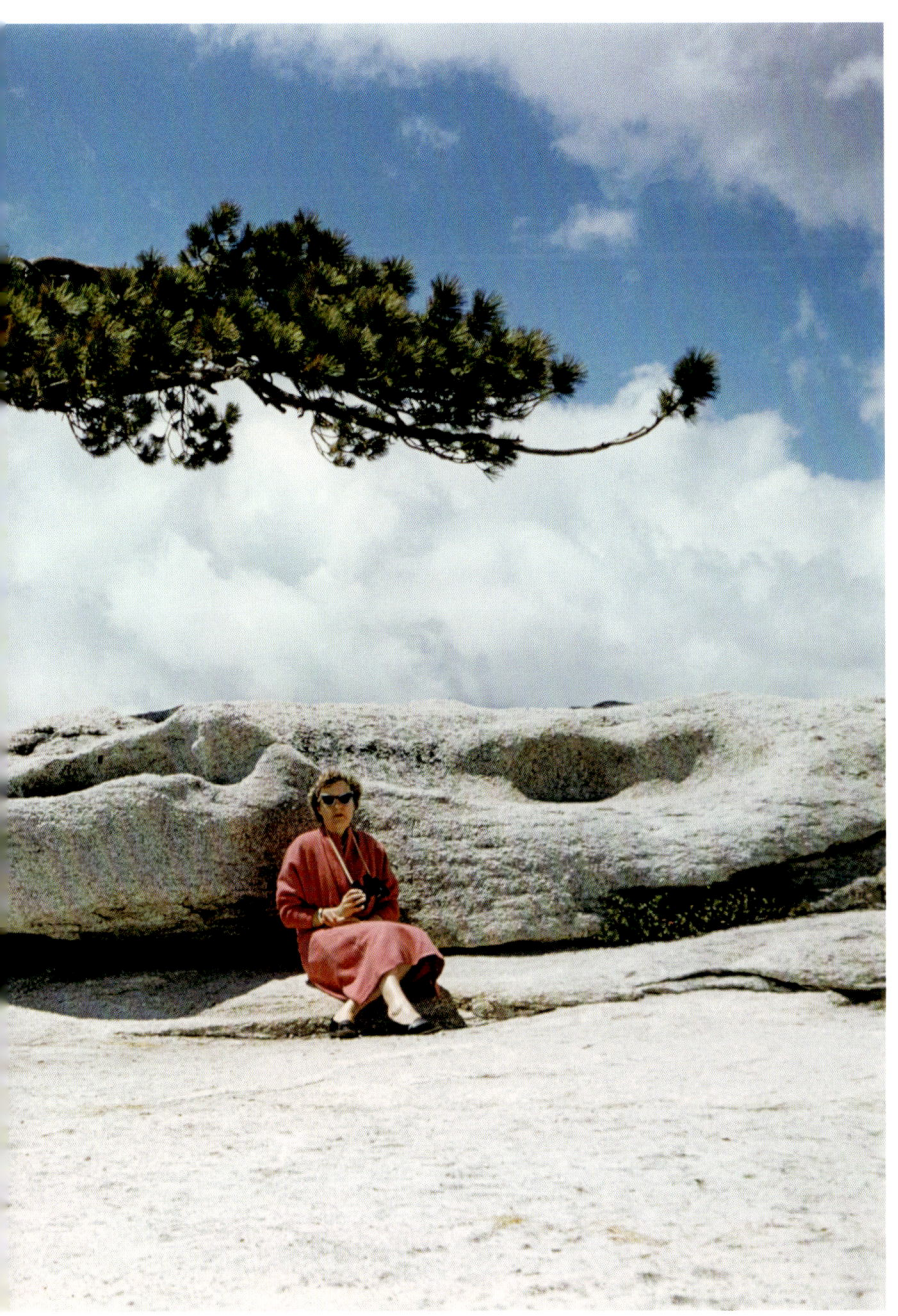

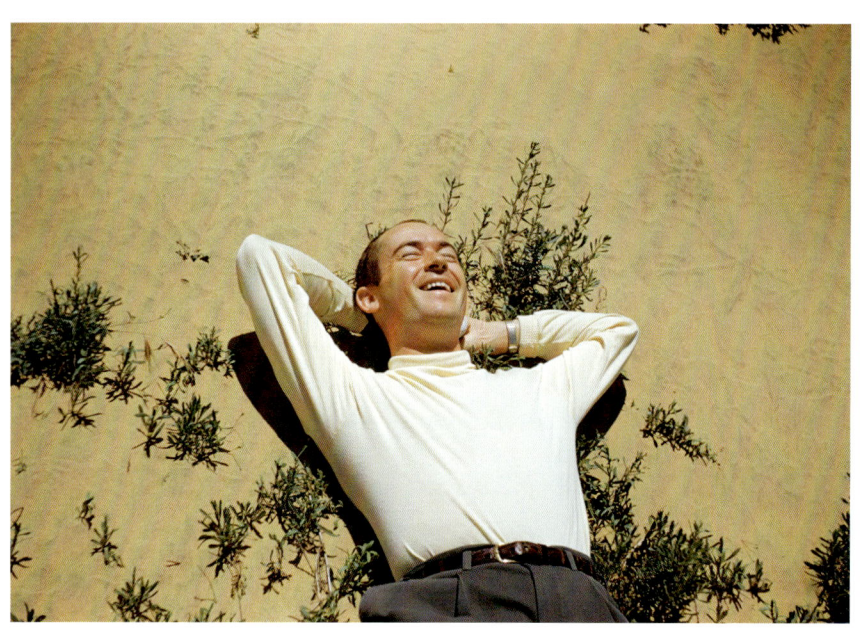

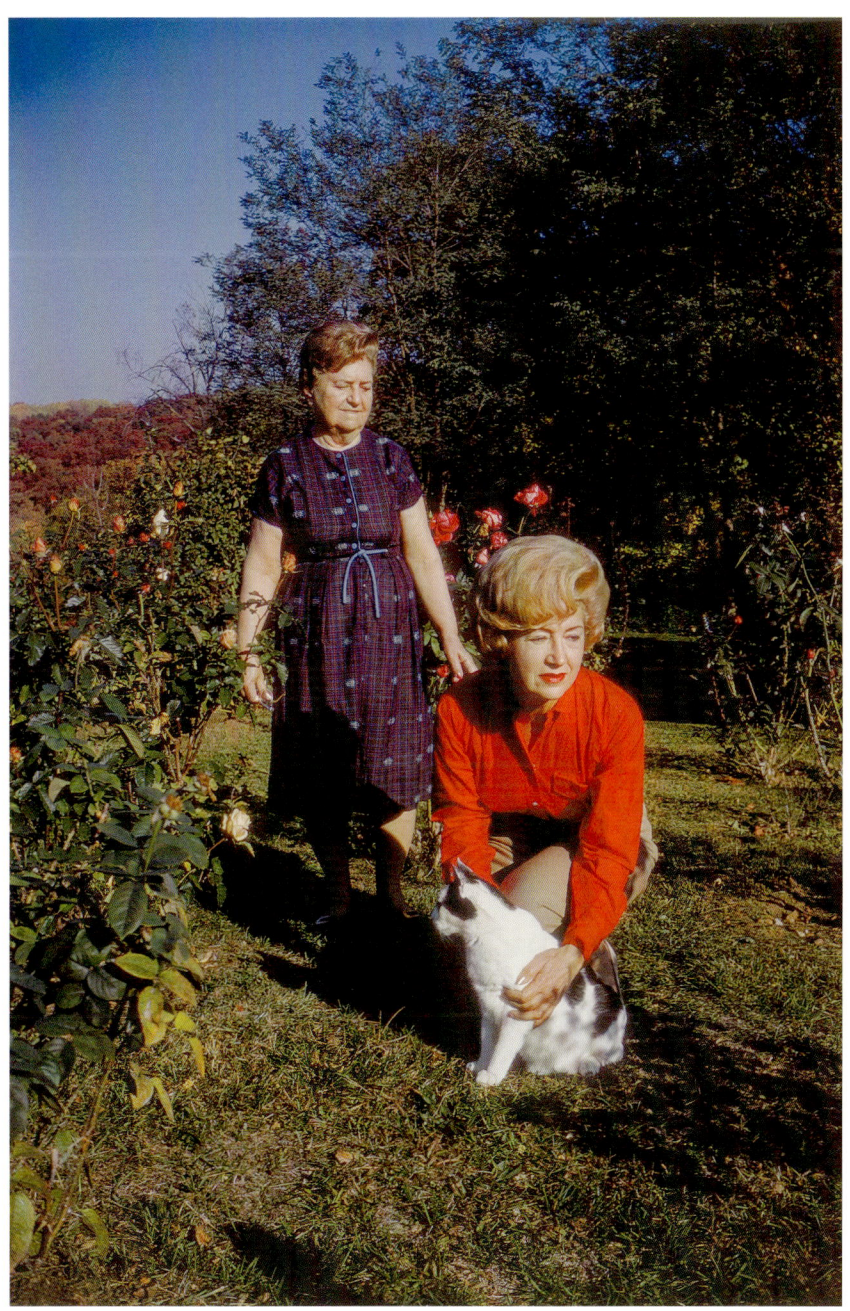

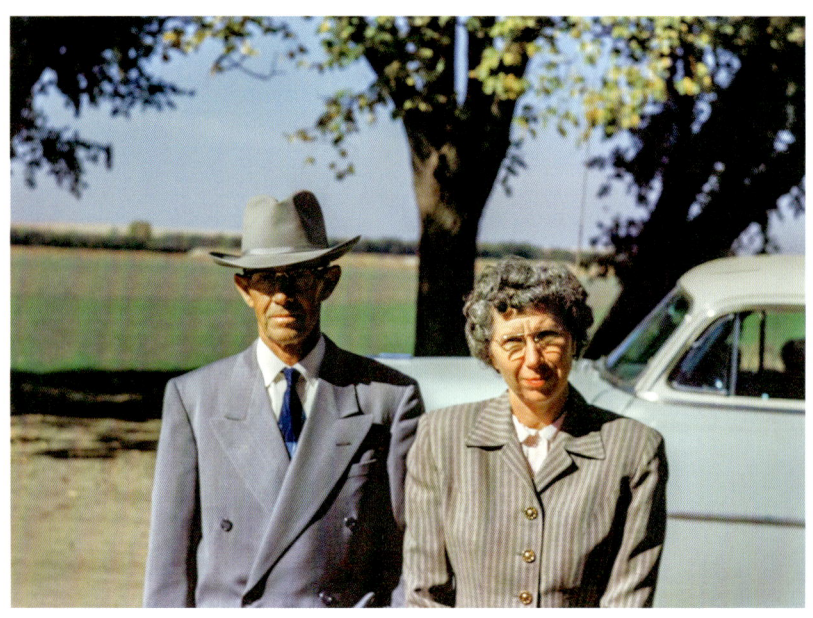

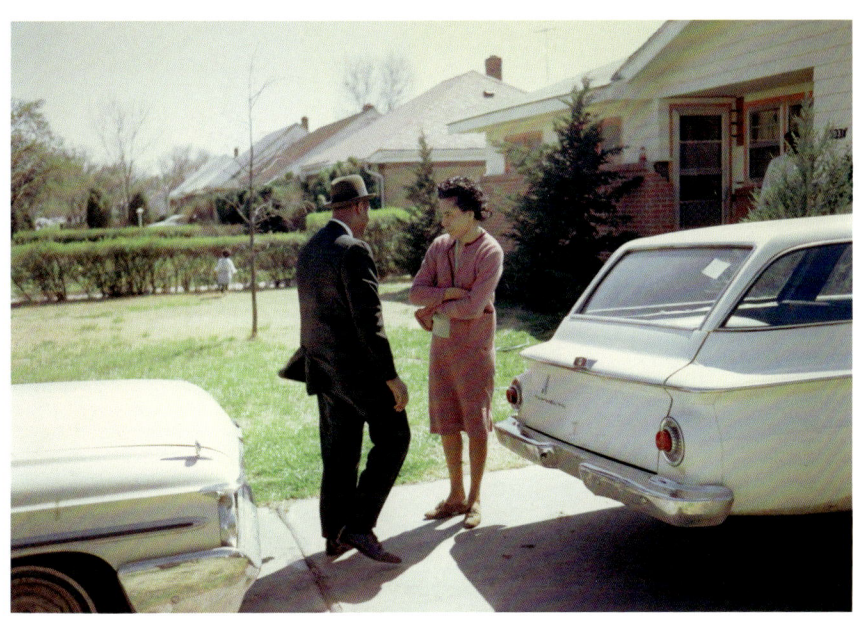

159

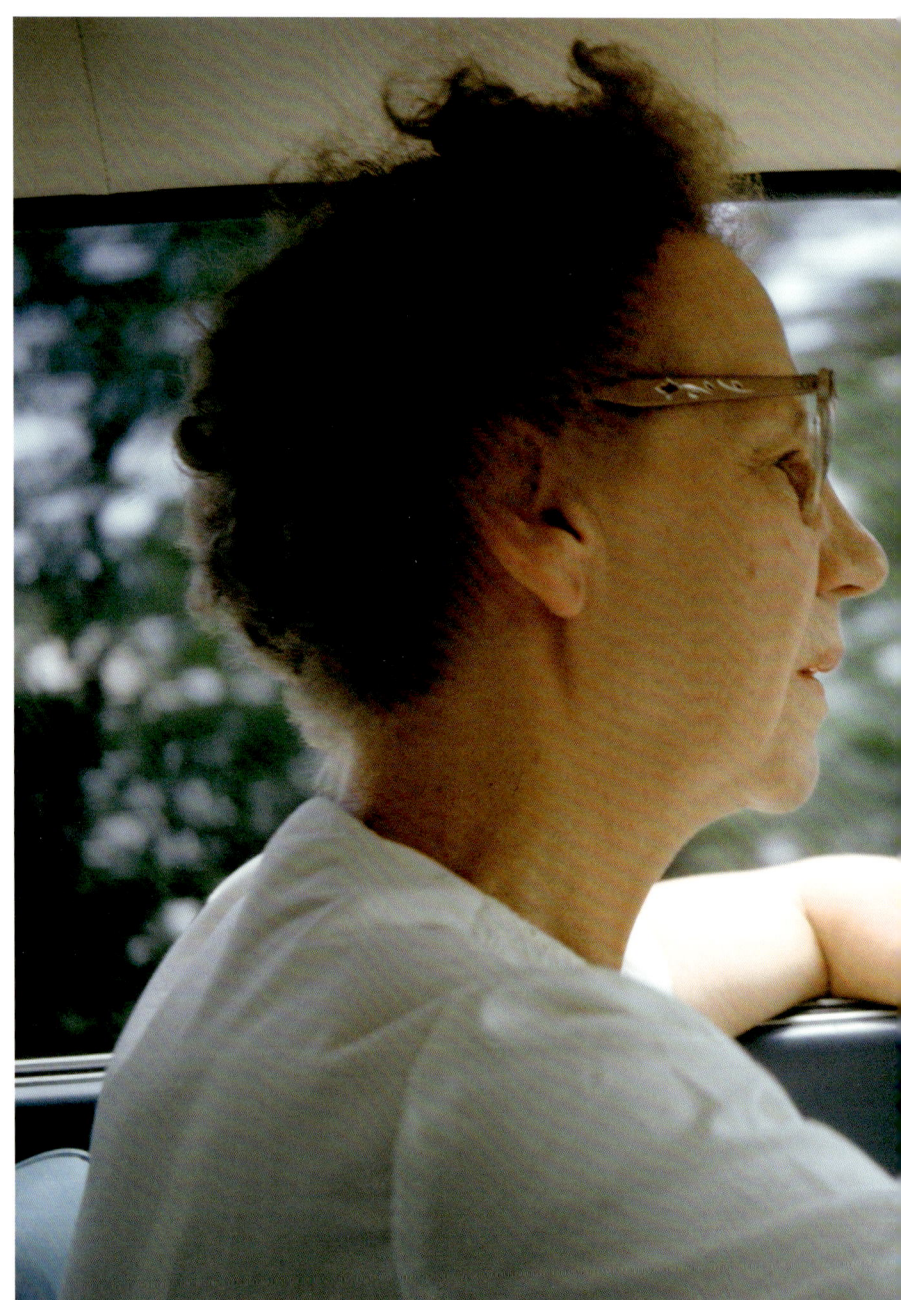

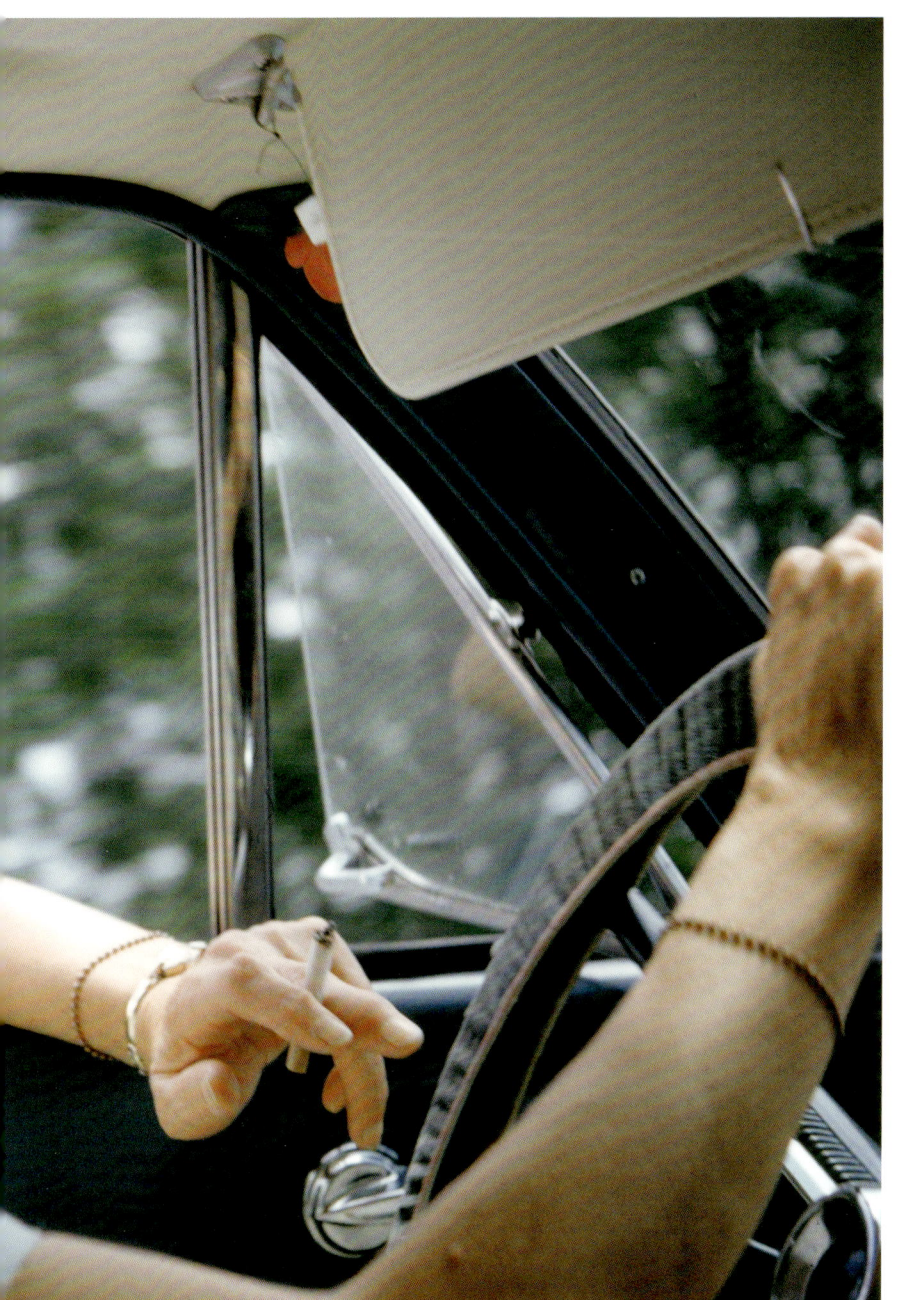

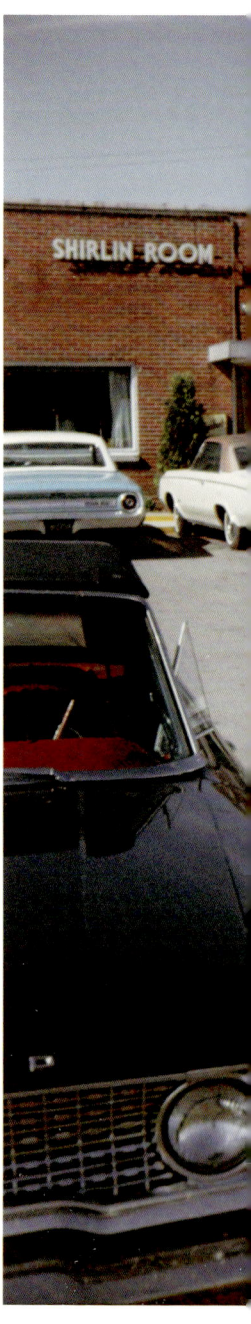

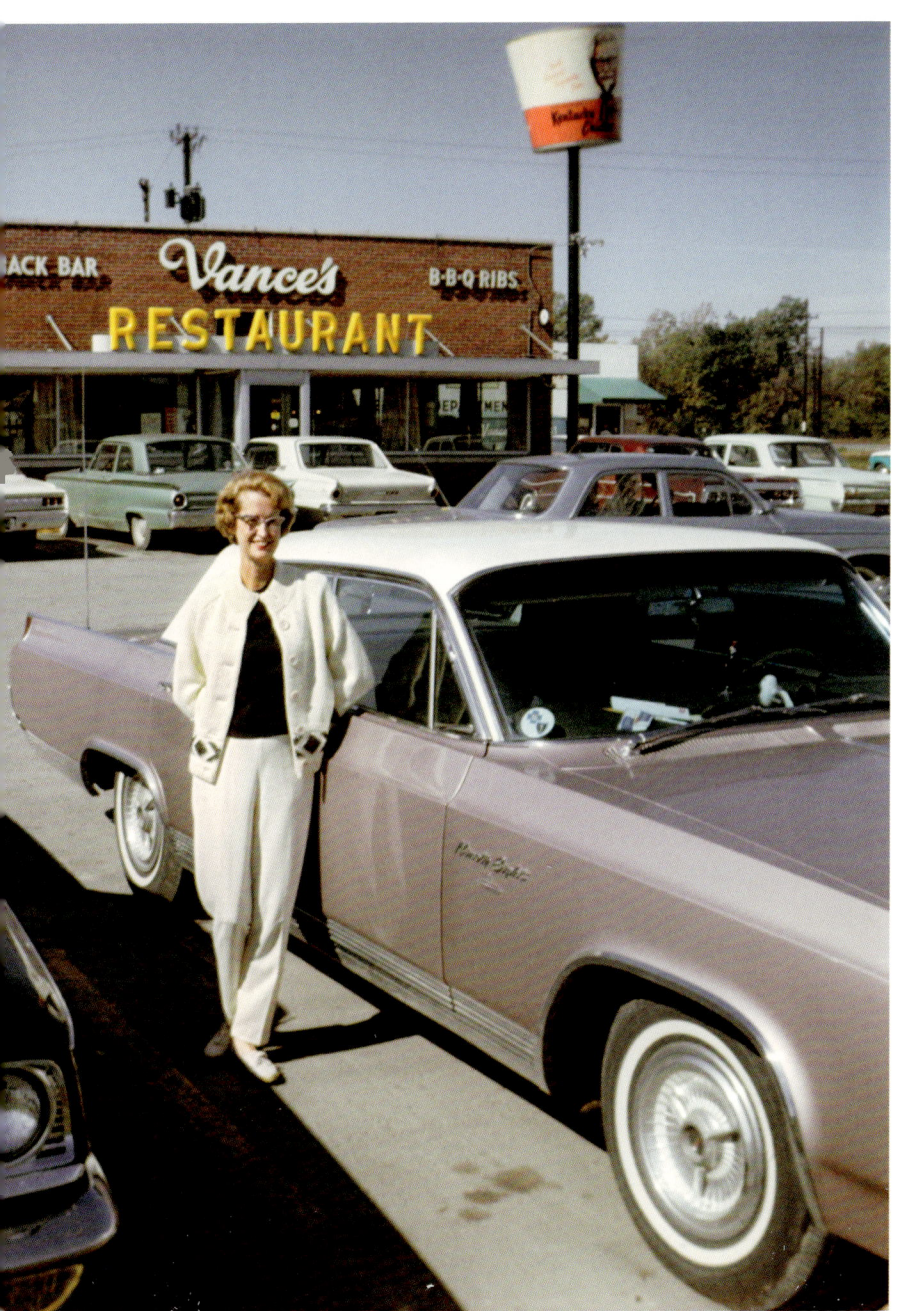

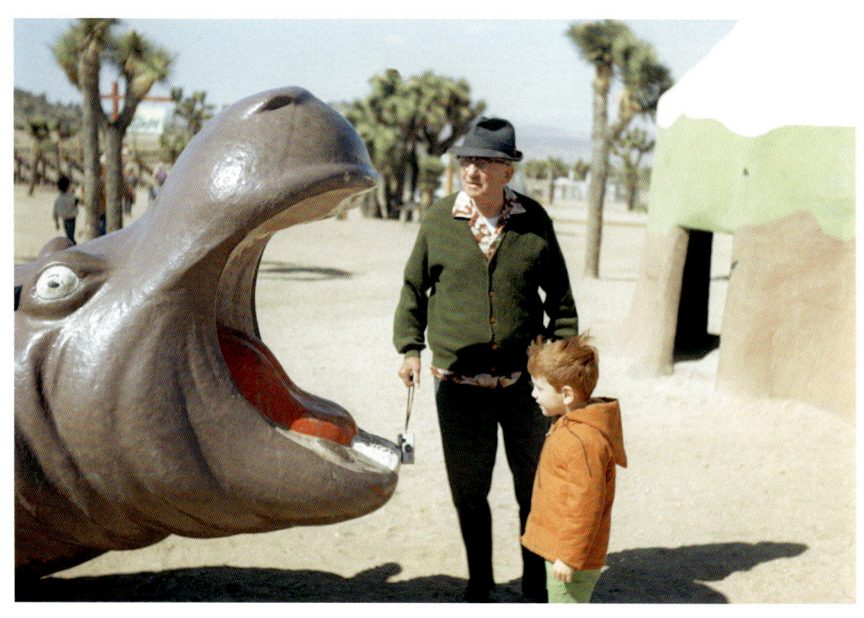

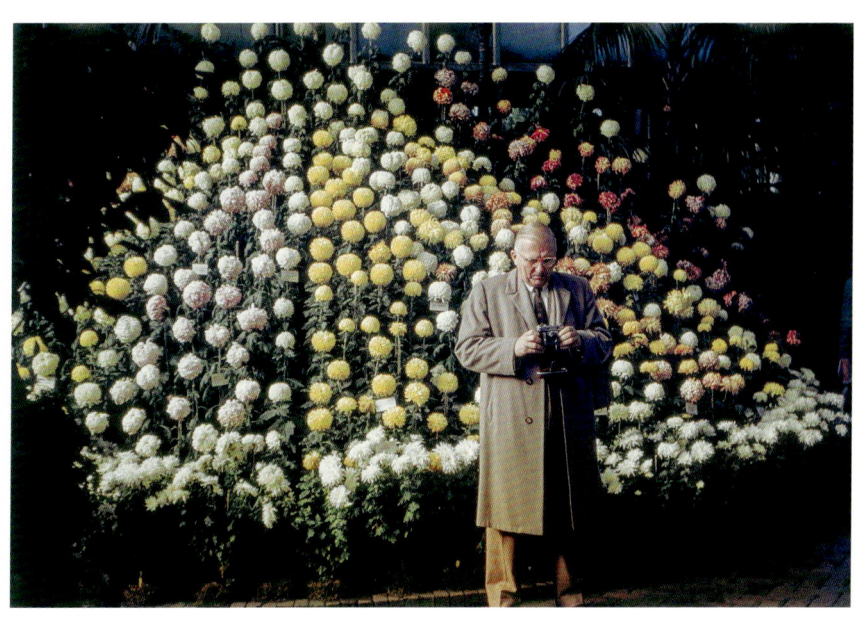

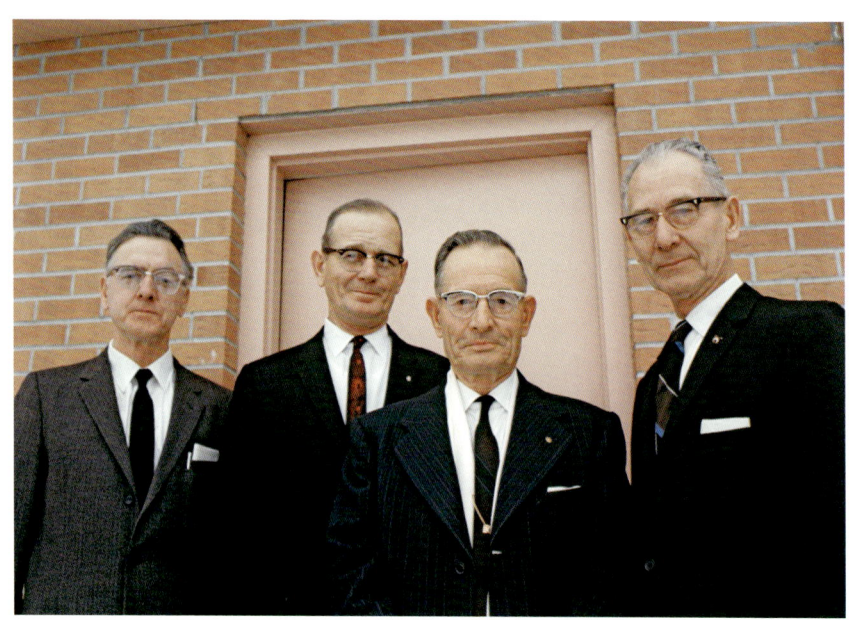

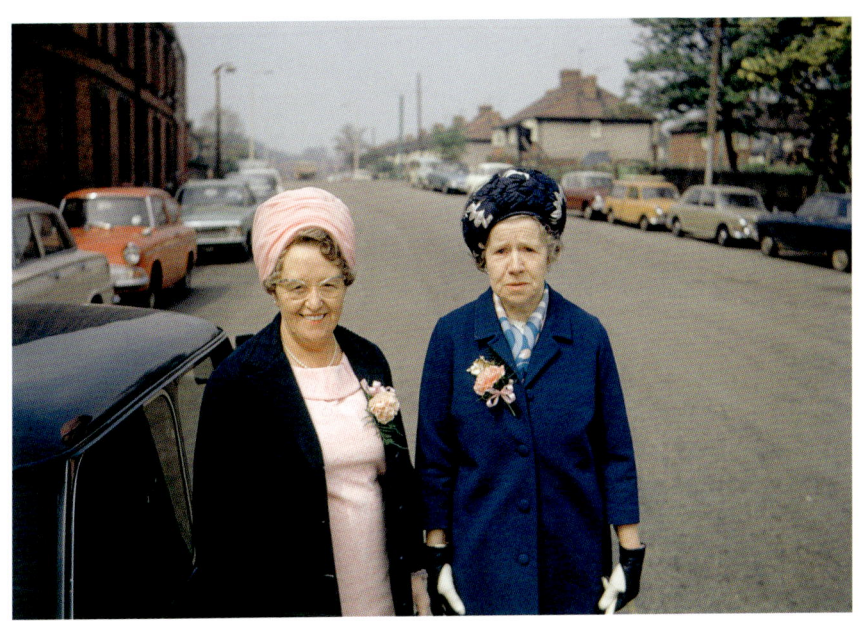

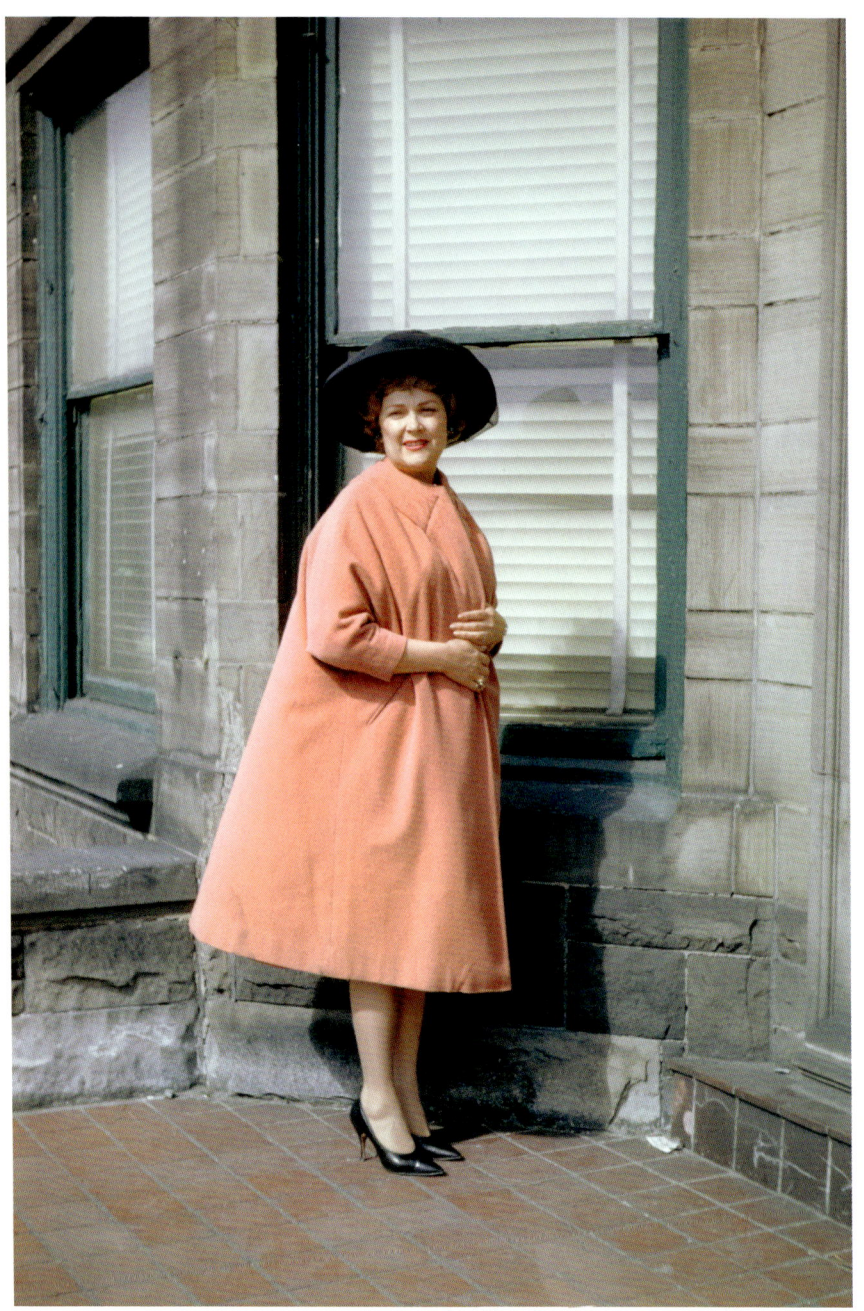

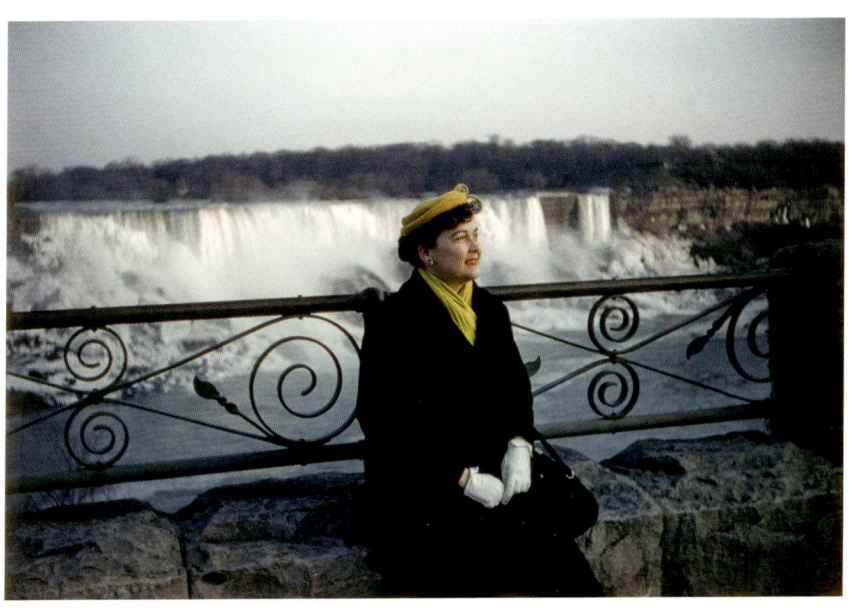

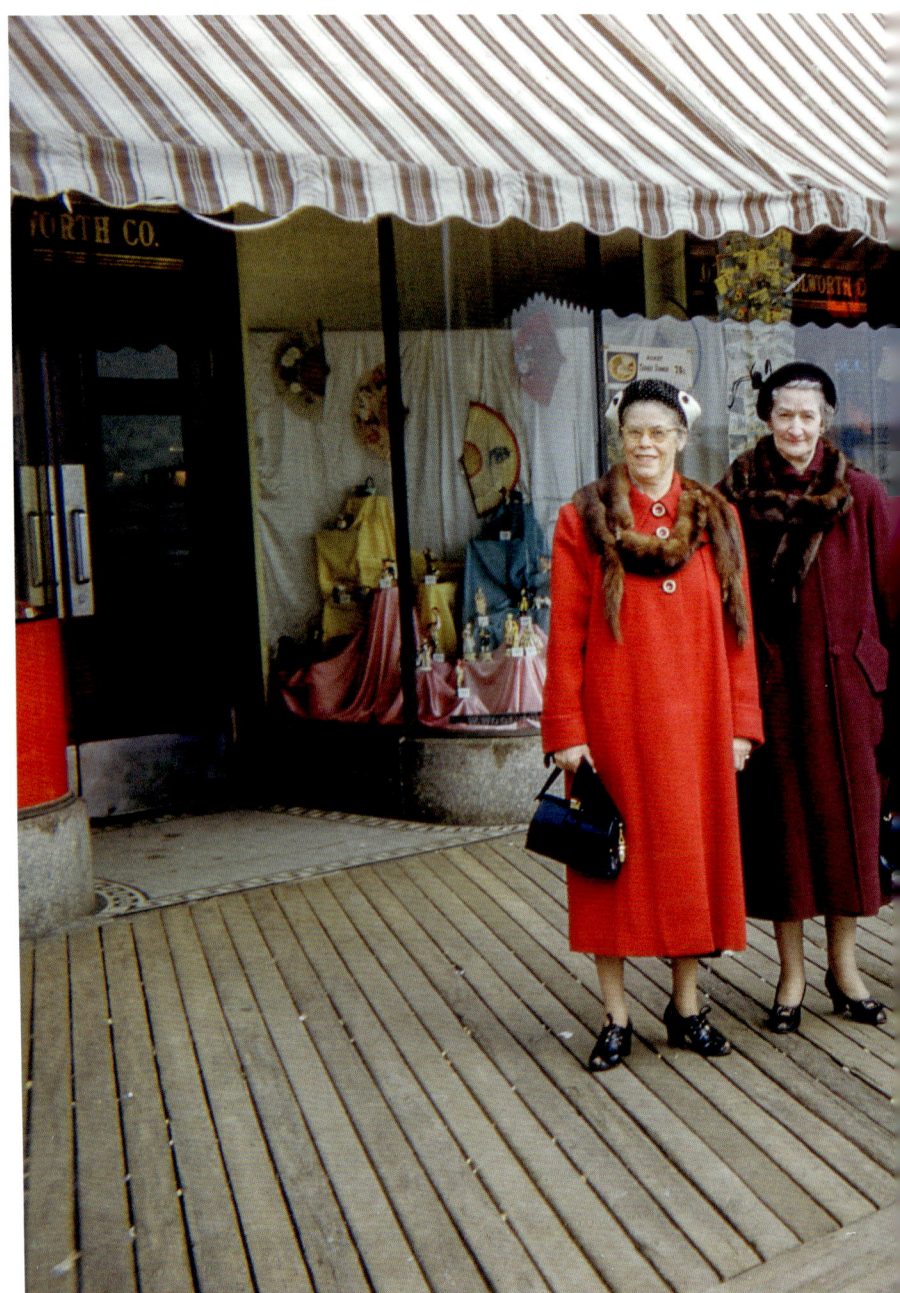

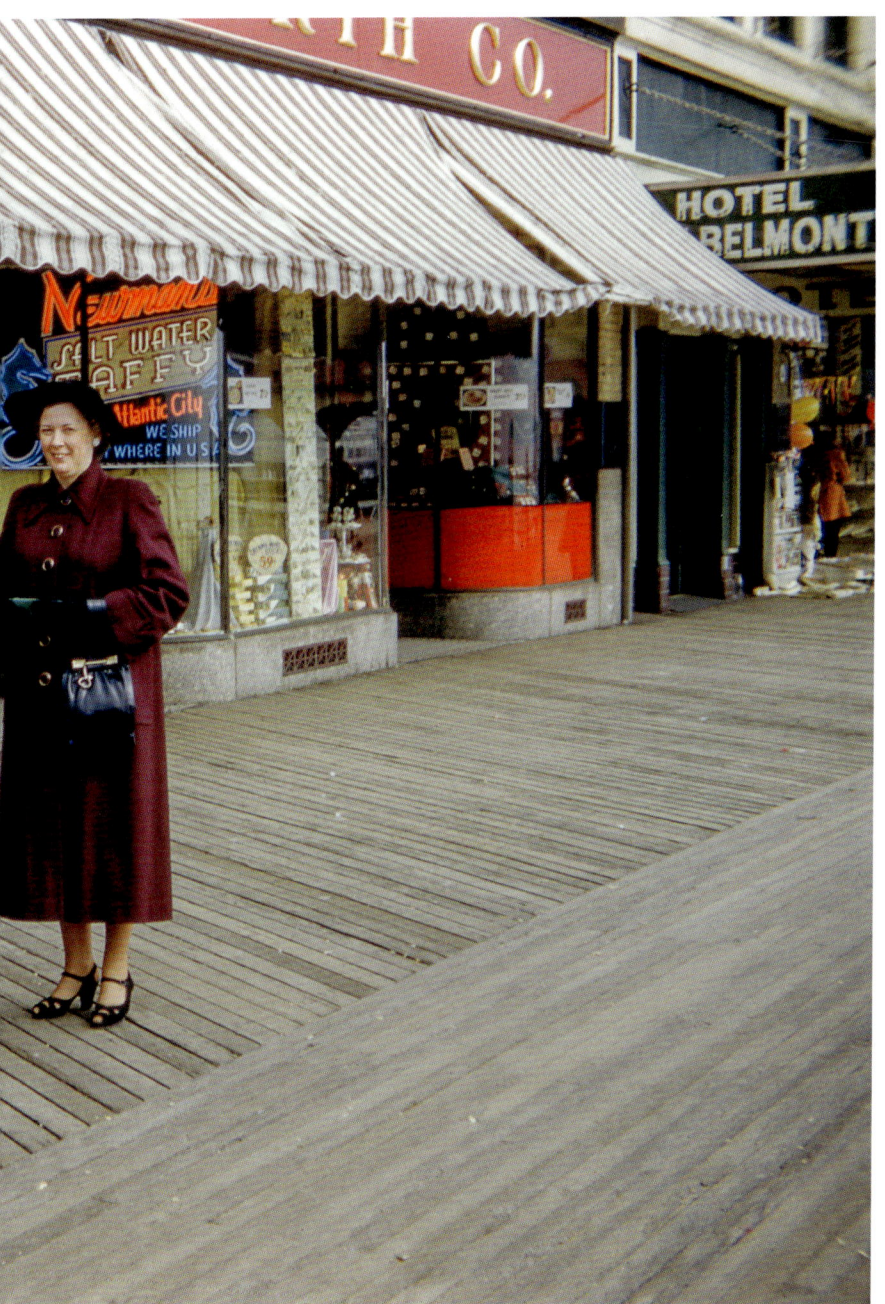

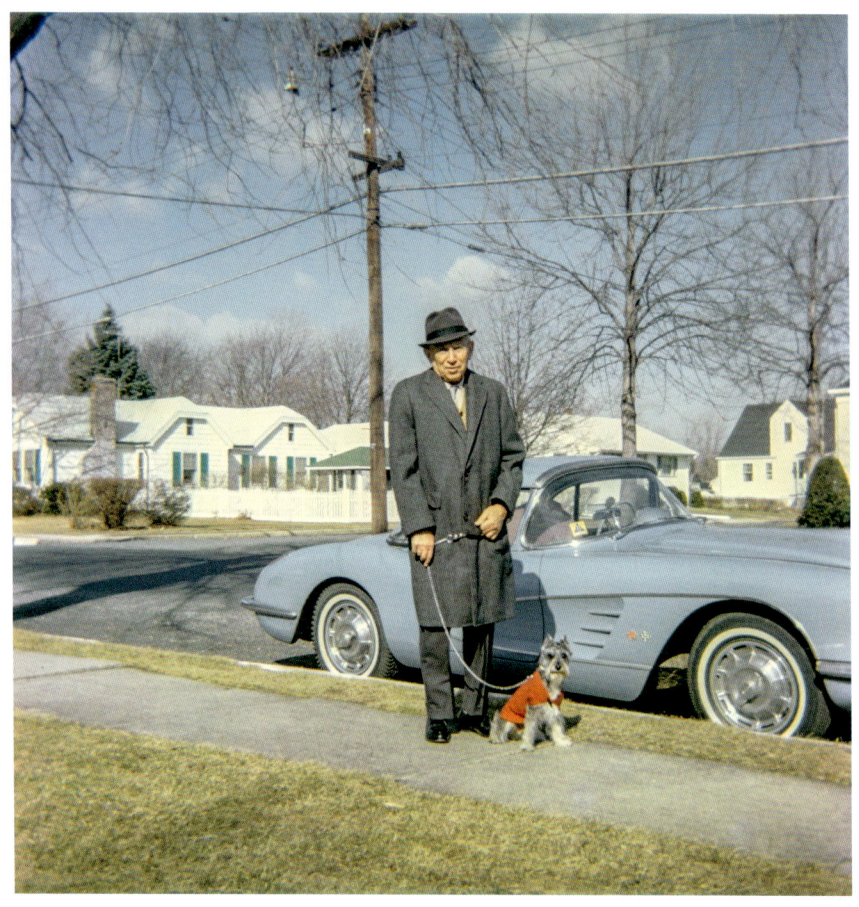

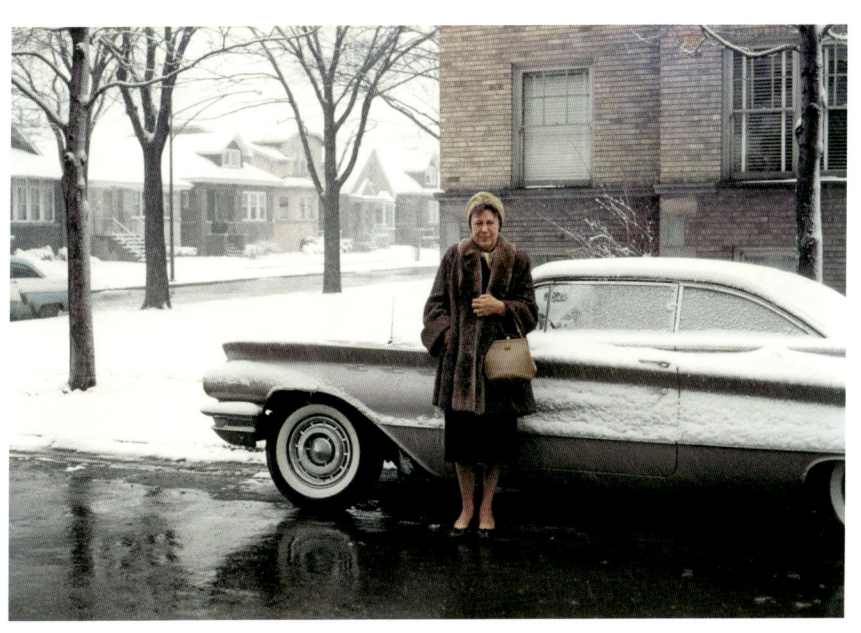

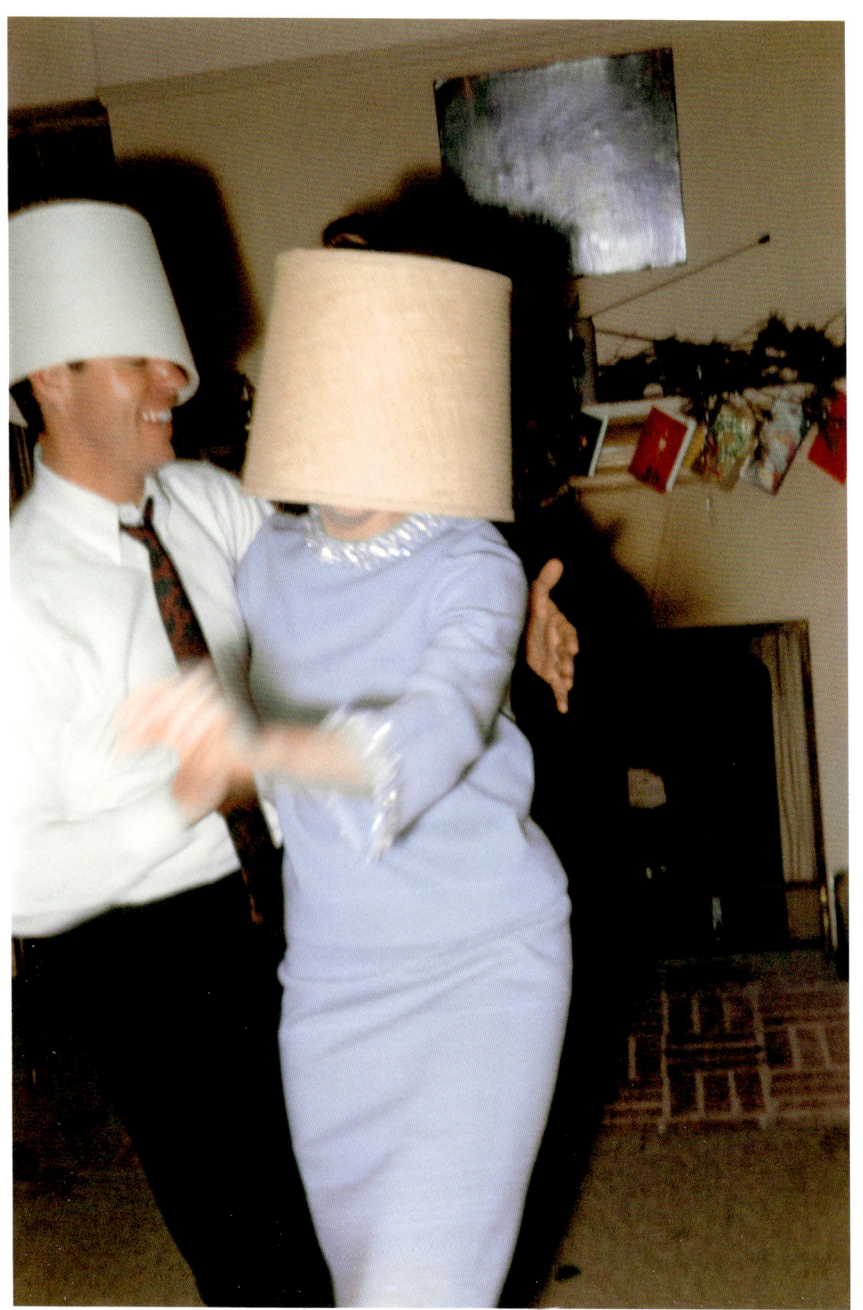

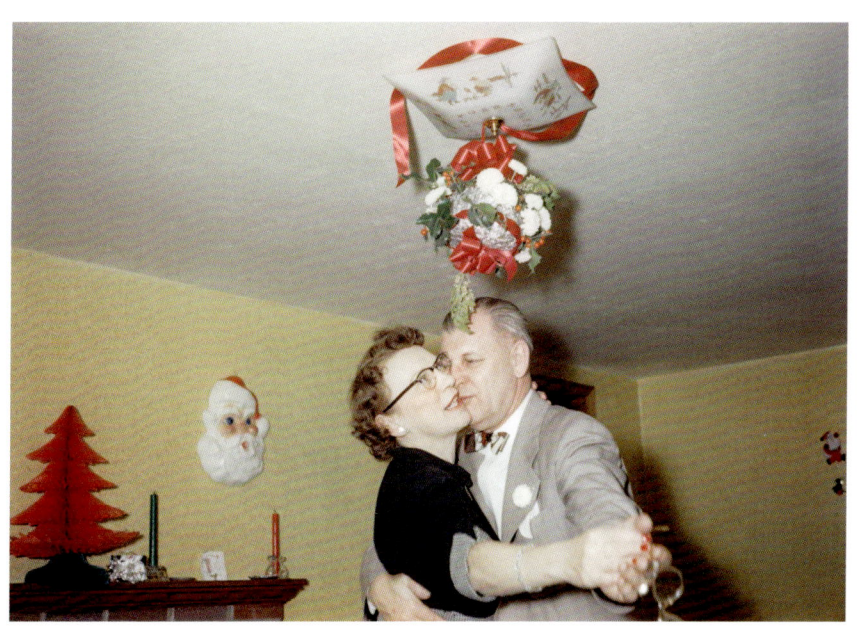

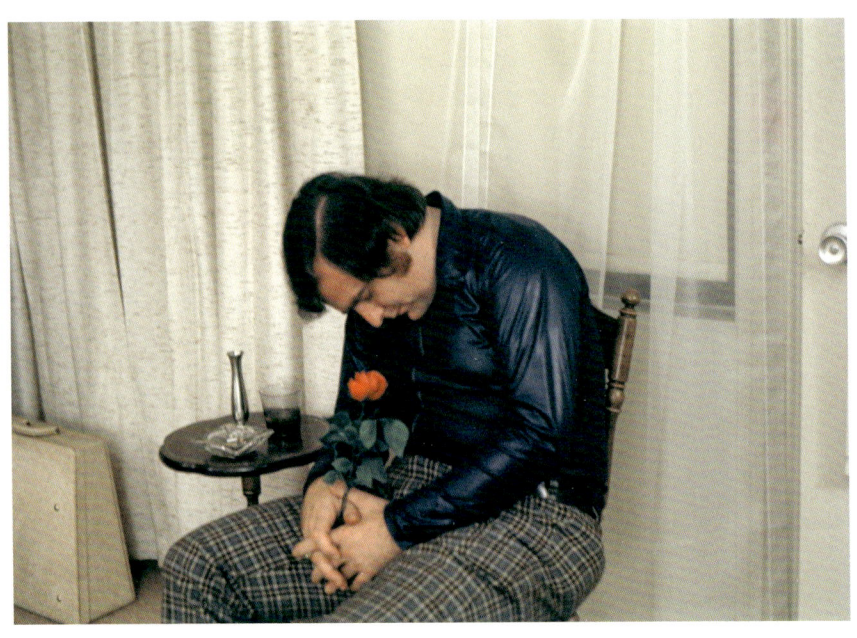

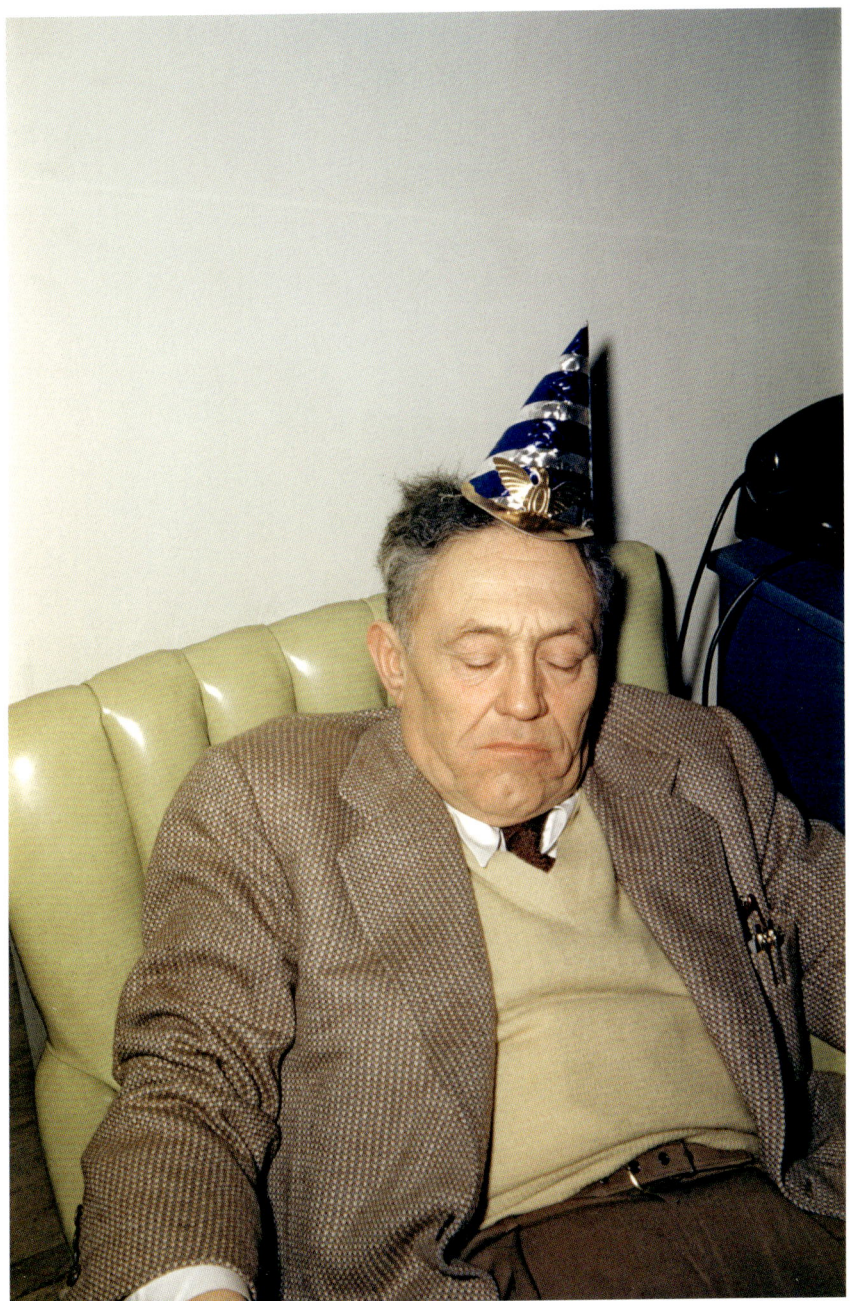

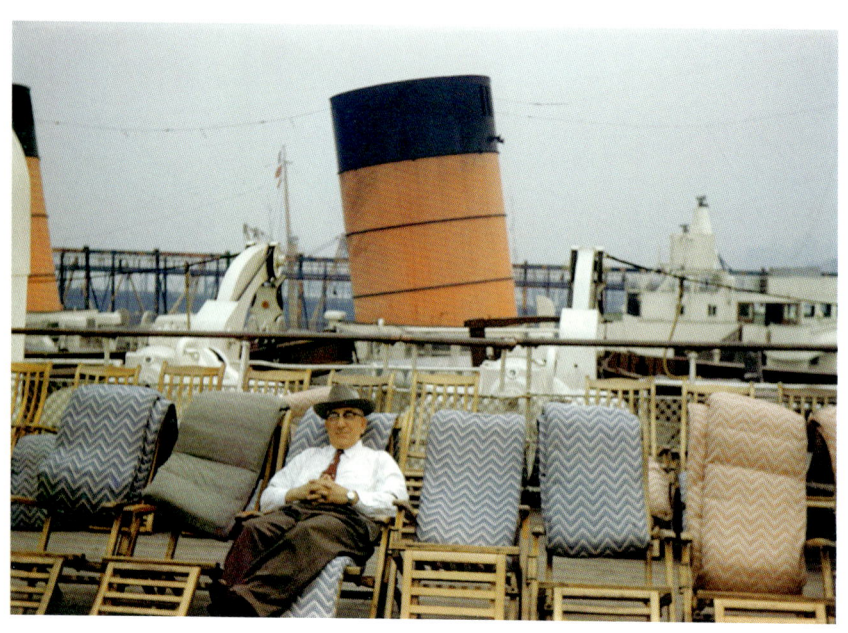

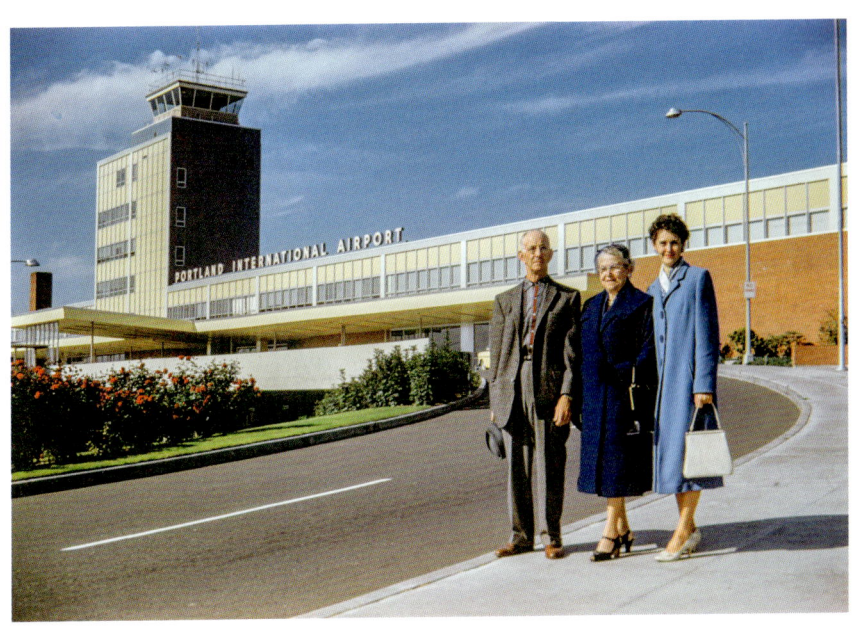

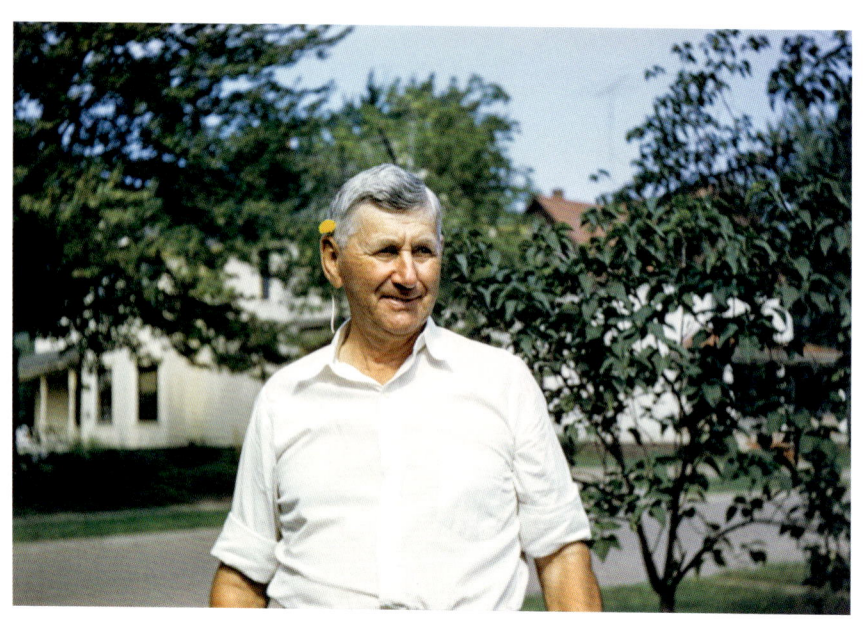

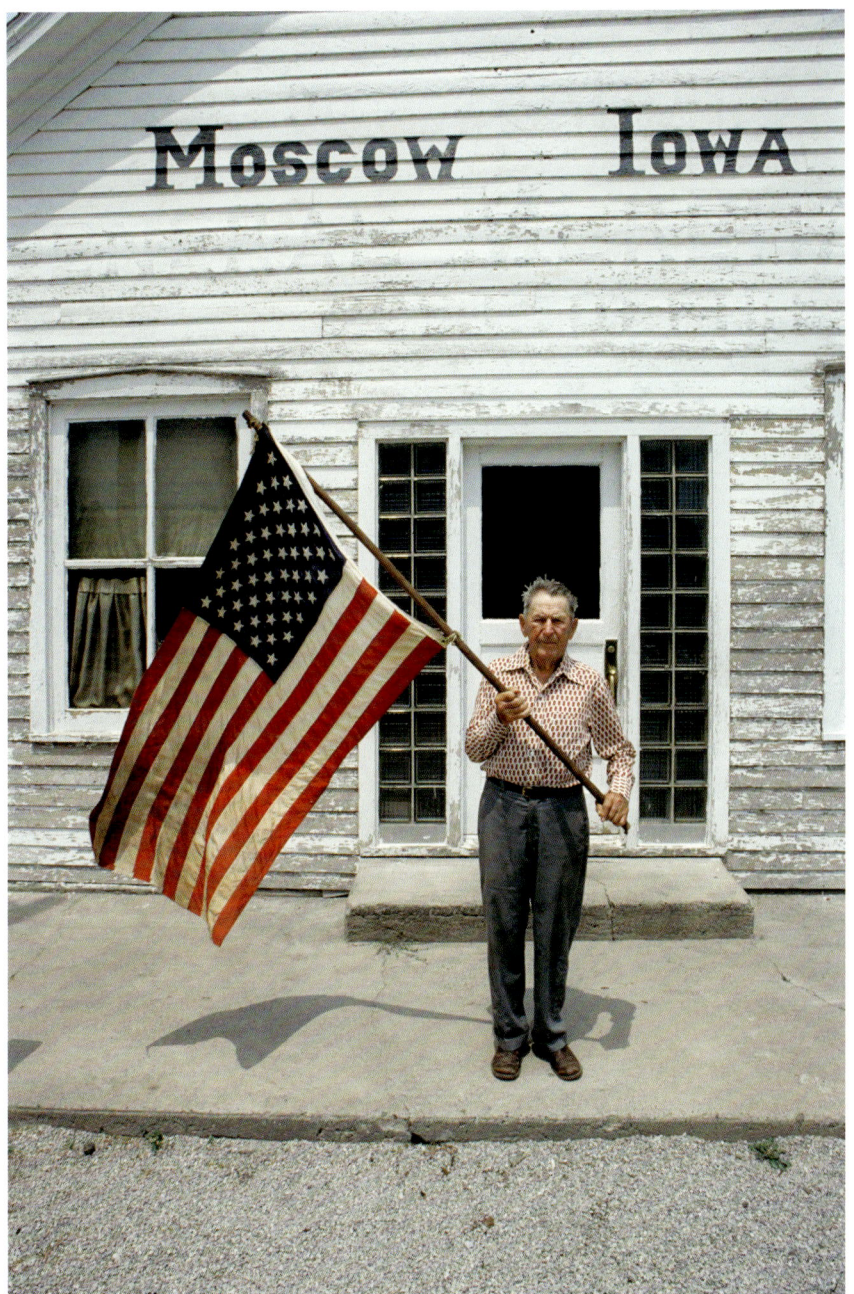

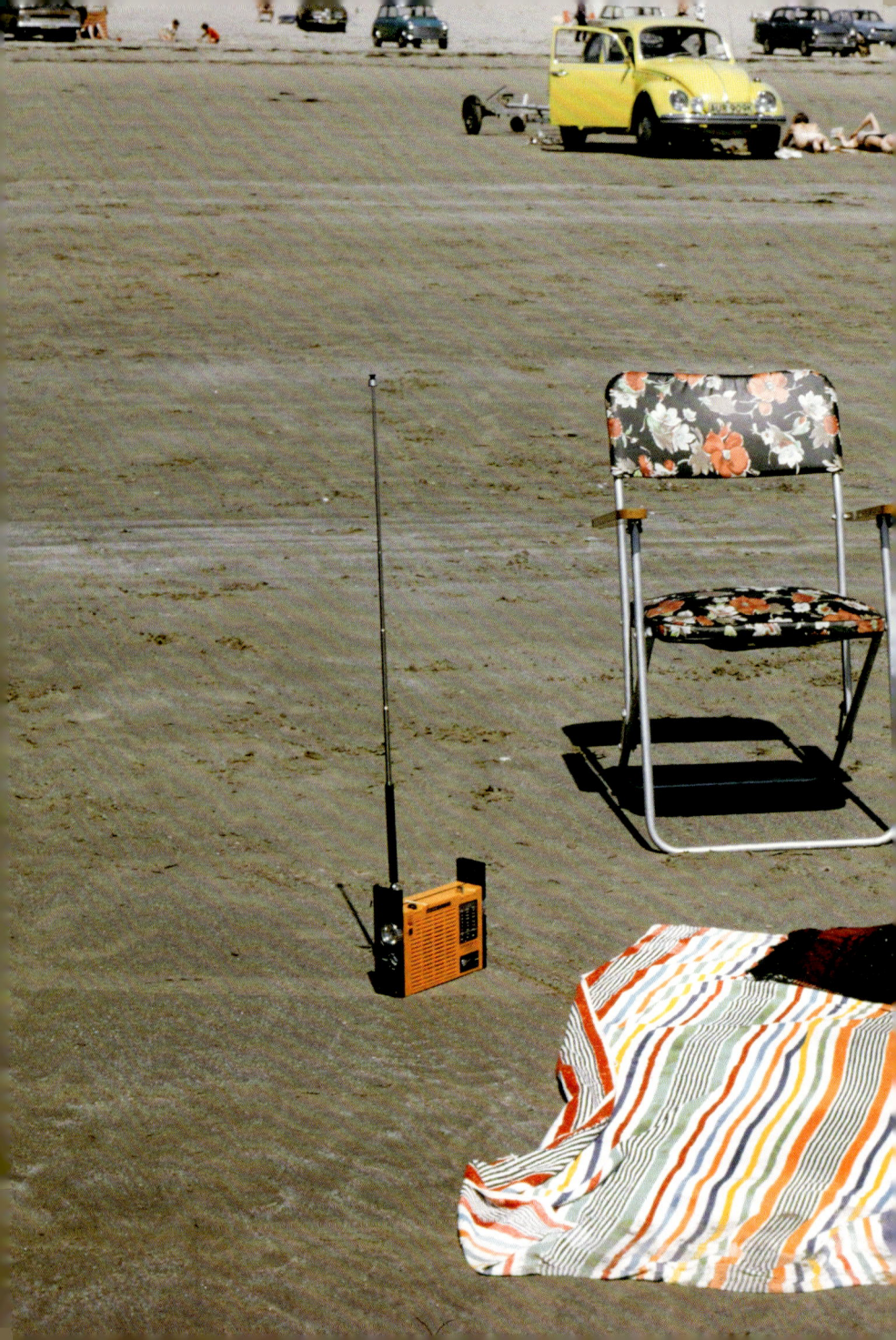

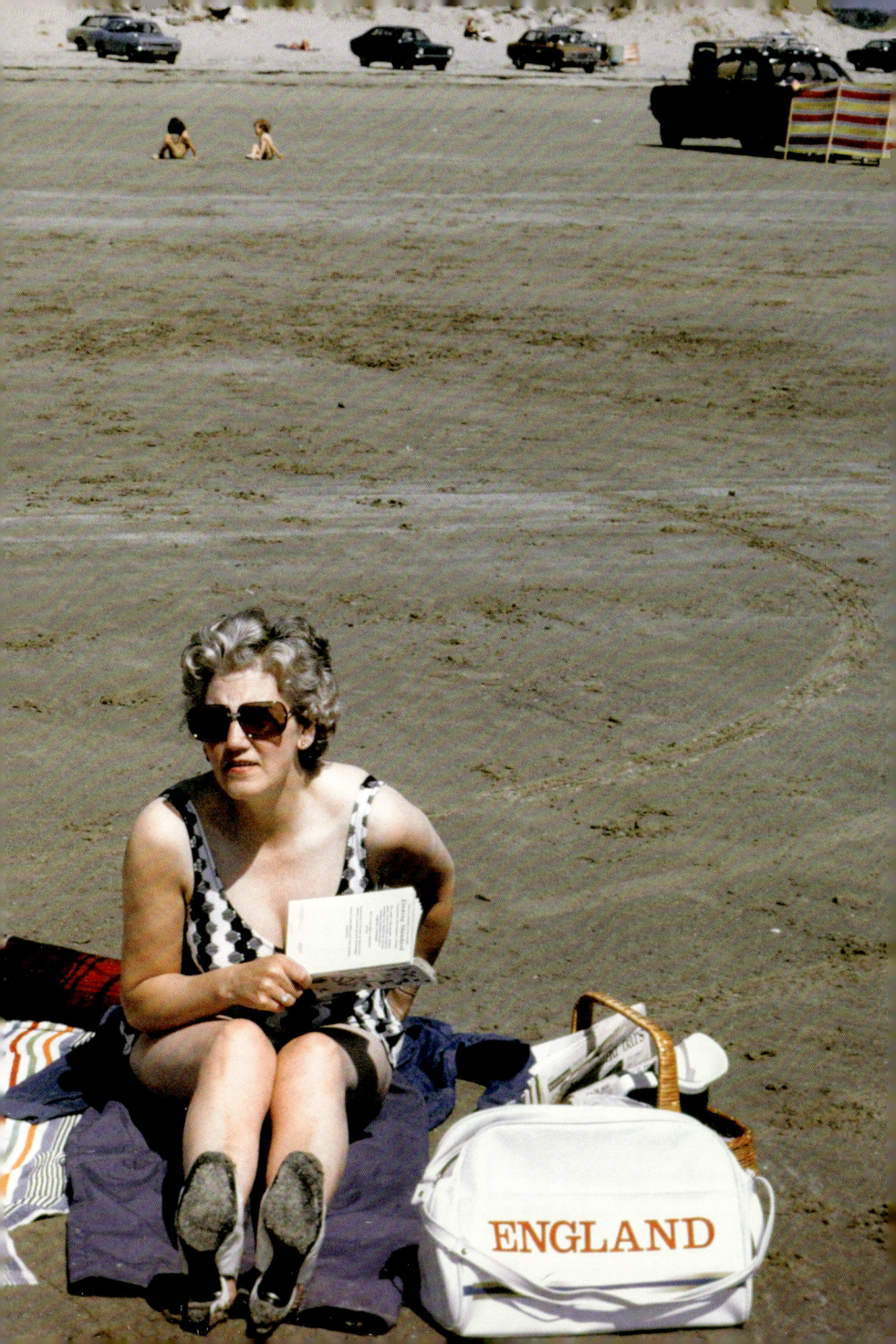

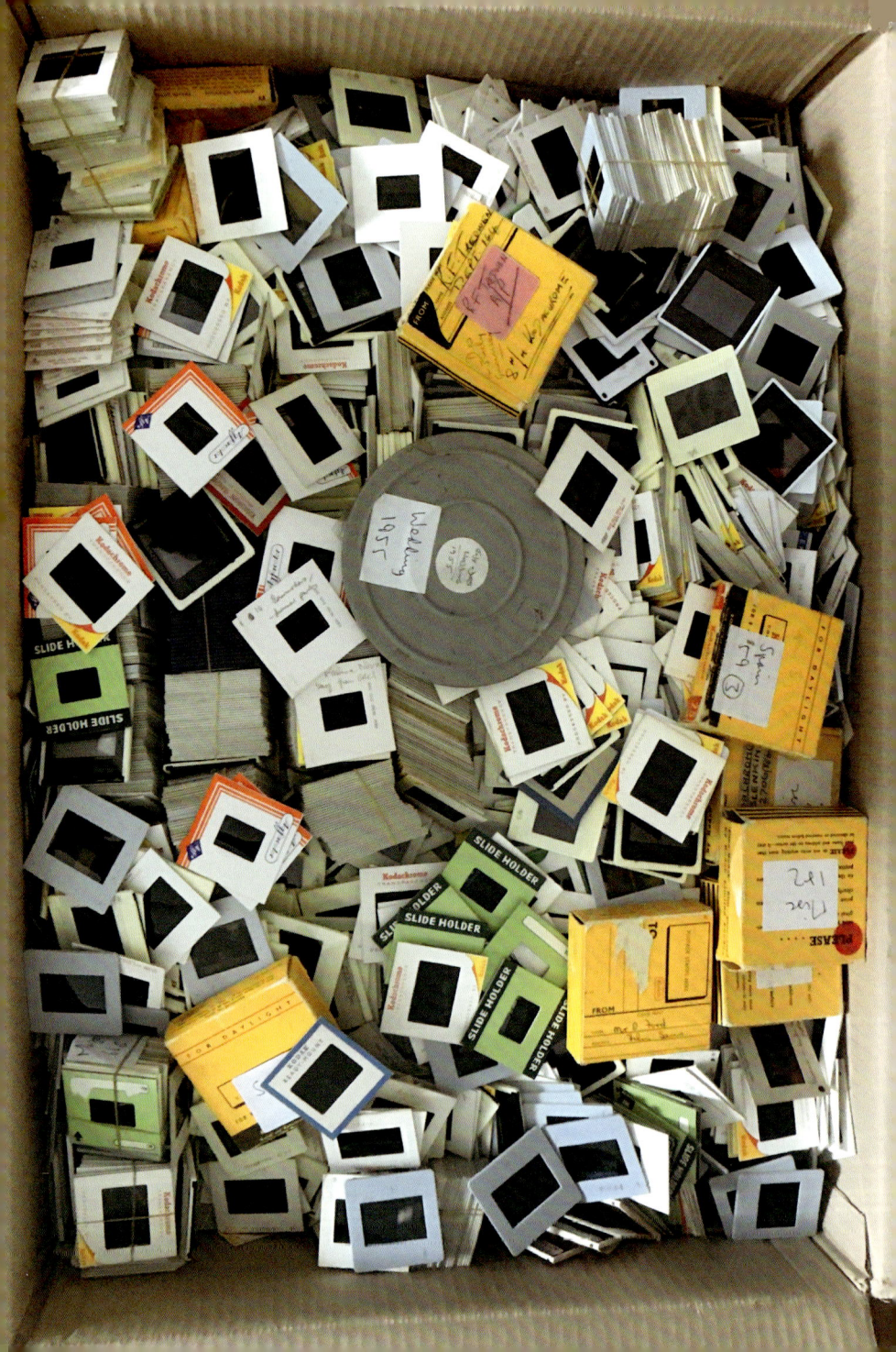

Slide into the Past

The founder and creative director of The Anonymous Project
on his collection and love for Kodachrome

Interview by Reuel Golden

*Born in London, Lee Shulman has a BA from the University of Westminster. He is an
award-winning film director working in advertising and music videos and lives and
works in Paris. In 2017 he founded The Anonymous Project, one of the most important
and unique collections of amateur photography slides in the world, with over 700,000
slides viewed and approximately 10,000 selected to be part of the collection. The project
has exhibited in Paris and Milan, and in 2019 The Anonymous Project was presented
at the prestigious Les Rencontres d'Arles Photography Festival in France.*

Why and when did you start The Anonymous Project?

I had always been a fan of slide photography. In fall 2016 I bought a random box
of vintage slides from the United States on a nostalgic whim. I remember the very
moment when I picked out the first one and held it up to the light. I was totally
blown away, not only by the incredible quality and color but by the intimate stories
revealed by these photographs. It was like discovering unique little windows into our
past. It was hard to believe that some of these these images were around 70 years
old, and yet they looked like they had been taken yesterday. I decided then that I
would take on the task of saving this lost collective memory. I immediately brought
in Emmanuelle Halkin, my good friend and publisher, and the project was born.

How does the project support itself, and what are your
ambitions for it?

This is very much a daily endeavor, but due to the amazing reception the project has
received worldwide over the last year, I have been able to support it through various
collaborations, publications, and exhibitions. We have been very lucky to have had
so much attention in the press. It's a constant struggle but a real labor of love. The
obvious next steps would be to get into mainstream museums and cultural spaces.

Why the focus on color slide film, namely Kodachrome?

Color slide film is unique in the world of photography. No cropping, no manipu-
lation, no printing or postproduction. What you see is what you get—unadulter-
ated imperfection at its best. It was so far ahead of its time in terms of technique,
quality, and color definition, especially Kodachrome, which through a unique
process gave the images a high definition that stands up to today's standards.

As a filmmaker I have always loved the projected image, and slide photography is undeniably unique in the way it combines photography aesthetics within the context of a cinematic experience.

What are your criteria for selecting an image from the thousands you view and making it part of the collection? What is your editing process?

This is very much a personal choice. It simply comes down to an intuitive feeling as I view each image. Often the images that make the cut are the ones to which I have some emotional connection. I definitely prefer images that capture an intimate family moment. For me the magic of amateur photography is the relationship between the photographer and the subject. In most instances, it is a close family member, a parent, a friend, or a lover, so these images are often charged with an emotional bond that we don't always find in professional photography. Emmanuelle and I have now viewed over 750,000 individual slides, and the process is the same as it was back in the day they were taken. Each frame is held up to the light with a viewfinder, there are no shortcuts. Time is our worst enemy.

What do you think the images tell us about how people lived their lives in the mid-to-late 20th century?

They lived it well is the short answer. Though this type of photography belongs to a middle-class society, it does represent an important document of its time. Postwar prosperity and a sense of community are very present in the collection; these intimate portraits show a society on the up. The family was and still remains the defining feature of human existence, and in these images this is very much the case. Though certain social and political barriers have shifted, we still continue to share the same goals and aspirations for ourselves and our loved ones. We definitely dressed better though.

In this age of Instagram and social media, do you think the project has taken on greater relevance?

Slide photography was one of the first examples of social media, with family and friends inviting one another over to watch an evening projection of family events, vacations, and celebrations. The idea of sharing images was one of the main advantages of slide photography. I often find exactly the same type of images that we see on Instagram, so in this respect not much has changed. We even have examples of selfies where people used time-release shutters to capture a moment. I am often asked if I prefer film to digital images with the expectation that I would instantly champion film. This project could only exist in a digital age, and if we didn't have these technologies at hand we would have never got it off the ground. Digital technology and social media have really given new life to film, especially in terms of archiving, preservation, and restoration.

Do you see yourself as a custodian?

I do feel a great sense of responsibility to the people in these images. For me they are like my huge extended family. I know them intimately. If I was to see myself as a custodian, it would not only be in terms of saving this once lost collective memory for future generations, but I must also think of myself as a storyteller and cultural archaeologist, unearthing these hidden gems from the past.

What do you hope people will derive from the book and the project?

That's a difficult one to answer as the experience of seeing these pictures is a very personal journey. Each person gets something different from every image, and that's what makes this project so meaningful to me. I hope that people will look past the vintage nature of the images and reflect on their personal and emotional content. By preserving this important part of our shared experience, we learn about each other and our differences, and, more importantly and to a much greater degree, we learn about our shared humanity.

What is your favorite photo in the book and why?

I love so many images, but I am especially fond of a photo where two ladies are relaxing in the living room sharing a beer, a cigarette, and a joke. I am not sure if they are reacting to a friend or just watching the TV, but it's such a great moment of complicity caught in time. It's natural and joyful, and it makes me smile every time. I often wonder what they are laughing about.

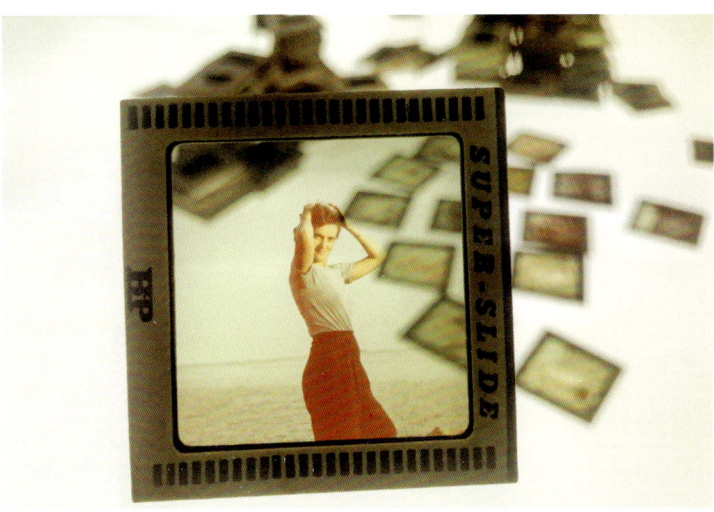

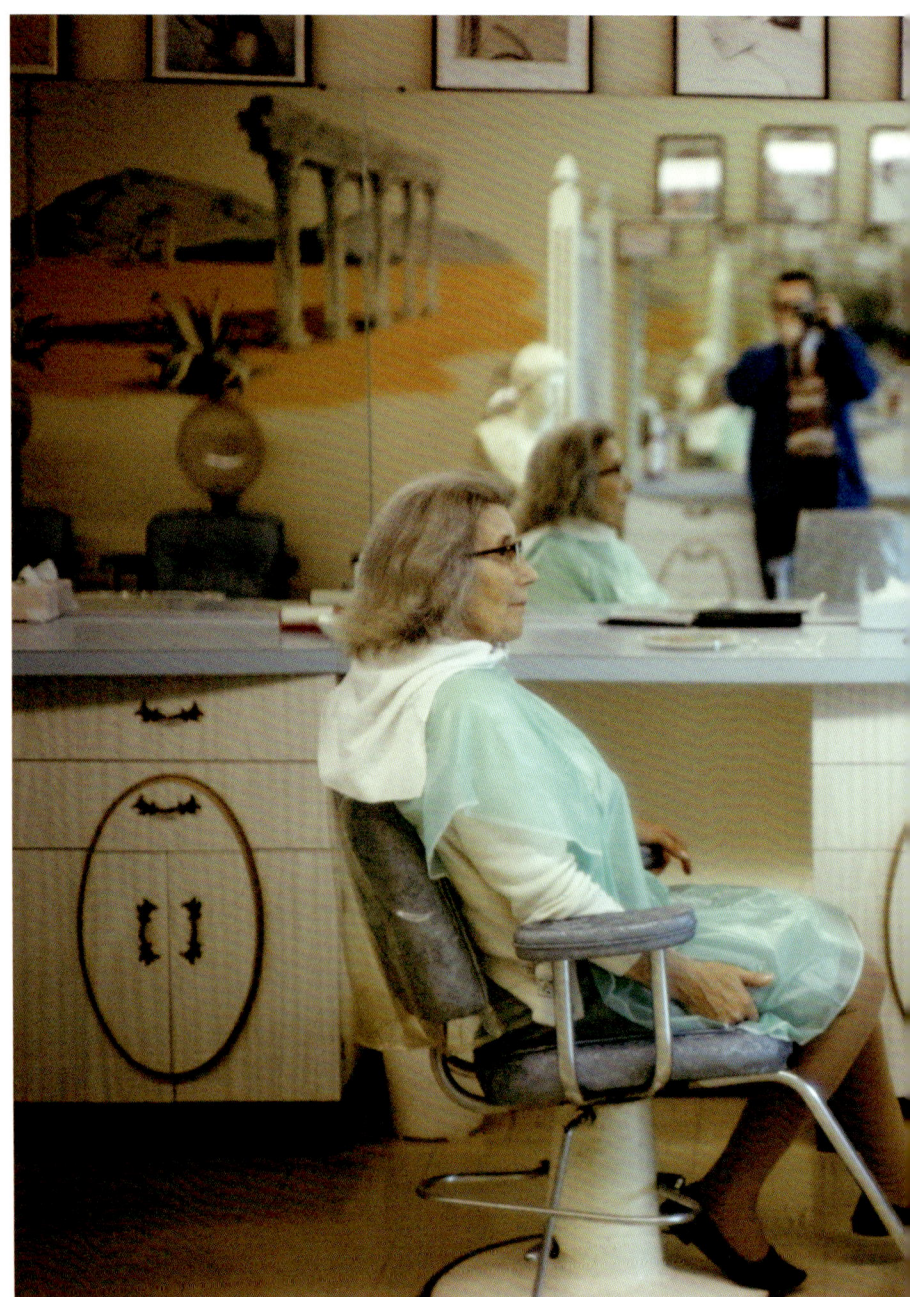

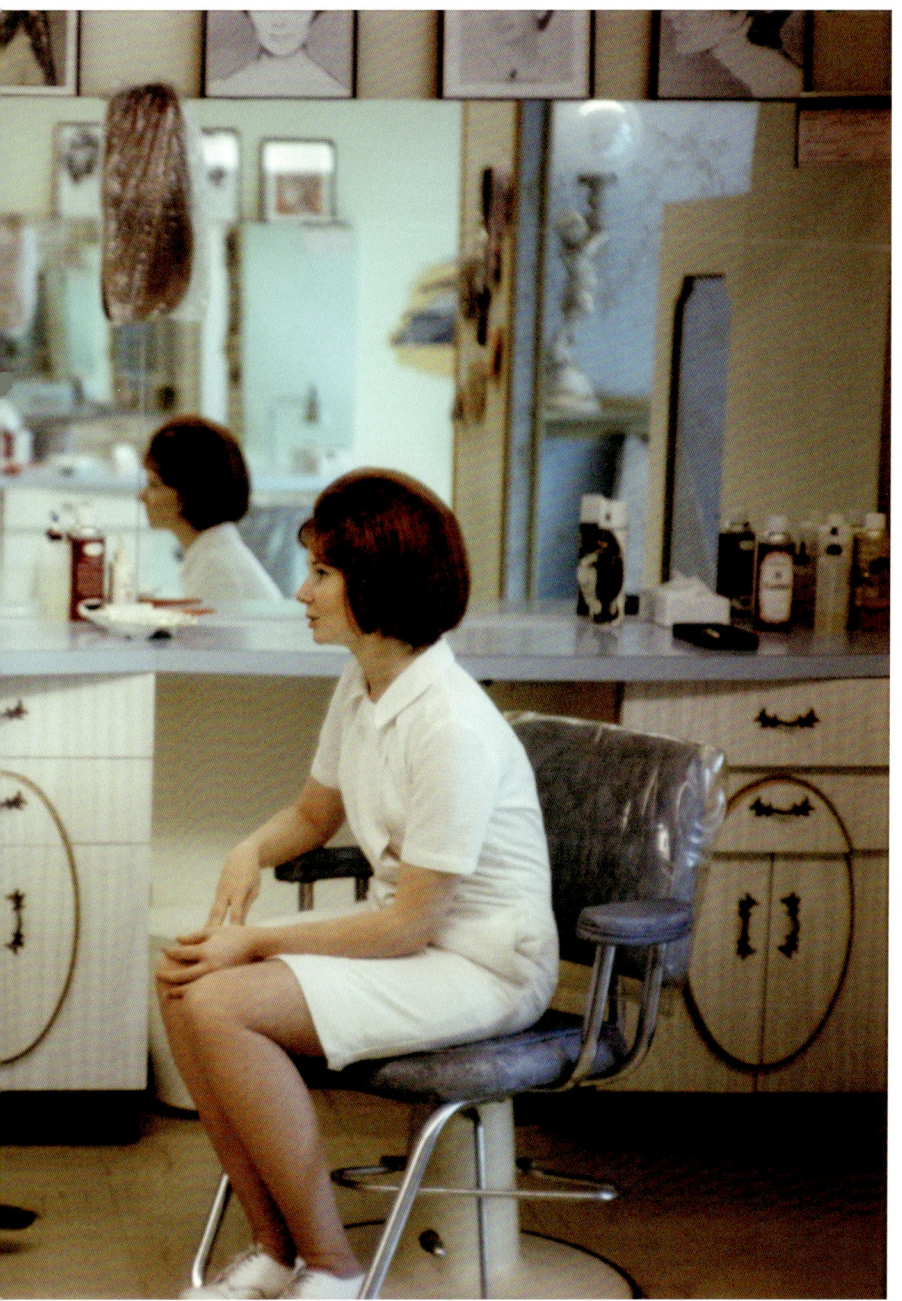

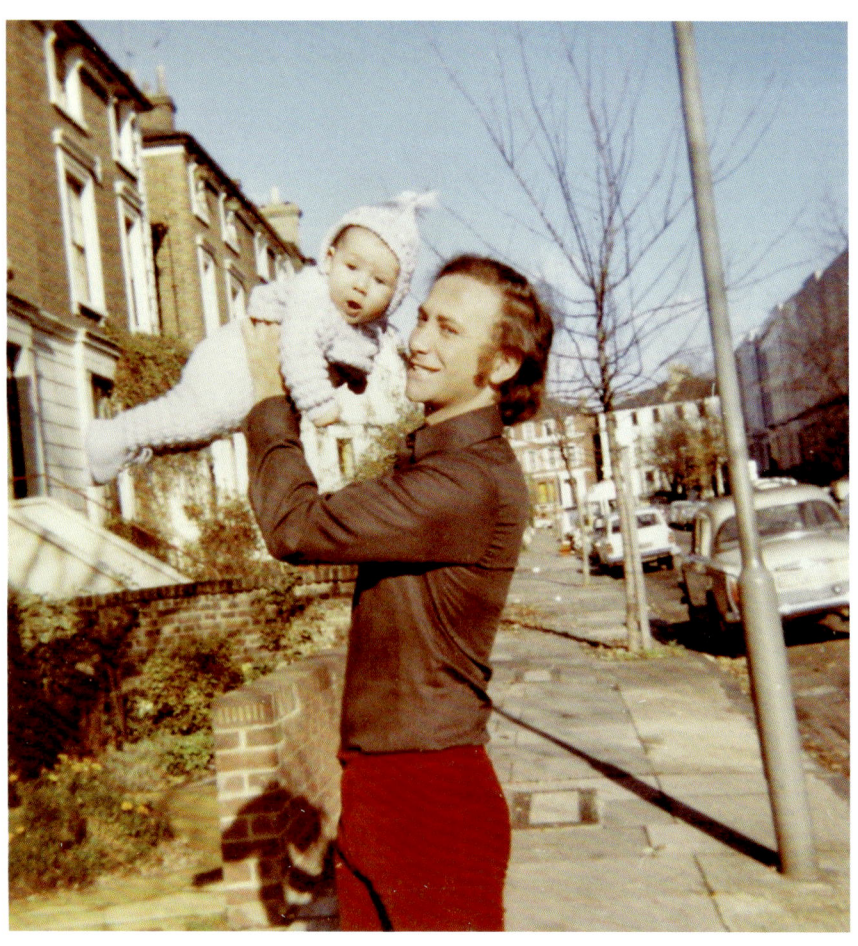

Lee Shulman and his father, London.

© 2023 TASCHEN GmbH
Hohenzollernring 53, D–50672 Köln
www.taschen.com

Original edition:
© 2019 TASCHEN GmbH

Photographs:
© 2019 The Anonymous Project
"Slide into the Past":
© 2019 Lee Shulman and Reuel Golden
"Collective Memories in Kodachrome":
© 2019 Richard B. Woodward
Endpapers, pages 4–5 and 184:
Photo by Leá L'Azou

Edited by: Reuel Golden, New York

Printed in Italy
ISBN 978–3–8365–9664–0

For my parents Emma & Neville
Shulman, thank you for the memories,
past, present, and future.

Very special thanks to Benedikt
Taschen, Reuel Golden, Josh Baker,
and Richard B. Woodward.

The Anonymous Dream Team:
Emmanuelle Halkin, Léa L'Azou,
and Matthieu Botrel.

Isabelle, Rose, and Olivia Shulman.

Alon Shulman and Lauren Hirschfield.

Natacha Wolinski, Picto.

I would especially like to thank all the
wonderful people in these images. Thank
you for letting me be part of your story.

—Lee Shulman, Paris 2019

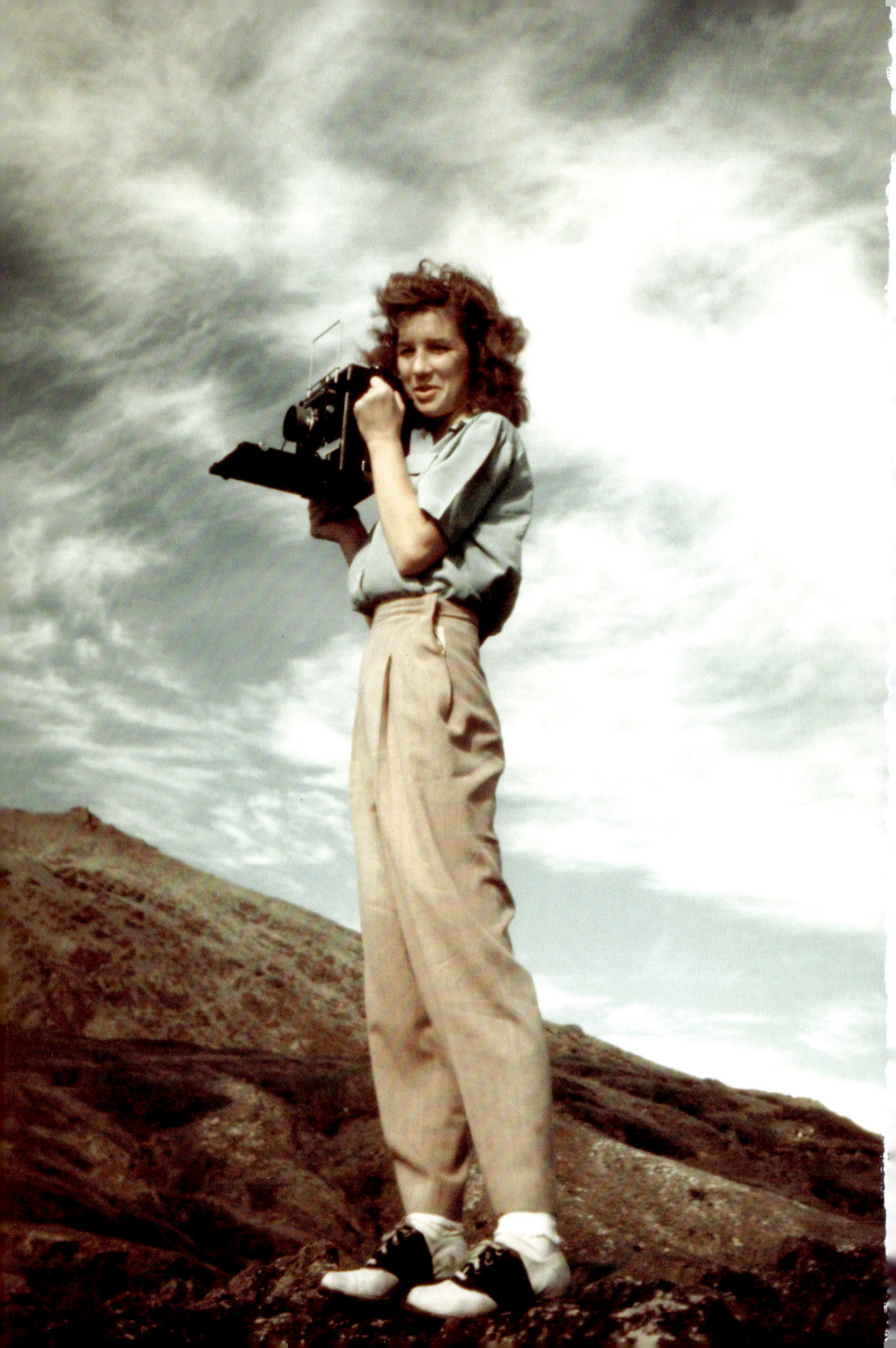

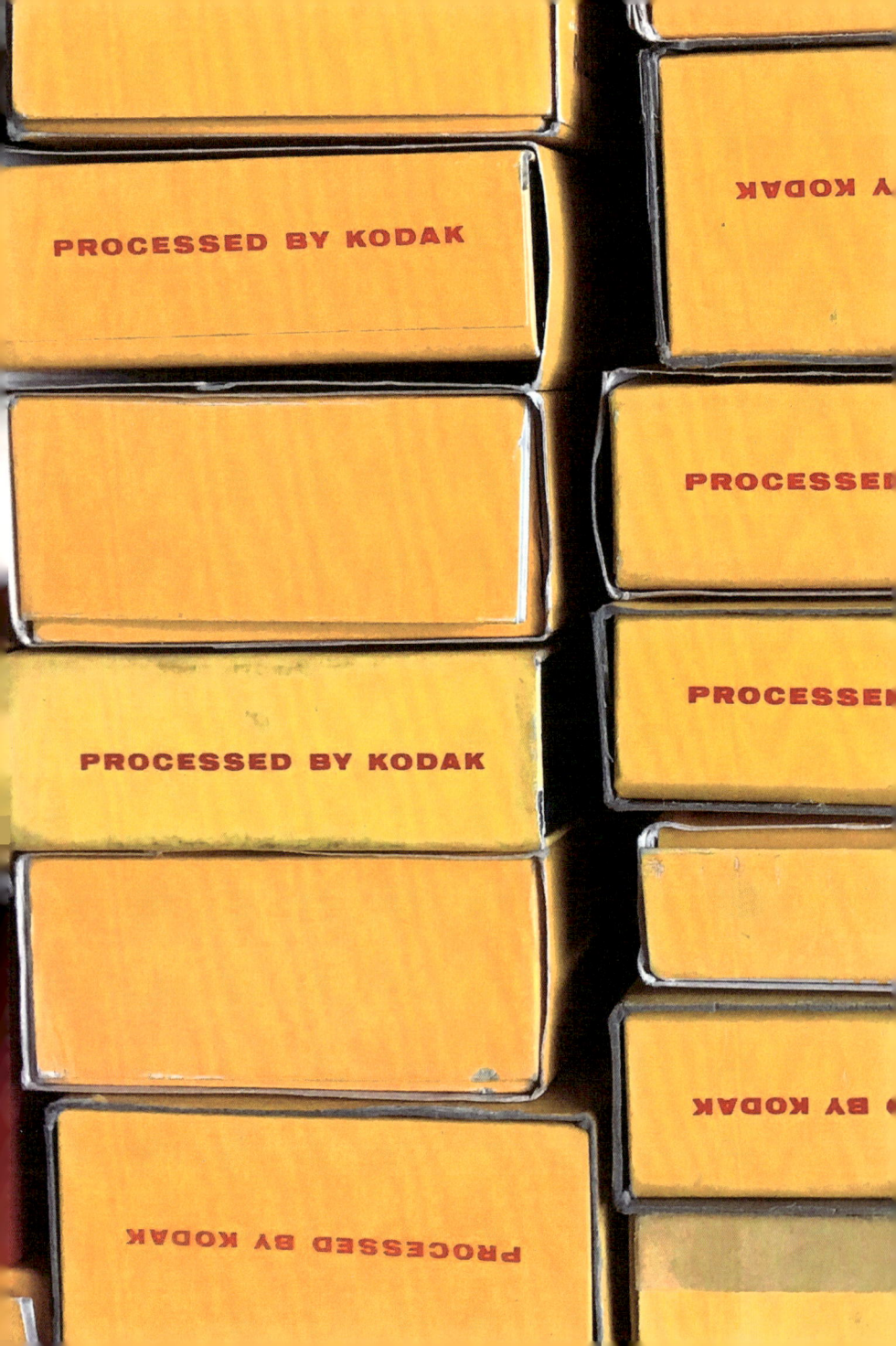